Insiders' Guide®

to the

Idaho Panhandle

Help Us Keep This Guide Up to Date

Every effort has been made by the author and editors to make this guide as accurate and useful as possible. However, many things can change after a guide is published—establishments close, phone numbers change, hiking trails are rerouted, facilities come under new management, etc.

We would love to hear from you concerning your experiences with this guide and how you feel it could be made better and be kept up to date. While we may not be able to respond to all comments and suggestions, we'll take them to heart and we'll also make certain to share them with the author. Please send your comments and suggestions to the following address:

The Globe Pequot Press
Reader Response/Editorial Department
P.O. Box 480
Guilford, CT 06437

Or you may e-mail us at: editorial@globe-pequot.com

Thanks for your input, and happy travels!

Insiders' Guide® Series

Insiders' Guide®
to the
Idaho Panhandle

Including Spokane
and
Coeur d'Alene

By Ellie Emmanuel

Guilford, Connecticut
An imprint of The Globe Pequot Press

The prices and rates listed in this guidebook were confirmed at press time. We recommend, however, that you call establishments before traveling to obtain current information.

Front cover illustration: Mark Gibson
Back cover illustrations (left to right): mountain bikers, courtesy of Coeur d'Alene Resort; winter street, courtesy of Duane D. Davis; radio flyer, courtesy of Marion Severuid; ranch, courtesy of Coeur d'Alene Resort.
Maps: Trapper Badovinac

ISBN 1-57380-185-2

Manufactured in the United States of America
First Edition/First Printing

Contents

Directory of Maps

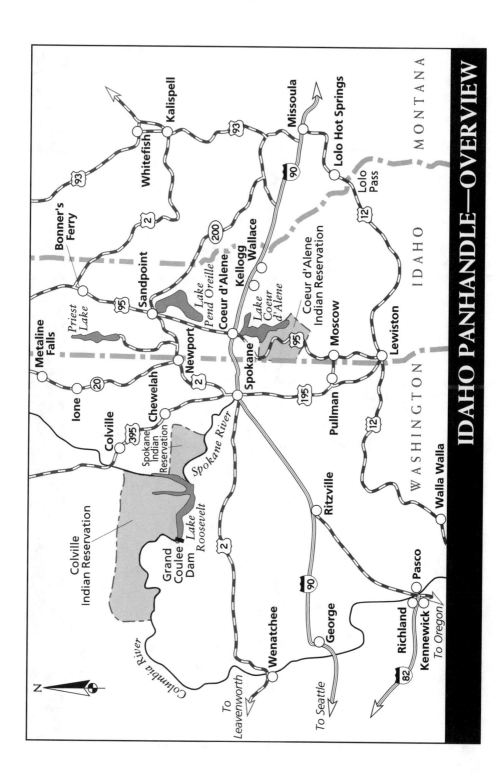

IDAHO PANHANDLE—OVERVIEW

SPOKANE AREA

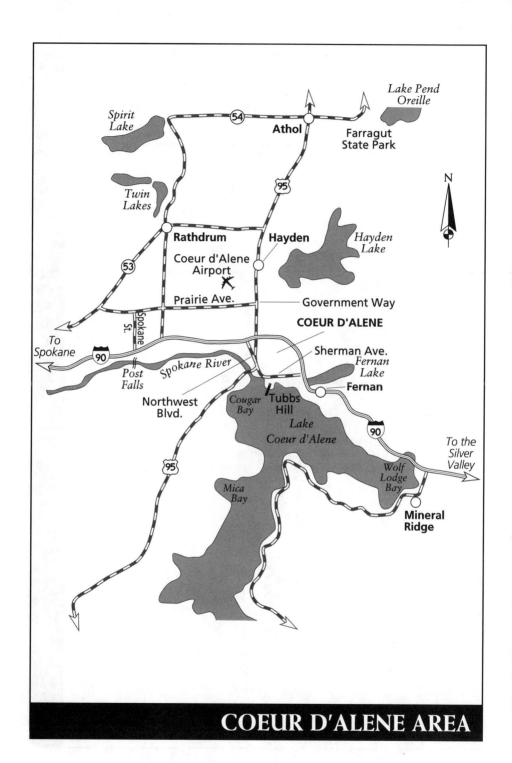

COEUR D'ALENE AREA

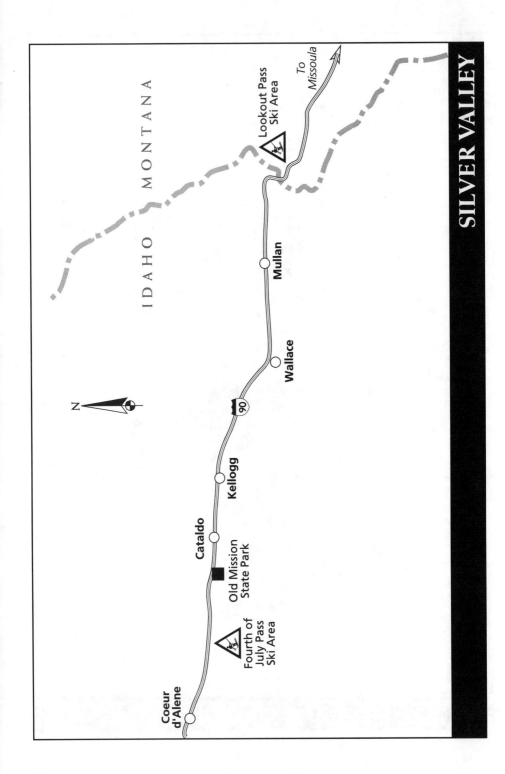

SILVER VALLEY

Preface

Spokane, Washington and Coeur d'Alene, Idaho are part of what's known as the Inland Northwest, an area that's a little obscure to many people in the United States. When we talk on the telephone to people from other places we're used to hearing "spo-kane" instead of the correct, "spo-CANN." Most people don't even try to pronounce Coeur d'Alene ("kore-da-LANE"). Many people think Spokane is just a short drive from Seattle (it's 280 miles), and they think it's overcast and rainy here all the time like Seattle (it isn't). Many refugees from California's problems move to Coeur d'Alene because it is still friendly, down-to-earth, and relatively unspoiled, and are shocked by the comparatively low wages and lack of job opportunities.

Our area has a fascinating geologic history, and you can see evidence of it everywhere. Black volcanic basalt usually found on the ocean floor is abundant in this area, evidence of former lava flows that once covered our land. Monstrous floods carved deep gorges, and glacier fingers reached down into this area, leaving behind our beautiful lakes. We are indebted to all of these prehistoric phenomena, for they created the beautiful and varied topography we enjoy today.

Spokane and north Idaho are still relatively uncrowded and unspoiled. Commute times are fairly short, except for people who choose to live in north Idaho and work in Spokane, or vice versa. Except in road construction areas, traffic usually moves along fine. Lines for movies aren't horrendously long, it's not too hard to find a parking place, and you can go to a park or walk on trails without being surrounded by people.

The Inland Northwest isn't without its problems. Natural resource-based jobs, especially mining and logging, were a mainstay of the economy until the 1980s, when a number of factors, including environmental problems and resource depletion, caused a lot of those jobs to go away. Many people were bitter, and a lot of small towns in the area have struggled to recover. Idaho's Silver Valley is focusing on tourism to replace good-paying mining jobs, but it hasn't been easy. In addition, while the mines paid well, they also left a legacy of toxic minerals in the streams and in the ground.

During the early 1990s, Spokane and Coeur d'Alene saw an influx of people from out of state—people who were attracted to the area's natural beauty and who brought the money with them to buy nice, lakefront homes or secluded mini-ranches. Increased demand drove up the price of housing, making it difficult for local people to afford to buy a home. Some of the new people have had to leave because they couldn't find good paying jobs. Economic development and job creation are one of this area's top priorities.

Despite some problems, the Inland Northwest is a place where people settle. Young adults often go away for a few years to experience working someplace else, but return when it's time to put down roots and raise a family. Friendships and family ties are considered the most important things here, over and above status and wealth.

Spokane and the Idaho Panhandle have one thing in common—each is geographically removed from their respective states' centers of political power, and each feels a little left out because of it. The "politicians in Olympia," as we call them, tend to forget about our needs in eastern Washington (or so we think anyway). Coeur d'Alene and northern Idaho are also a long way from Boise, Idaho's largest city and state capital; locals up here think Boise politicians focus all their energy on the southern half of the state. This common feeling of isolation drives people in our area together.

The Inland Northwest is a great place to live, and it's a fun place to visit. You are welcome to come and see our mountains, lakes, rivers, and natural beauty. Come and enjoy our shopping, cultural activities, and friendly people. You'll be delighted with your "find," and you'll be able to tell others about us. Perhaps, too, you'll fall in love with our area and want to stay—it's happened to many people already. If you do, you'll find it easy to fit in and make friends. You won't be a stranger for long.

Acknowledgments

I've lived in the Inland Northwest for more than 12 years, and I've watched things change tremendously during that time. Spokane and Coeur d'Alene are growing and changing—in most ways for the better, I think. This area has a unique topography—to the east lie arid, rocky plains, and to the west lie the mountains. It is beautiful and green, and has four distinct seasons that change quickly so you never get tired of the weather. The many lakes make this area different from others in the Rockies.

The people in the Inland Northwest make it really special. Through ice storms and fire storms, people pull together, help their neighbors and friends, and really make it a warm and friendly place to live. During the time I've been writing this book, all my friends and family have been so understanding and supportive. My husband Nick has kept himself busy and out of the way, and many times has kept me on task. The kids, Scott, Todd, Jessie, Jared, and Mark, and Jessie's boyfriend, Aaron, have given me ideas and suggestions and helped when I was stuck. And my dog, Dover, has helped me think by taking me for long walks.

My friends Debbie, Bonnie, Marcia, Pat, and Jenny have been so understanding when I ignored them for long periods as I worked feverishly to meet deadlines. Beau, with his love of Idaho and the northwest, donated books and stories that helped me get started. The Mayfields in Wallace, Idaho, were so nice to take me on a personal tour of the Oasis Bordello Museum and tell me stories from the past. There were many other business people who gave suggestions and helped me dig up information for the book, and I'd like to thank them all.

How to Use This Book

Most Insiders' Guides cover one city or one area of a state. This guide covers an area that crosses state lines—the Idaho Panhandle and Northeastern Washington. However, there is a strong regional identity here, independent of political boundaries. Distant from both Washington's and Idaho's state capitals, the Inland Northwest is unique. It is relatively undiscovered, yet has much to offer both tourists and residents.

Most information in this book is arranged geographically within each chapter, starting in Spokane and northeast Washington, and moving into Coeur d'Alene and north Idaho. You'll be introduced to the area's background and history, and learn what makes us unique. Practical information about hotels and motels, camping, resorts and guest ranches, restaurants, and sightseeing attractions will help those visiting the area for the first time. For active visitors and residents I've included information about golf, skiing and other winter sports, hunting and fishing, biking, and water activities. Prospective and current residents will find chapters on real estate, education and child care, the arts, and retirement helpful.

Beginning with overviews that introduce you to some of the unique features of our area, the book then tells you how to get here, and how to get around once you're here. You can read it straight through, or more likely skip around, looking for the information you need at the moment. Take your time as you read through the chapters—I know the area well and share many details you won't find in other sources.

If you've visited here before but not in the last ten years or so, you'll be amazed at the changes. The region has embraced the new century with gusto, sprucing up downtowns, making attractions and recreation areas more accessible, and attracting new businesses and residents. There's more to do now, for everyone from children to senior citizens, and you'll find many great ideas in this book. Whether you're a prospective visitor or already a resident, this is one book you'll use a lot.

As you travel around our area you'll make your own observations and discoveries. If you find places that should have been included in this book but weren't, please write and let us know about them. We'd love to hear your suggestions and comments. You can reach us online at our website (www.insiders.com), or write to us at this address:

Insiders' Guides
c/o The Globe Pequot Press
P.O. Box 480
Guilford, CT 06437-0480

Area Overview

The Inland Northwest, which includes Spokane, Coeur d'Alene, and other towns in northeastern Washington and northern Idaho, is still largely rural. There are many small communities, and many people living on a few acres of land, enjoying the natural beauty of the area. Most of the countryside is either farmland or forest. Away from town it isn't uncommon to see deer, coyotes, bears, and sometimes even cougars. While the wilderness isn't as pristine as it was 200 years ago, it still supports a lot of wildlife.

Much of our claim to fame lies in our lakes, rivers, and mountains. Over 50 lakes within an easy drive of Spokane or Coeur d'Alene make it easy to enjoy fishing, swimming, boating, and other water activities. Ski mountains range from low-key, family areas to world-class resorts. The same mountains offer great hiking and mountain biking in summer. Our rivers and streams are great recreation areas too. Larger rivers like the Spokane and Pend Oreille are used for everything from boating and water-skiing to kayaking and canoeing. Many smaller streams are great for fishing too. However, the Coeur d'Alene River and some smaller streams leading away from the Silver Valley have high levels of lead and other dangerous minerals, so eating fish from these streams isn't a good idea.

This chapter is an introductory tour of the cities and towns in the rugged Inland Northwest. After learning a little about the history, geography, and personality of the region, you'll be better able to plan your own travels, using the in-depth information further in this book.

Spokane

Spokane is the largest city in eastern Washington, currently second largest in the state (with Tacoma a close runner-up), Spokane (pronounced spo-CANN) is the business, academic, and health center for a wide geographic area. People come to Spokane from Idaho, Montana, Oregon, British Columbia, and even Alberta, to shop, attend to medical needs, and take care of business. For people from surrounding farms, ranches, and small towns, Spokane is a big city. However, the city is somewhat isolated and just a little defensive about always being compared to big, cosmopolitan, liberal Seattle.

The city of Spokane grew up around waterfalls on the Spokane River. The area had been a fur trading and then lumbering settlement when James Glover arrived in 1872 to establish a town. He platted the town and brought the railroad in; by the mid-1880s it was a bustling commercial center. Wealthy mine owners who didn't want to live out in the wilds of Idaho built beautiful mansions in gracious neighborhoods—today, some of these remain private homes while others have become restaurants, apartments, churches, and meeting facilities.

Spokane sits on the cusp of two very different geographic areas. To the west, the endless, dry plains of central Washington stretch all the way to the Cascades. To the east and north, you can see the mountains, lush and green in the summer, covered with snow in the winter. Two rural cultures meet in Spokane: farmers and ranchers from the flat, open prairies, and loggers and miners from the mountains and foothills. Yet the city also includes many urban folks who don't know anything about farming or forestry. Natural wonders are never far away, however, and most people here feel some kind of attachment to the outdoors and especially to the area's mountains and lakes.

Interstate 90 connects Spokane with the "west side"; it continues on into Idaho, bisecting Post Falls and Coeur d'Alene. From there it heads into the mountains across Fourth of July Pass, down through the Silver Valley, up over Lookout Pass, and on into Montana. I-90 is the only interstate in the area, although Spokane has a "north-south" freeway in the planning stages. Other major highways are Idaho Highway 95, which leads north from Coeur d'Alene to Sandpoint, and south to Moscow; Washington Highway 395, which goes north from Spokane to Colville, and south to Pullman; and Washington Highway 2, which branches off from Highway 395 in north Spokane to go to Newport.

South of Spokane

As you head south on Highway 395 from Spokane, you'll soon enter the region known as the Palouse. This is farm country, known for its loess soil, one of only two such areas in the world (the other is in China). Wheat is the major crop here, although soybeans, peas, lentils, and grass seed are also common. Small farming communities dot the landscape, in between rolling hills covered with green in the spring, gold in late summer.

About 50 miles south of Spokane you come to Steptoe Butte, named after Colonel Edward Steptoe, whose defeat by the Cayuse Indians here in 1858 is commemorated with interpretive signs and a state park. The butte itself is a quartzite mountain—the only one for miles around—that's over 600 million years old. Today you can drive to the top for views of the farming country all around.

Further south lies Pullman, home of Washington State University, "Wazzu," the state's primary land-grant institution and temporary home to about 17,000 students. Pullman is a clean, prosperous town with a stream running through it; many university alumni stay after graduation. As a result, residents here have one of the highest education levels in the United States; over 36% have at least a four-year degree.

North of Spokane

Taking any road north out of Spokane brings you to vastly different country from the area to the south. Even before you leave the city the landscape begins to change. Pine, cedar and fir trees replace the maples, chestnut, and birch that are common further south. Soon you're driving through evergreen forests and passing settlements almost hidden by the trees.

Highway 395 north will lead you through Chattaroy and Deer Park, small communities that have almost become commuter suburbs of Spokane (although the drive can be harrowing in winter). Further north lies Loon Lake, one of the area's most popular for summer cabins. Chewelah (chew-EE-lah) is the next town of any size; a logging community far enough from Spokane to support all the necessary services, it was the first town in the Inland Northwest with a Wal-Mart.

East of Spokane

Post Falls

Driving east from Spokane on I-90 you cross the Spokane Valley and enter Idaho just where the freeway crosses the Spokane River. You're likely to encounter road construction on this drive, as sections of the freeway are constantly being widened and repaved, and new interchanges added, to accommodate the tremendous population growth we've seen in the past nine years. As you drive through Post Falls you'll see many new businesses and lots of new housing construction. There's an outlet mall just off the freeway, and parks and a beautiful resort on the river. The mountains begin here, and they make a lovely backdrop to the town.

Frederick Post, a German immigrant, purchased the site by the falls from Andrew Seltice, a Coeur d'Alene tribal chief, in 1871.

Spokane's Riverfront Park is a top area attraction. PHOTO: COURTESY SPOKANE CHAMBER OF COMMERCE

The contract was validated with a unique pictograph painted on a granite rock, still visible at Treaty Rock Park. Post built sawmill operations at the site, and there is still a significant forest products industry in Post Falls.

In addition to driving from Spokane to Coeur d'Alene, you can walk, bike, or rollerblade the entire distance on the Centennial Trail, a paved pathway that extends 63 miles from the west side of Spokane through Coeur d'Alene and along the lakeshore. Much of the trail runs along the Spokane River; in Post Falls it runs right by the outlet mall. The Centennial Trail is one of our area's most popular amenities; see the Recreation chapter for more detail.

Coeur d'Alene

Post Falls and Coeur d'Alene (core-da-LANE) almost run together these days, but from the freeway you can still see the Louisiana-Pacific lumber mill operations through the forest (along with the fences and housetops of new subdivisions) as you drive between the two towns. Nearby is a new family fun center with laser tag and go-carts. In Coeur d'Alene, take the Northwest Blvd. exit (Exit 11), which will take you right down to the lake, the park, the floating boardwalk, and the downtown shopping area, all in close proximity. This is a beautiful resort town and on sunny summer days the area is packed with people, both locals and tourists. Surprisingly, there is usually plenty of free parking on the street, and there is a big public parking lot on the other side of the Coeur d'Alene Resort.

Mountains surround the lake—not stark and rocky, but rounded, green, and inviting, giving Lake Coeur d'Alene one of the most beautiful settings in the world. A boat cruise (leaving from the city dock), is a relaxing way to enjoy the lake and see some of the interesting homes along the shore.

Coeur d'Alene is part of an area that originally belonged to the Coeur d'Alene Indians. These were Salish-speaking people whose name, Schee-Chu-Umsh, was changed by French fur traders to Coeur d'Alene, meaning "heart like an awl," supposedly for their sharp trading skills.

According to tribal legend, Circling Raven, a Coeur d'Alene chief, had a vision that men in black robes would come to his people. When the Coeur d'Alenes heard that Father Peter DeSmet, a Jesuit missionary, was with the Flathead Indians in Montana, they sent a message asking him to come. When he did, they readily embraced Christianity and built several missions, including the Cataldo Mission still standing east of Coeur d'Alene.

Sandpoint

Leaving I-90 for awhile, head north on Idaho 95 toward Sandpoint. This road is heavily traveled and narrows to two lanes after Hayden, so it's best not to be in a hurry. As you drive north you'll see all kinds of stores and restaurants, plus the Silver Lake Mall, Coeur d'Alene's largest. Fifteen miles north of Coeur d'Alene you'll pass Silverwood, a late-1800s mining town theme park with rides and attractions, restaurants, and shopping.

Near the small community of Athol is the turnoff for Farragut State Park, one of Idaho's finest. On the shores of Lake Pend Oreille (pronounced ponderay), the park has miles of forest trails, clean campgrounds, and fishing and swimming areas.

The southern entrance to Sandpoint is spectacular. Highway 95 leads across Lake Pend Oreille on the two-mile Long Bridge. Right beside the bridge is an older span that's now used as a bike and walking path. Lake Pend Oreille is one of the largest lakes in the west, with over 100 miles of shoreline. Its also one of the deepest; the U.S. Navy operates a deep-water testing facility near Farragut.

Sandpoint is an artists community and a resort town, with an outstanding ski mountain right outside the city limits. There's an interesting variety of downtown shops, museums, a summer concert series, and endless outdoor recreation.

Heading west from Sandpoint, Highway 2 follows the Pend Oreille River to Oldtown and Newport, on the Idaho/Washington state line.

The Mission of the Sacred Heart is the oldest standing building in Idaho. PHOTO: COURTESY COEUR D'ALENE CHAMBER OF COMMERCE.

Silver Valley

Back on I-90 driving out of Coeur d'Alene, the freeway hugs the shoreline, providing beautiful views of the lake. Soon you'll be gaining altitude as you wind through the mountains up to Fourth of July Pass. On the other side is the Silver Valley, known for over 100 years as one of the world's largest silver producing areas. You'll see stark evidence of the years of mining activity as you enter the valley, passing the ongoing Bunker Hill Superfund Site cleanup efforts. Despite the legacy of toxic minerals left by mining operations, most people in these parts remain loyal to the mines, and get a little defensive when outsiders make comments about local environmental problems. In any case, the air is fresh and clean up here in the mountains.

Today, most of the mines have shut down and the region is focusing on its other resources; the abundant forests and mountains are prime recreation areas. Even the hundreds of miles of unpaved logging roads that crisscross local forests are used primarily for recreation now; they make this one of the prime ATV and snowmobile playgrounds in the west.

Kellogg

The town of Kellogg is named after Noah Kellogg, the miner who found the largest silver strike in the area. Legend has it that Kellogg's jackass wandered off during the night, and was found in the morning standing beside a great outcrop of silver— Kellogg's great strike. The jackass is still a local symbol, and plays a part in many local jokes.

As the mines closed down in the 1980s, citizens of Kellogg looked for a way to save the town and create new jobs. They came up with the idea of making Kellogg over into a Bavarian village, reminiscent of Leavenworth, Washington's successful transformation. Kellogg hasn't had quite the same success as Leavenworth, but they're still working on it. The biggest attraction here is the world's longest gondola, built by one of Europe's top gondola companies, which takes passengers to the top of Silver Moun-

Insiders' Tip

In 1996, the movie *Dante's Peak*, about a volcanic eruption, was filmed in Wallace, even though the surrounding mountains aren't really volcanoes.

tain for skiing in winter and hiking and concerts in summer. There is a nice restaurant at the top too, and the ride, in comfortable, enclosed cars, is a lot of fun.

Downtown Kellogg has some interesting specialty shops, and as you drive or walk around town you'll see local artist David Dose's "junk-art sculptures."

Wallace

Don't pass up pretty little Wallace; the whole town is listed in the National Register of Historic Places, and it's a fun place to explore. Once known as the Silver Capital of the World, the town now relies mostly on tourism.

Wallace has a character and charm not found in many other mining towns. It sits right at the foot of steep mountains; stairs and steep streets climb up to houses built into the hillsides. Lucky for Wallace you can't see evidence of mining from here. You can, however, take a mine tour, putting on a hard hat and walking through old mining tunnels in the hillside. You can also visit the Oasis Bordello, the last one in town to be shut down (in 1988!) and now a museum.

Hollywood took over the town of Wallace in 1996 for the filming of the movie *Dante's Peak* (actually, though, none of the local mountain peaks are volcanic). Locals were recruited as extras and the town basically became a movie set during the months of filming.

Wallace takes advantage of its proximity to mountain trails by allowing ATVs to be ridden on certain streets in summer, and snowmobiles in winter. Several companies rent both.

Vital Statistics

Mayor/Governor:
Mayor of Spokane: John Powers
Mayor of Coeur d'Alene: Steve Judy
Mayor of Sandpoint: Paul Graves

Governor of Washington: Gary Locke
Governor of Idaho: Dirk Kempthorne

Capital/major cities/outlying counties

Largest city in eastern Washington: Spokane
Largest city in northern Idaho: Coeur d'Alene
Spokane is in Spokane County
Coeur d'Alene is in Kootenai County
Sandpoint is in Bonner County
Kellogg and Wallace are in Shoshone County

Population (city/metro area/state)

Washington State: 5,700,000
Idaho: 1,011,900
City of Spokane: 189,000
Spokane County, Washington: 415,000
Coeur d'Alene: 32,000
Kootenai County, Idaho: 104,000
Sandpoint: 7,900
Bonner County, Idaho: 34,000
Kellogg, Idaho: 2,500
Wallace, Idaho: 1,000
Shoshone County, Idaho: 14,000

Area (sq. miles)

Spokane County: 1,758 square miles
Kootenai County: 5,400 square miles

Nickname/motto

The whole area: The Inland Northwest or Inland Empire
Spokane: The Lilac City
Coeur d'Alene: The Lake City
Kellogg, Wallace area: The Silver Valley
Idaho: The Gem State
Idaho State motto: Esto Perpetua (It is forever)
Another Idaho motto (on license plates): Famous Potatoes
New Idaho motto: Idaho: The Human Rights State (proposed by the Kootenai County
Task Force on Human Relations in response to the bad publicity brought to the state by
   groups like Richard Butler's Aryan Nations)
Washington: The Evergreen State
Washington State motto: Alki (Chinook Indian word meaning "bye and bye")

Average Temperatures (Hi/Lo), July   Hi: 85   Lo: 52

Average Temperatures (Hi/Lo), January   Hi: 34   Lo: 22

Temperatures are about the same for Spokane and Coeur d'Alene. Temperatures in the
Silver Valley are usually colder, as it is higher in the mountains. Temperatures north of
Coeur d'Alene and Spokane are also colder.

Average rain/snowfall/days of sunshine

Average rain: 16 inches
Average snowfall: 51 inches (200-400 inches in the nearby mountains)

Average days of sunshine: 161

Coeur d'Alene area:
Average rain: 29 inches
Average snowfall: 50 inches (200-400 inches in the mountains)
Average days of sunshine: 161

City/state founded

Village of Spokan Falls founded in 1871. (The final "e" in the name was added in 1881, and the "Falls" was dropped in 1891.)
In 1878, James Glover, "father of Spokane," filed a townsite plan for Spokane
Washington Territory was created in 1853
Washington became a state in 1889
In 1863, Idaho Territory was created out of the eastern part of Washington Territory
Idaho became a state in 1890
Fort Coeur d'Alene built in 1878
Town of Coeur d'Alene incorporated in 1887
In 1880, Robert Weeks opened a general store in Pend Oreille, just to the east of Sandpoint.
In 1898, railroad agent L.D. Farmin filed the original Sandpoint townsite.

Major universities

In/near Spokane:
Gonzaga University (private, Jesuit)
Whitworth College (private, Presbyterian)
Eastern Washington University, Cheney, Washington (also a Spokane campus downtown)
Washington State University, Spokane campus
Community Colleges of Spokane
In/near Coeur d'Alene
University of Idaho has classes in Coeur d'Alene
North Idaho College (2-year community college)

Important dates in history

80 million years ago: ocean covered the area
35 million years ago: this area gradually rose out of the ocean
Between 75 million and 10 million years ago, lava flowed out of huge cracks in the earth and covered eastern Washington.
1 million years ago: glacial ice sheets reached almost as far south as Spokane and Coeur d'Alene
13,000 to 15,000 years ago: An ice dam had formed in what is now Montana, creating a huge inland sea, Lake Missoula. Water eroded it from underneath, and it broke and released the water from the lake in a major catastrophe called the Missoula Floods. The lake emptied in two days as water up to 400 feet deep raced across Idaho and Washington, following the course of the Columbia River to the Pacific and creating many of the geologic features found today in eastern Washington.
Over 10,000 years ago: The first people came to the area
1805: Lewis and Clark came through the area
1809: David Thompson explored the area and established a fur trading post on Lake Pend Oreille
1810: Canadian fur traders (Hudson's Bay Company) opened a trading post on the Spokane River near present-day Spokane
1840: Cataldo Mission built
1858: Colonel Steptoe lead troops north of the Snake River in violation of a promise made by the governor of Washington Territory. Combined forces of Spokane, Coeur d'Alene, and Palouse Indians attacked and defeated the troops. This lead to retaliatory strikes by the U.S. Army, ending with the hanging of Chief Qualchan and others at Hangman Creek.

1862: Mullan Road completed—major commercial route for Coeur d'Alene/Silver
   Valley area
1877: Gonzaga University established in Spokane
1880: Frederick Post established a sawmill on the Spokane River (at present-day Post Falls)
1881: Spokane Indian Reservation established
1883: Northern Pacific Railroad arrived, linking Washington with the east
1889: Fire destroyed 32 blocks of Spokane's business district
1939: Grand Coulee Dam finished and Lake Roosevelt began filling
1972: Ninety-one miners died in the Sunshine Silver Mine fire in the Silver Valley
1974: Riverfront Park built in Spokane for Expo '74.
1980: Mount St. Helens erupted, covering the Inland Northwest with volcanic ash

Major area employers

Spokane County top employers:
Fairchild Air Force Base, 5,217 employees
Spokane School District #81, 3,169 employees
Sacred Heart Medical Center, 2,931 employees
State of Washington, 2,478 employees
City of Spokane, 2,082 employees
Kaiser Aluminum & Chemical Corp., 2,001 employees
Empire Health Services, 1,973 employees
Spokane County, 1,910 employees
U.S. Federal Government, 1,592 employees
U.S. Postal Service, 1,294

Kootenai County top employers:
Hagadone Hospitality, 1,500 employees
Kootenai Medical Center, 1,200 employees
North Idaho College, 1,034 employees
Coeur d'Alene School District #271, 838 employees
Kootenai Rehab Center, 750 employees
U.S. Government, 655 employees
Kootenai County, 561 employees
GTE Northwest, 380 employees
Coldwater Creek, Inc., 375 employees
Silver Lake Mall, 300 employees

Famous sons and daughters

Spokane area: Former House Speaker Tom Foley, Bing Crosby, Sherman Alexie (Spokane/
Coeur d'Alene Indian writer)
Idaho: Lana Turner (actress) from Wallace
Sacagawea (Shoshone woman born in present-day Idaho)

Chamber of Commerce (phone number and address)

Spokane Area Chamber of Commerce
801 West Riverside Avenue
Spokane, WA 99201
Tel: (509) 624-1393
Fax: (509) 747-0077
E-mail: info@chamber.spokane.net
Website: www.spokanechamber.org/

Coeur d'Alene Area Chamber of Commerce
P.O. Box 850
1621 N. 3rd Street
Coeur d'Alene, ID 83816
Tel: (208) 664-3194

Fax: (208) 667-9338
E-mail: info@coeurdalenechamber.com
Website: www.coeurdalenechamber.com

Greater Sandpoint Chamber of Commerce
P.O. Box 928
Sandpoint, ID 83864
Tel: (208) 263-2161
E-mail: chamber@netw.com
Website: www.sandpoint.org/chamber/

Wallace Chamber of Commerce
P.O. Box 1167
Wallace, ID 83873
Tel: (208) 753-7151

Kellogg Chamber of Commerce
608 Bunker Ave.
Kellogg, ID 83837
Tel: (208) 784-0821
Fax: (208) 783-4343
E-mail: Kellogg@nidlink.com
Website: www.kellogg-id.org/index.htm

Public transportation

Spokane Transit Authority (STA) operates buses in the Spokane/Spokane Valley area.
Adult/child fare is $.75
Over age 65 or disabled, fare is $.35
STA also operates a paratransit service that offers door-to-door pickup and delivery for
    qualified people who cannot ride the regular bus. Fare is $.35.
Spokane International Airport has flights from Delta, Horizon, Alaska, Southwest,
    United, and Northwest airlines.
Amtrak serves Spokane; the Empire Builder train departs for points east and west
    sometime between 1 and 3 A.M. daily.

Military bases

Fairchild Air Force Base (10 miles west of Spokane)

Driving laws (seat belts, car seats, speed limits, wipers/headlights, HOV lanes, etc.)

Washington:
Seat belts required for all passengers in all seats
Children younger than one year or less than 20 lbs. must be in a rear-facing child seat
Children 1-3 years or 20-40 lbs. must be in a rear or forward facing child seat
Children 4-5 years or 50-60 lbs. must be in a child booster seat
Adult safety belts permissible for children 6-15 years and over 60 lbs.

Speed limits
Rural interstates: 70
Urban interstates: 60
Other limited access roads: 55
Fines are doubled for speeding in road construction zones

All motorcycle riders must wear helmets
Studded tires are legal in Washington State from November 1 through March 31
    (unless dates changed by Washington DOT, depending on weather)
No HOV lanes in this area
Headlights must be on one hour before sunset and one hour after sunrise.

Idaho:
Seat belts are required for people ages 4 and up in the front seat
Children ages 3 and younger or less than 40 lbs. must be in an approved child restraint
New residents must get an Idaho driver's license within 90 days.

Speed limits
Rural interstates: 75
Urban interstates: 65
Other limited access roads: 65

Motorcycle riders under age 18 must wear helmets. Riders 18 and older are not required to wear helmets.
Studded tires are legal from October 1 to April 15.
No HOV lanes in this area

Alcohol laws (age, DUI limit, buy on Sundays, bars open til, buy in supermarkets, etc.)

Idaho:
DUI limit: .08
Age limit: 21
Only state-run stores can sell liquor by bottle. They can be open Monday through Saturday, no restriction on hours. Sunday sales prohibited.
Retail stores may sell beer and wine Monday through Sunday, 6 A.M. until 1 A.M.
Bars/taverns may sell beer and wine Monday through Sunday 6 A.M. until 1 A.M.
Bars/taverns may sell liquor Monday through Saturday, 10 A.M. until 1 A.M.

Washington:
DUI limit: .08
Age limit: 21
State liquor stores closed on Sunday. Hours vary by store; most in Spokane open 10 A.M. to 6 P.M. or 11 A.M. to 7 P.M.
Retail stores can sell beer/wine 6 A.M. until 2 A.M.
Bars/taverns can sell alcohol Monday through Sunday 6 A.M. until 2 A.M.

Daily newspapers

Spokesman-Review (has Spokane and North Idaho editions)
Coeur d'Alene Press

Sales tax (how much and on what goods) (Room tax/meal tax/etc.)

Spokane County
Sales tax: 8.1%
Exempt categories: drugs, groceries, medical services
Lodging tax: 2%

Kootenai, Shoshone, and Bonner counties
Sales tax: 5%
Exempt categories: drugs, medical services
Lodging tax: 2%

Time/Temp phone numbers

Current local time/temperature: (509) 324-8800 x1234

Getting Here, Getting Around

Spokane and north Idaho are a little bit out of the way, but we can still be reached by air, rail, and road. As the largest city within an almost 300-mile radius, Spokane is the transportation hub for the Inland Northwest.

Winter weather sometimes makes things difficult; highway travelers from Seattle have to cross Snoqualmie Pass to get to this side of the Cascades. From Montana travelers must cross both Lookout and Fourth of July Passes in Idaho to get to Coeur d'Alene. And winter fog sometimes slows down air travel at the Spokane International Airport. Still, winter storms don't usually last too long, the roads get cleared, and travel resumes.

Unless you're here for winter sports, summer is the best time to visit for sightseeing. Spokane has an efficient bus system and north Idaho is developing one, but you'll need a car to see outlying areas. Car rental companies abound, and it's fairly easy to find your way around.

The Inland Northwest also presents wonderful opportunities to use human-powered transport. The downtown areas of all our cities are great for walking, and you can ride a bike all the way from Spokane to Coeur d'Alene on a paved trail. Hiking trails and mountain bike trails cover the mountains, and canoes and kayaks can be used on most of our rivers and lakes.

Roadways

Interstate 90 is our main thoroughfare; it leads into Spokane from the west, goes through the Spokane Valley, into Idaho, through Post Falls and Coeur d'Alene, over Fourth of July Pass and through the Silver Valley, and on into Montana. Unfortunately, we don't yet have a freeway running north and south, although Spokane has one in the planning stages. I-90 has seen major construction work in recent years; it seems like as soon as one project is finished another is begun. Be alert for possible traffic slowdowns anywhere between Spokane and the Post Falls/Coeur d'Alene area.

In Spokane, two major roadways are Division Street, which runs north/south and divides the city into eastern and western halves, and Sprague Avenue, which runs east/west and is the north and south dividing line. All city addresses begin at these two streets, so for instance you would know that 500 North Monroe is five blocks north of Sprague Avenue. One quirk you many notice in older listings of Spokane addresses: they used to be written with the direction before the number, as in East 1300 Rockwell. The post office objected, saying that made it

Insiders' Tip

If you're traveling on I-90 into Idaho from Washington or vice versa, be sure to stop at the Visitor Information Centers on each side of the border for maps and brochures covering many of the local attractions.

hard for their machines to read our addresses, so now most of us write our addresses the conventional way, with the number first.

Division Street is also Highway 395, which heads north out of Spokane to Deer Park, Chewelah, and the Canadian border. On North Division, past Francis Avenue, Highway 2 branches off to the right (this is called the North Division "Y") to Newport. Sprague Avenue is the alternate I-90 business route through Spokane, and it is sometimes faster than the freeway when construction narrows the freeway to one lane. Another major east/west route is Trent Avenue, which becomes State Route 290 and goes all the way to Idaho.

Going west from Spokane, Highway 2 is an alternate to I-90. It leads to Fairchild Air Force Base, and from there through farming country to the apple growing area around Wenatchee and across the Cascades on Stevens Pass (often closed in winter) to Seattle.

The main southern route out of Spokane is Highway 195, which is the road to Pullman, home of Washington State University. On football weekends this road can be crowded, and it's two-lane much of the way. This is also the road to Steptoe Butte (see the Attractions chapter).

In north Idaho, the main north/south route is Highway 95, which leads all the way from the Canadian border south to the Boise, Idaho area. It is a main business route in Coeur d'Alene and is lined with shopping malls, stores, and restaurants. Highway 95 leads from Coeur d'Alene to Sandpoint, and it can be slow with traffic. There are four lanes near Coeur d'Alene but it narrows to two lanes the rest of the way; however there are occasional passing lanes. The entry into Sandpoint from the south is beautiful, going across the Long Bridge, which spans the northwest end of Lake Pend Oreille. On the other side of Sandpoint is the turnoff for Schweitzer Mountain Resort.

Our roads take a beating in the winter, with a constant cycle of freezing and thawing, which causes a lot of potholes to develop in the spring. We also allow studded tires in this area, so some roads develop ruts that can be disconcerting to drive on. Maintaining the roads is an ongoing job, and some visitors from milder climates have commented that our roads seem to be in poor condition. However, our winters may be hard on roads but they're easier on people—instead of a winter-long freeze, we get breaks from the icy-cold weather.

Airports

Spokane International Airport
9000 West Airport Drive, Spokane
(509) 455-6455
www.spokaneairports.net

Spokane International is the only major airport in the Inland Northwest. As this area has grown, so has the airport; passenger traffic has increased over one hundred percent since 1991, and the airport is undergoing a major expansion. Non-stop service is available to Minneapolis-St. Paul, Chicago, Denver, Calgary, Oakland, Salt Lake City, San Francisco, and of course Portland and Seattle. Airlines serving Spokane include Air Canada, Alaska, Big Sky, Delta, Horizon, Northwest, Southwest, and United.

All the major car rental agencies service Spokane International, as do buses, hotel shuttles, and taxis. Parking costs $4 a day or $24 a week in the outside shuttle lot, $4.50 a day in the economy lot, and $6.50 a day in the parking garage. The parking complex accepts major credit cards.

Felts Field
6105 East Rutter Avenue, Spokane
(509) 535-9001

If you want to fly into Spokane in your own plane, this is the airport to call. Located in Spokane at the north end of Fancher Way, Felts Field is an active general aviation airport. It was Spokane's municipal airport in the '30s and '40s, and was also the first home of the Washington Air National Guard. The terminal building and several others are listed on the National Register of Historic Places.

Coeur d'Alene Airport
11401 Airport Drive, Hayden Lake
(208) 772-7838

There is a small airport serving private aircraft in Hayden Lake, just north of Coeur d'Alene. It is planning for expansion and hopes to offer scheduled passenger service in the next few years. Currently, north Idaho residents use Spokane International for passenger flights.

Buses

Spokane Transit Authority
1230 West Boone, Spokane
(509) 325-6000 or (509) 328-RIDE for schedule information
www.spokanetransit.com

The Spokane Transit Authority, known as STA, provides fixed route buses, paratransit for the elderly and disabled, and ride share/vanpools. Fares are very reasonable compared to many cities: children ages 6-18 and adults pay $.75, while up to three children ages 5 and under can ride free with a person paying full fare. Ages 65 and older and qualifying disabled pay $.35, and the paratransit vans, which provide door to door service, also cost only $.35. (For more information about transportation services for the elderly, see the chapter on Retirement.)

The STA hub is the Plaza, located in downtown Spokane on Wall Street, between Sprague and Riverside. The showpiece transportation center was completed in 1995 and has shops, a Burger King restaurant, and a police substation. At the Plaza you can buy bus passes and tokens, get route maps, and catch a bus anywhere in Spokane.

North Idaho Community Express
137 Spruce, Coeur d'Alene
(208) 664-9769 in Coeur d'Alene
(208) 263-7287 in Sandpoint

Also known as NICE, the Community Express serves all of north Idaho. It operates 33 vehicles on both fixed routes and curb-to-curb for those with special needs. Constantly growing, NICE plans to connect with the Spokane Transit Authority to form a regional network.

Greyhound
221 West First Avenue, Spokane
(509) 747-3766
www.greyhound.com

The Greyhound terminal, which is in the same building as the Amtrak station, provides full service ticketing, baggage, and package express service. It is open 24-hours a day. From the station, Greyhound provides eleven departures daily to Seattle, Portland, Ellensburg, Missoula, Butte, and Billings.

Northwest Trailways
4711 South Ben Franklin Lane, Spokane
(800) 366-6975

Northwest Trailways (NWL) provides scheduled and charter service linking cities and towns around the northwest. There is daily service between Spokane and Wenatchee, Omak, Oroville, Winthrop, Everett, Seattle, Tacoma, and Pullman in Washington, and Moscow, Lewiston, and Boise in Idaho.

Trains

Amtrak
221 West First Avenue, Spokane
(509) 624-5144
Railroad Avenue, Sandpoint
www.amtrak.com

If you don't mind arriving in the middle of the night, the train might be a fun way to get here. Amtrak's Empire Builder train serves Spokane, but it arrives around midnight and departs between 1 and 3 A.M. The station building is open 24 hours but only comes to life during train arrival and departure times. It offers ticket sales, checked baggage, and full accessibility for people in wheelchairs.

The station in Sandpoint is unstaffed, but you can catch the Empire Builder there also. Trains arrive and depart just before midnight.

Taxis and Shuttles

Most Spokane hotels and motor inns offer free airport shuttle service, and there are commercial services as well. Taxi service is available 24 hours a day in Spokane, Coeur d'Alene, and Sandpoint. Unlike larger metropolitan areas, our cabs are dispatched to most fares; don't expect to hail a cab from the street.

Spokane Cab
Spokane
(509) 568-8000

Providing 24-hour service, Spokane's white and green cabs can take you anywhere around town, as well as Fairchild Air Force Base and the airport. Posted fare from the airport to downtown Spokane is $15.

Taxi by Hall
Coeur d'Alene
(208) 664-2424

With round-the-clock service in the Coeur d'Alene area, Taxi by Hall offers senior and handicapped discounts and sightseeing.

Spokane Airport Shuttle
Spokane International Airport, Spokane
(509) 276-9177

With home or hotel pickup seven days a week, 24 hours a day, Spokane Airport Shuttle charges by the trip, so the more people you have the cheaper it is. In addition to serving the airport, they take people to appointments, shopping, and special events. There are discounts for seniors on request.

Moose Express
Coeur d'Alene
(208) 676-1561

Sandpoint
(208) 255-2755

Offering a shuttle service to the Spokane International Airport from Coeur d'Alene, Sandpoint, Bonners Ferry, Hayden Lake, and Post Falls, Moose Express also carries freight around the northwest. Seniors and children may get discounts off regular passenger fares.

Bike Rentals

Bicycling is a leisurely way to see the Panhandle, especially on one of the many bike paths. In addition to the Centennial Trail connecting Coeur d'Alene and Spokane, a paved path begins at the corner of Appleway and Highway 95 in Coeur d'Alene and continues north for 10 miles. Many area roads are safe for riding also.

If you're going to bike anywhere in the Inland Northwest, be sure to wear a helmet. You can rent bikes at several places in Spokane and Coeur d'Alene, and most places will provide helmets also. It's an important safety precaution. Follow the same rules of the road that apply to cars, stopping at lights and stop signs. Be sure to signal turns. Paved trails have their own etiquette. Pedestrians should keep to the right and bikes should pass on the left. It helps to call out "On your left!" as you approach pedestrians to let them know you're coming. Be especially careful around children; they may unexpectedly run or ride their bikes right in front of you. Slow down and check for traffic wherever the trail crosses a roadway.

Bike rentals are primarily offered in the summer months.

Spokane Area

Quinn's Wheel Rentals
Riverfront Park, Spokane
(509) 456-6545

In the summer you can rent every kind of pedaled vehicle from Quinn's. Bicycles are available if you want to see more of the city, but to tool around the trails in Riverfront Park, why not try something different, like a 4-person buggy? Quinn's is located close to the Carousel on the walking bridge.

North Idaho

Island Rentals
200 Sherman Avenue, Coeur d'Alene
(208) 666-1626

Island Rentals has a convenient downtown location, offering mountain bikes ($8 per hour), roller blades ($6 per hour), and mopeds ($15 per hour), as well as various motor boats and jet skis from $55 per hour.

Sandpoint Recreational Rentals
Lakeside Inn, 106 Bridge Street,
Sandpoint
(208) 265-4557

Offering a full line of recreational rental equipment including bicycles, paddle boats, canoes, fishing boats, and jet skis.

U-Save
302 Northwest Boulevard, Coeur d'Alene
(208) 664-1712

U-Save rents various make and model bicycles at $4 per hour with a two-hour minimum, or $15 per day. They also have child carriers.

Tours

Rather than driving or biking on your own, sometimes you can see more by taking a tour. Especially when the tour takes you to places you couldn't go otherwise, like up in the air or out on the water. For a different sightseeing experience, try one of these interesting modes of travel and see our area a new way!

Cavanaughs River Queen
Cavanaughs Templin's Resort, Post Falls
(208) 773-1611

Daily public cruises on the Spokane River begin near the end of May and last through the summer. The basic cruise cost is $12 for adults and $7 for children. You can buy tickets at the Gift Shop in the resort, seven days a week.

Brooks Seaplane Service
City Dock at Independence Point,
Coeur d'Alene
(208) 664-2842

A seaplane ride is a fast but pricey way to tour Idaho's lake country. Soar above Lake Coeur d'Alene and view forested coves, rugged cliffs, islands, and wildlife. Open mainly in summer. A 25-minute tour costs $40 for adults, $20 for children under 12.

Lake Coeur d'Alene Cruises
City Dock at Independence Point,
Coeur d'Alene
(208) 765-4000

See the famous floating golf green and secluded lakeside homes on one of three daily 90-minute cruises during the summer. Also featuring an all-day, shadowy St. Joe River cruise, dinner cruises, and holiday lights cruises in the winter.

Iron Horse
(208) 667-7314

Tour Coeur d'Alene (summer only) on an authentic English double-decker bus. The bus leaves from the North Idaho Museum (at 115 Northwest Blvd. in Coeur d'Alene) at 10 A.M. and 4 P.M. daily. Tours end Labor Day weekend.

North Pend Oreille Valley Lions
Excursion Train
Ione, WA
(509) 442-5466
www.povn.com/byway/train/lions.html

Here's a different way to see the rugged and beautiful scenery of northeastern Washington. On summer weekends, the North Pend Oreille Lions Club operates this rail tour from Ione to Metaline Falls and back. You'll cross deep mountain gorges on high trestles and ride over the historic Box Canyon Dam. Afterward, you can look around Ione or stop and take a walking tour of Metaline Falls, named one of the top small art towns in America. Tours run at 11 A.M., 1 P.M., and 3 P.M., but only on selected weekends so be sure to call first for dates and to make reservations. Tickets are $6.

Biking is a good way to experience the natural beauty of North Idaho. PHOTO: COURTESY COEUR D'ALENE CHAMBER OF COMMERCE

Accommodations

Accommodations in Spokane and the Idaho Panhandle run the gamut from simple rooms in budget motels to elegant and unique bed and breakfast inns and hotels. We have a good selection of both budget and upscale national chains; they're pretty much the same everywhere, so I haven't included reviews of most of them. Instead, you'll find in these pages some of our best, one-of-a-kind places, where you won't forget whether you're in Coeur d'Alene or Cleveland. Experience authentic Inland Northwest hospitality and try one or more of these special places.

As in other parts of the book, I've arranged this chapter starting with Spokane and northeast Washington, then moving into Post Falls and Coeur d'Alene, north to Sandpoint and beyond, and last, to the Silver Valley. Take a look through these listings before you decide where to stay; you may find a place that captures your imagination, a place that will make your stay a memorable one.

Price Code

To make it easy to compare accommodations in northeast Washington and the Idaho Panhandle, I've created a dollar-sign key showing the approximate average cost of a double occupancy room with two double beds for one night during the summer. Peak season is summer, so prices are a bit higher, but winter is growing in popularity too, so rates vary throughout the year. Weekends may be higher, and there will usually be extra charges for more people in the room, efficiency apartments, or pets (when they're allowed). These prices do not include state and local taxes. Unless otherwise noted, all properties accept major credit cards. Reservations are always recommended, especially in the summer. Here is the breakdown:

$	$60 or less
$$	$61–$80
$$$	$81–$125
$$$$	$126 and up

Spokane

Apple Tree Inn
9508 North Division
(509) 466-3020
$

Located near the North Division "Y," where Hwy 2 branches off to Newport and Hwy 395 heads north to Colville, the Apple Tree is close to the Northpointe shopping area with stores like Shopko and Target and many chain restaurants. If you are in Spokane to ski at Mt. Spokane or 49 Degrees North, or prefer to stay away from the downtown area, this is a good choice.

The Apple Tree has 71 rooms, including two and three bedroom units with kitchens. There is a heated outdoor pool, and free continental breakfast for guests.

Best Western Peppertree Airport Inn
3711 South Geiger Blvd.
(509) 624-4655
www.peppertreeinns.com/spokane1.htm
$$-$$$$

This airport motor inn is in a convenient location for people visiting Fairchild Air Force Base, Eastern Washington University, the Boeing facility in Airway Heights, or the new Northern Quest Casino, yet it's only ten minutes from downtown Spokane.

The Peppertree has 100 minisuite guest rooms with microwaves and refrigerators, hair dryers, irons, and ironing boards. Each room has cable television and a VCR, with movie rentals available. There are two phones in each room, each with voice mail and data ports. A pool, spa, and exercise room are next to the restaurant and lounge. For those who cannot manage stairs, an elevator is available for upper floor access, and there are wheelchair-accessible suites. The hotel has a complimentary airport shuttle and offers free parking. To get to the Peppertree, take I-90 to Exit 276.

Fotheringham House Bed & Breakfast
2128 West 2nd Avenue
(509) 838-1891
www.fotheringham.net
$$$

In Spokane's historic Browne's Addition, Fotheringham House has won several awards for historic preservation. When you walk in you'll feel like you've stepped back in time to another era, with the home's traditional Victorian architecture and period furnishings. Each elegant bedroom is furnished with a queen-sized bed covered with an antique quilt. One guest bedroom has a private bath, and the other three share two bathrooms. Hosts Graham and Jackie Johnson deliver freshly brewed coffee or tea to each guest room in the morning, which is followed by a gourmet breakfast in the main floor dining room.

On chilly days, many guests enjoy a cup of tea in front of the fireplace, and in the summer a porch swing awaits. Gardeners and flower lovers will enjoy the 55 varieties of old garden roses, as well as hundreds of other perennials and annuals. Coeur d'Alene Park, Spokane's oldest, is right across the street. Children under twelve are not allowed. Reservations are recommended.

Kempis Hotel Suites
326 West 6th
(509) 747-4321, (888) 236-4321
www.thekempis.com
$$$$

The Kempis was a turn-of-the-century apartment building before renovation. The rich woodwork and hand-painted murals in this European-style boutique hotel add to the charm. In the sunlit atrium a fountain bubbles, and you can sit in antique chairs and enjoy the atmosphere. The Kempis offers 14 unique suites with kitchens and elegant dining areas. You can have your dinner catered right in your room by the hotel's restaurant, the Winged Lion (see the Restaurants chapter for more information). Rooms are furnished with antique furniture and fixtures, but have TVs and VCRs, and air conditioning. Business travelers will appreciate the two line phones, programmable voice mail, and data ports in each suite. Reservations are highly recommended.

Hotel Lusso
North One Post
(509) 747-9750
www.hotellusso.com
$$$$

One of downtown Spokane's elegant boutique hotels, the Hotel Lusso has 48 guest rooms in the historic Whitten and Miller buildings, joined by the beautiful lobby. In addition, the hotel has four large penthouse suites decorated with Italian marble and wood, and featuring gas fireplaces.

All guest rooms have televisions, high speed data ports, ironing boards, and terry cloth robes for guests to use. Complimentary limousine service transports guests to and from the airport and throughout the downtown area for shopping or entertainment. Valet parking is also available.

The Lusso's restaurant, Fugazzi, offers creative and outstandingly prepared dishes. It is open for breakfast Monday through Friday for hotel guests only, and for lunch and dinner Monday through Saturday (see the Restaurants chapter for more information). The Cavallino Lounge has a martini bar, with many unique variations of the classic drink.

Reservations are recommended at the Hotel Lusso. There are special room packages offered throughout the year; call for more information.

Marianna Stoltz House
427 East Indiana
(509) 483-4316, (800) 978-6587
$$-$$$

This classic home was built in 1908 and is listed on the Spokane register of historic homes. Guests have exclusive use of the parlor, dining room, and sitting room, all furnished in period style. There are four guest bedrooms on the second floor, with king, queen, or single beds and private or shared baths. In the morning, guests enjoy a tasty and generous breakfast.

The Marianna Stoltz House is located in the shady Gonzaga University district, close to the Centennial Trail, downtown, and many restaurants and shops. Reservations are recommended.

Shilo Inn
923 3rd Avenue
(509) 535-9000, (800) 222-2244
$$$

This Northwest chain advertises "affordable excellence," and it does offer hotel amenities at a lower price. In Spokane, the Shilo Inn was recently remodeled and is convenient to downtown (though not within walking distance). The hotel has an atrium pool and spa, a fitness center, steam room, and sauna. Rooms have ironing boards, irons, hair dryers, and data ports. A restaurant and lounge are on the premises. Pets are accepted and there is a free airport shuttle to the Spokane International Airport.

Solar World Estates
North E. 20 Pine Ridge Court
(509) 468-1207, (800) 650-6530
1832 S. Lawson, Airway Heights
(509) 244-3535, (800) 650-9484
$$-$$$$

With two locations in the Spokane area, Solar World Estates offers executive suite accommodations by the day, week, or month. Rental sizes range from townhouse apartments to three bedroom homes, with everything furnished including linens and housewares. All utilities are included. Each rental is equipped with cable TVs and VCRs, and on-site laundry facilities are free.

Rental rates vary depending on the size of the accommodations and the length of stay. The rate per day goes down a lot if you're staying for a month. Daily rates range from $114 to $200 for two people, while monthly rates start at $850 and go up to $1400 for a three bedroom house.

WestCoast Grand Hotel at the Park
West 303 North River Drive
(509) 326-8000, (800) 325-4000
$$$-$$$$

Location is what makes this large hotel special—it is right across the river from Riverfront Park and downtown Spokane. Paved walking paths lead right from the hotel, across the river, and through the park to the Imax Theater, Opera House, and other attractions. The hotel has over 400 rooms and 28 large suites, all with Internet access, hair dryers, and irons and ironing boards. Room service is available for all guests. The heated indoor and outdoor pools are popular, and a fitness center will help you stay in shape. The hotel has two restaurants: Windows of the Seasons features fresh seafood and USDA choice beef, while the Atrium Café and Deli specializes in sandwiches and salads. The Park Place Lounge has an outside deck overlooking the Spokane River.

WestCoast Ridpath
515 West Sprague
(509) 838-2711, (800) 325-4000
$$$-$$$$

Although the Ridpath is now owned by the WestCoast hotel chain, it has been in Spokane since the early 1900s and is a downtown landmark. It has 342 guest rooms and over 16,000 square feet of meeting and banquet space. Rooms have TV, high speed Internet access and data ports, hair dryers, ironing boards, and coffeemakers. The hotel has a fitness center and a seasonal rooftop swimming pool. Two restaurants are on the premises, including Ankeny's, one of Spokane's most elegant dining establishments.

The Ridpath offers complimentary transportation to and from the Spokane International Airport, or valet parking for those who are driving. It has room packages for holidays and special events, and shopping packages that include gift certificates at local stores, movie passes, and discount meals. Reservations are recommended.

Newport

Inn at the Lake
581 South Shore Diamond Lake Road
(509) 447-5772, (877) 447-5772
www.povn.com/inatlake/
$$$$

Located 35 miles north of Spokane and eight miles south of Newport, the Inn at the Lake overlooks Diamond Lake. The Inn's four suites all have private bathrooms, cable TV and VCR, and views of the lake. Most suites also have Jacuzzis. In the shared family room there is a 27-inch TV and fireplace, and just outside is an expansive deck with steps down to the lake. A full breakfast is served to guests each morning, and rates also include snacks and drinks. In the winter the Inn offers snowmobile packages, and in summer rents canoes.

The Inn at the Lake accepts adults only. Reservations are recommended. Weekly and monthly rates are available.

Post Falls

Riverbend Inn
4105 West Riverbend Avenue
(208) 773-3583
$$

The Riverbend Inn motel is in a convenient location for auto travelers, just off I-90 via Exit 2 in Idaho. It's right next to the Post Falls Outlets shopping mall, and there are lots of fast food restaurants close by. Rooms are basic but do offer cable television with free movies. An outdoor heated pool is open in the summer.

Coeur d'Alene

Baragar House
316 Military Drive
(208) 664-9125, (800) 615-8422
www.baragarhouse.com
$$$-$$$$

Baragar House is in the historic Fort Sherman residential district of Coeur d'Alene, close to downtown and only about a block from the lake and Centennial Trail. It has three air-conditioned guest rooms, furnished with period antiques. A big, family-style breakfast is served in the dining room, and before breakfast you'll find a coffee tray outside your bedroom door. Baragar House has a parlor for socializing, and guests have use of an indoor spa and sauna.

All of the guest rooms in Baragar House have a professionally applied solar system by Stellar Vision on the ceiling, giving the effect of sleeping under the stars. Rooms also have cable TV and VCRs, and terry cloth robes are provided for guests. Baragar House does not allow smoking inside or pets, and discourages children. Reservations are required. They are open year-round.

Flamingo Motel
718 Sherman Avenue
(208) 664-2159
$$

This small, older motel is nicely kept up and furnished, and it is close to downtown and the lake. It's adjacent to a city park with basketball and tennis courts, and a playground. Cable television is available in all rooms, and some rooms have microwaves and refrigerators or small kitchens. An outdoor heated pool is open in the summer.

Insiders' Tip

Don't forget your camera and binoculars when going for a cruise on Lake Coeur d'Alene. There are beautiful views and birds and wildlife to see.

Baragar House is only a block away from Lake Coeur d'Alene and the Centennial Trail. PHOTO: ELLIE EMMANUEL

Gregory's McFarland House
Bed & Breakfast
601 Foster Avenue
(208) 667-1232, (800) 335-1232, ext. 5
$$$-$$$$

McFarland House has won awards for preservation of the turn-of-the-century home, which was built for Robert Early McFarland, one of Idaho's early Attorneys General. It is lovingly decorated with period furnishings and Gregory family heirlooms, from the foyer to the five guest suites. In the family entertainment room, guests may enjoy watching television, browsing through the library, playing pool, or visiting. A delicious gourmet breakfast is served in the conservatory overlooking the deck and lush yard.

Children over 14 are welcome at McFarland House. A two-night minimum stay is required in the summer high season and on holidays. Rooms have alarm clocks, air conditioning, and robes for guests to use. Reservations are required.

Silver Lake Motel
6160 Sunshine Street
(208) 772-8595
www.slmotel.com
$-$$$

The Silver Lake Motel is located in the north part of Coeur d'Alene, near Silver Lake Mall. It has a convention center on the premises. Rooms have basic furnishings, but some have full-size Jacuzzi hot tubs or kitchens. There is a separate data line to every room, and all have cable television, refrigerators, and microwaves. A heated outdoor pool is open in the summer, and the motel offers a tanning salon, exercise facility, coin-operated laundry, and video game room. To get there, take Hwy 95 north from I-90; the motel is 2.2 miles north on a side road next to Hwy 95.

Wolf Lodge Creek Bed & Breakfast
715 North Wolf Lodge Creek Road
(208) 667-5902, (800) 919-9653
www.wolflodge.com
$$$-$$$$

Sixteen miles outside of Coeur d'Alene, Wolf Lodge is a secluded hideaway deep in the forest. It features suites and rooms furnished with log or brass beds and down comforters. Guests gather around the stone fireplace or in the outdoor hot tub, hike in the woods, or snowshoe in winter. A hearty breakfast buffet with homemade breads and muffins is served every morning. The owners will also make up picnic baskets or sack lunches on request.

Hayden Lake

Clark House
East 4550 South Hayden Lake Road
(208) 772-3470, (800) 765-4593
$$$-$$$$

The Clark House is the renovated F. Lewis Clark Mansion, also called Honeysuckle Lodge. Its 12-acre estate sits on the shores of Hayden Lake, surrounded by forest. It was built as a summer home by F. Lewis Clark and his wife in 1910, and at the time was the most expensive home in Idaho. Its 15,000 square feet were filled with Italian marble, Oriental rugs, and crystal chandeliers and fine furnishings from Europe. The estate even had its own zoo. However, in 1914 Lewis mysteriously disappeared and his wife was unable to hold on to the family fortune. In 1922 the bank took over the estate, and in the ensuing years it was home to church groups, homeless boys, the U.S. Navy, and a restaurant. By 1988 it was in such poor condition that it was scheduled to be burned down in a training exercise for the local fire department.

In 1989, the current owners, Monty Danner and Rod Palmer, bought the estate and began renovations. Today it is operated as an elegant bed-and-breakfast inn. Rooms are furnished with queen or king feather beds. Some have extra-large Roman tubs and fireplaces. The inn also has a private veranda overlooking Hayden Lake and a reservation-only restaurant that serves six-course gourmet dinners.

Children under 12 and pets are not allowed at Clark House. There is no smoking allowed inside the building. Reservations are highly recommended.

Sandpoint

Blue Heron Bed and Breakfast
1026 Glengary Bay Road, Sagle
(208) 263-2809, (800) 504-2455
$$$

The Blue Heron is owned by retired professor Hal Hargreaves, and his wife, Ruth, who is a retired nurse. After traveling the world, they chose to build a house on a bluff overlooking Lake Pend Oreille and Gamlin Lake, and opened the Blue Heron, with two guest rooms. It's a beautiful, modern house with lots of wood, stone and glass, and views all around. They offer refreshments by the fire in winter, or outside in the summer. Guests may use the indoor hot tub in a windowed room with views of the forest. In the summer, there's swimming in the lake.

The Blue Heron is right next to the Gamlin Lake Special Management Area, an area set aside for wildlife preservation. Hiking, birdwatching, fishing, and canoeing are all nearby activities. Guests have a choice of a full, hearty breakfast or a continental breakfast and sack lunch. Children under 12 are not allowed unless one party is reserving both rooms, and pets are not allowed. The Blue Heron is smoke-free. Reservations are required.

The turn off to the Blue Heron is five miles south of Sandpoint on Hwy 95. From there, it is 13 miles east, toward the shore of Lake Pend Oreille.

Edgewater Resort Motor Inn
56 Bridge Street
(208) 263-3194, (800) 635-2534
$$$

The Edgewater's beachfront location is perfect for summer water activities. In addition, it's only a block from Sandpoint's main downtown shopping district. There are 55 guest rooms, all with a private balcony or patio overlooking Lake Pend Oreille. Rooms also have air conditioning and cable television. Jacuzzi and fireplace suites are available.

The Edgewater has a sauna and whirlpool, and is close to sightseeing, boat rentals, and shopping. Their Beach House restaurant and lounge offer regional cuisine, and in nice weather you can dine outside on the deck. Reservations are suggested.

Lakeside Inn
106 Bridge Street
(208) 263-3717, (800) 543-8126
$$-$$$

The Lakeside Inn sits at the edge of Lake Pend Oreille, adjacent to City Beach. It's only a block to downtown Sandpoint, with it's many shops and restaurants. It offers complimentary boat moorage and docks, rooms with balconies and lake views, an outdoor hot tub, sauna and spa, kitchen suites, guest laundry facilities, and on-site lake cruises and boat rentals. A complimentary breakfast is served each morning.

Schweitzer Mountain Bed & Breakfast
110 Crystal Court
(208) 265-8080, (888) 550-8080
www.schweitzermtnbb.com/
$$$-$$$$

This lovely lodge on Schweitzer Mountain has a Bavarian look and is an especially nice place for snow lovers to stay. Both downhill and cross-country skiers will like the ski-in and ski-out access. In addition, there are horse-drawn sleigh rides, sledding, tubing, and snowmobiling available close by. After a day on the slopes guests can come back and enjoy a soak in the hot tub overlooking the ski area. Those who'd rather just hang out can curl up by the fire with a book or enjoy a game of pool or checkers in the game room. In the summer there is hiking, mountain biking, or shopping in Sandpoint.

Schweitzer Mountain has five guest rooms with queen- or king-size beds, plus a suite with a loft sleeping area. A gourmet breakfast is served each morning.

Bonners Ferry

Bear Creek Lodge
5952 Highway 95
(208) 267-7268
$-$$

Bonners Ferry is a small town north of Sandpoint, near the Canadian border. Located close to downtown, Bear Creek Lodge is a very nice, modern log motel with a hot tub for guest use, and a restaurant specializing in Northwest cuisine, including steaks, chops, and fresh seafood. Motel rooms are comfortably furnished in northwest style. A complimentary breakfast is served to motel guests.

Best Western Kootenai River Inn
7160 Plaza Street
(208) 267-8511
$$$

The Kootenai River Inn is just two blocks from downtown shopping, and has a

Insiders' Tip

On warm summer days at the lake or river, be sure to use a sunscreen or other sun protection. Our weather may not be as hot as Arizona or Florida but the sun can burn just as badly.

The Kingston 5 Ranch bed-and-breakfast offers spacious rooms with balconies overlooking the Idaho countryside. PHOTO: COURTESY KINGSTON 5 RANCH

casino on the premises. It overlooks the Kootenai River, which is known for fishing and rafting. There is a heated indoor pool, steam room, and fitness center, and an adjacent restaurant and lounge. Babysitting services are available, and kids under 12 stay free. Rooms have cable television and hair dryers, and each room has a balcony with views of the mountains.

Paradise Valley Inn
300 Eagle Way
(208) 267-4180, (888) 447-4180
$$$-$$$$

This secluded inn overlooks an expansive valley and the Kootenai National Wildlife Refuge. It's about 10 minutes outside of Bonners Ferry. The lodge has five luxury suites, all with private bath and lovely views, which sleep from two to five people. In addition, there are two private cabins sleeping from two to six. Lodge rates include a hearty breakfast. By special arrangement the chef can prepare picnic or box lunches or gourmet dinners using fresh local ingredients.

This isolated area offers a multitude of outdoor activities year-round. The inn can arrange horseback riding, golf, mountain biking, kayak touring, rafting, jet ski rentals, cross-country and downhill skiing, and snowmobile touring for guests. Many people enjoy visiting in the great room, relaxing in the spa, or sitting on the deck and taking in the view.

Silver Valley

Beale House Bed & Breakfast
107 Cedar Street, Wallace
(208) 752-7251, (888) 752-7151
$$$-$$$$

Beale House was originally the home of mining attorney Charles Beale and his family. Hosts Jim and Linda See bought Beale House in 1987, restored it, and opened a bed-and-breakfast. They maintain contact with Beale family members, as well as members of the other three families

Enjoy a hearty breakfast Idaho-style. PHOTO: COURTESY KINGSTON 5 RANCH

who owned the home, and can tell you all about the history of the house. Guests are also welcome to view the historic photos collected from former owners. Each of the five guest rooms are unique—with a fireplace, balcony, or other feature. The house is furnished with period antiques.

Downtown Wallace is close by, for shopping or sightseeing. Guests can relax in the backyard hot tub, or visit on the front porch. Children under twelve are not allowed. A friendly cat lives in the house. Reservations are recommended.

Best Western Wallace Inn
100 Front Street, Wallace
(208) 752-1252, (800) 643-2386
$$$-$$$$

The Wallace Inn sits at the western edge of Wallace, but all the town amenities are within walking distance. The 63 guest rooms have cable television, data ports, and alarm clocks. A nice indoor heated pool and whirlpool are complemented by a sauna and steam room and exercise facility. The inn also has its own restaurant and lounge.

Jameson Restaurant, Saloon, and Inn
Corner of 6th and Pine Streets, Wallace
(208) 556-6000, (800) 556-2544
$$$-$$$$

The historic Jameson Hotel in downtown Wallace has six rooms for rent on the third floor, each furnished in turn-of-the-century Victorian style. The rooms do not have private bathrooms, but there are two "water closets" and two bathing rooms for guests on the third floor. One of the rooms is allegedly haunted by Maggie the ghost, an 1890s guest who liked her third floor room so much she never left.

The cost of a room at the Jameson includes a full country breakfast in the Jameson's restaurant. The dining room is open to the public for lunch and dinner, and the saloon is a lively place to spend the

Sun on the deck of the Kingston 5 Ranch bed-and-breakfast beckons to guests. PHOTO: COURTESY KINGSTON 5 RANCH

evening. All downtown Wallace attractions and shops are within walking distance.

Kingston 5 Ranch Bed & Breakfast
P.O. Box 130, Kingston
(208) 682-4862, (800) 254-1852
www.k5ranch.com/index.htm
$$$-$$$$

The Kingston 5 Ranch lies in a picturesque valley not far from I-90. In the large, modern farmhouse, private suites for guests offer fireplaces, jetted tubs, and private outdoor spas. Terry robes and slippers are available for each guest to use, and in-room refrigerators are stocked with complimentary juice and soda. Guests may also help themselves to the coffee and tea bar, a bottomless cookie bar, or a fruit basket. A healthy and hearty gourmet breakfast is served each morning.

The ranch has ski packages in winter and special deals and packages at other times of the year. Rental bikes are available for the Hiawatha Trail (see the Recreation chapter for more details) or just to explore country roads. Kellogg is only 10 minutes away, and Coeur d'Alene, with excellent dinner restaurants, is only 25 minutes away on the freeway.

Reservations are required. To get to the ranch, take I-90 east from Coeur d'Alene to the Silver Valley and turn off on exit 43.

The Mansion on the Hill Bed & Breakfast
105 South Division Street, Kellogg
(208) 786-4455, (877) 943-4455
www.mansionbnb.com
$$$-$$$$

The Mansion sits on land originally owned by Noah Kellogg, who lived there with his family from 1893 to 1897. The current house was built in 1944, and was restored in 1998. The main home has two guest suites, and there are also two beautifully furnished guest cottages nearby. The comfortable common area has a river rock fireplace, television, and games. A delicious breakfast is served each morning. Packages are available for skiers, or with massages and steam baths at Kellogg's Reflections Salon and Day Spa. Children are welcome in Carla's Cottage only. Reservations are recommended.

Guest Ranches and Resorts

As in other parts of the book, I've arranged this chapter starting with Washington and ending with Idaho. Guest ranches and resorts are more plentiful in north Idaho, which is an up and coming Western vacation destination. Eastern Washington is not as well known but has several ranches and resorts worth visiting. Priest Lake, in northern Idaho, has been a favorite family vacation destination for generations, and its resorts are often booked a year ahead of time for the summer months.

Washington

Bull Hill Ranch & Resort
3738 Bull Hill Road, Kettle Falls
(509) 732-6135, (877) 285-5445
www.bullhill.com

Owned by the Guglielmino family, this guest ranch is part of an old, working cattle ranch. You can enjoy a true Western experience here, especially if you're interested in unlimited horseback riding and fly fishing, the ranch's specialties. Bull Hill has more than 40 horses, and they'll give you one that matches your riding experience and ability. For beginning riders, they offer lessons and trail rides, while more experienced riders can participate in cattle drives. In addition, you can try trap shooting, archery, fishing, hiking, cross-country skiing, and swimming, all included in the daily rate. For an additional charge there are guided river fishing trips, snowmobile rentals, downhill skiing, and airplane tours.

The ranch has seven comfortable cabins for guests. The cookhouse serves as the meeting place for meals, bar service, planning, and entertainment. It overlooks the ranch valley. Two hot tubs are available for guest use, and there is a shower house and laundry nearby. In the horse barn, guests learn how to groom and saddle up their own horses.

Summer rates at Bull Hill are $155 per person, per night, and $85 for kids ages 5-12. This includes lodging, meals, ranch activities, horseback lessons and riding, fishing, and cattle drives. The summer season runs from May through October. The ranch is also open for a winter season during January and February.

K Diamond K Guest Ranch
15661 Hwy. 21 South, Republic
(509) 775-3536, (888) 345-5355
www.kdiamondk.com

The K Diamond K is a family-owned, working cattle ranch. Located in rolling hill

Insiders' Tip

Many area resorts recommend making summer bookings as far ahead as a year. It is impossible to know what the weather will be like a year ahead of time, but August seems to bring more consistently nice weather to north Idaho and northeastern Washington than June or July. However, sunny weather isn't guaranteed!

country 125 miles north of Spokane, the ranch offers a real western experience. It is open year-round, and offers ranch activities that vary with the seasons. Riding lessons and horseback rides are very popular from April through October. You can fish or pan for gold in the river that runs through the ranch, hike, or go birdwatching. There are hayrides and roping lessons. In the spring calves and foals are born, there's a spring roundup, branding, and the timber harvest. In the fall, guests can watch or participate in the autumn roundup, hay harvest, and hunting. During the winter, help with winter hay feeding and snowshoe, cross-country ski, or snowmobile. There are maintenance activities year-round for guests who want to participate.

Lodging is right in the log ranch house, which offers four bedrooms and two bathrooms for guests. Meals are served with the family. Rates include lodging, three meals per day, riding, and all ranch facilities. From April through October, adults are $115 per person per night, and children ages 3 to 5 are $65. From November through March the rate is $75 per person per night. Horseback riding isn't available in the winter.

Idaho

BC & M Houseboat Vacations
Hope
(877) 909-BOAT
www.galaxymall.com/entertainment/ vacation

For an alternative vacation stay, you can rent a houseboat on Lake Pend Oreille for three, four, or seven days. Starting out in the small town of Hope, you can explore the 43 miles of the lake, fish, swim, lie in the sun, read, and generally enjoy a relaxing vacation. Houseboats sleep either eight or ten people, and have full kitchens, bathrooms, living areas, and full-length sundecks on top. Each boat has a swim ladder and waterslide for even more fun. The family-owned business will show you how to operate everything and give you cruise charts and a fish finder.

During July and August, the high season, weekly rentals are $1,250 for the smaller boat and $1,700 for the larger one. Weekend rentals are $795 and $995. Low season rates, during May, June, and September, are $100 to $200 less.

Best Western Templin's Resort
414 East First Avenue, Post Falls
(208) 773-1611, (800) 283-6754

Templin's overlooks the Spokane River in a beautiful location with its own beach and marina. An indoor heated pool, fitness center, and spa are available for guests to use. Play tennis, or take lessons from the staff tennis pro, or rent a boat and explore the river. Mallards restaurant offers gourmet selections and a popular Sunday brunch, and there are tables out on the deck in nice weather. The lounge offers live entertainment on Friday and Saturday nights.

Guest rooms offer cable television and movies, refrigerators and microwaves, and room service. Children under 18 stay free at Templins, and a shuttle is available to the Spokane International Airport. During the summer high season, rooms for two adults range from about $100 to $120 per night.

Coeur d'Alene Resort
(208) 765-4000, (800) 688-5253
www.cdaresort.com

The award-winning Coeur d'Alene Resort is one of the top resorts in the northwest. It receives the AAA Four Diamond Award and Mobil Four Star Award annually, has been rated highly by readers of *Conde Nast Traveler Magazine,* and has won an award as a top facility for meetings. The resort's incredible golf course has also won numerous awards. If you can afford it, you can't go wrong staying here.

Resort amenities include four restaurants (including Beverly's, detailed in the Restaurants chapter); a lounge with live music Tuesday through Saturday; a full service spa with massages, facials, aromatherapy, wraps, and a hair and nail salon; a fitness center with racquetball courts; tennis courts; shopping; and a kid's camp. The golf course has the famous floating green (for more details, see the Recreation chapter). Lake cruises leave from the resort's own dock. Parks, beaches, and downtown shopping and restaurants are all within walking distance.

Accommodations range from standard hotel rooms to deluxe suites with fireplaces, lanais, and separate sitting areas. All rooms include minibars, hair dryers, robes, irons, movies, and video games. Most offer high-speed Internet access. During the summer, high season room rates are between $150 and $300 per night. In the winter (except during the holidays) rates may be half that. Executive and penthouse suites range from $600 to $2,500 per night. The resort offers various seasonal packages that can be a good deal; check the website under accommodations for more information.

You can reserve van transportation to and from the Spokane Airport to the Coeur d'Alene Resort by calling the resort.

The fee is $40 per person round trip. Guests may park in the resort's parking garage for $12 per night.

Elkins Resort
404 Elkins Road, Nordman
(208) 443-2432
www.elkinsresort.com

Elkins has been a favorite Priest Lake resort since 1932. Its beautiful, rustic lodge and cedar log cabins are a fun place to spend a week in the summer. Cabins have stone fireplaces, fully equipped kitchens, bed linens, and firewood. Activities here include swimming and boating, fishing, hiking, mountain biking, snowmobiling, and snow shoeing. The resort offers packages that include cabins plus boat or snowmobile rental.

Elkins' acclaimed restaurant is open for breakfast, lunch, and dinner, and you'll find interesting choices at each meal. (See the Restaurants chapter for more information.) Cabins are rented weekly from mid-July through the end of August, and range from $835 to $2,225

Hill's Resort, overlooking Priest Lake, is open all year. PHOTO: NICK EMMANUEL

per week. Daily rates during the rest of the year (there is a two-night minimum) are between $100 and $305. The largest, most expensive cabin sleeps 14.

Grandview Resort
Reeder Bay, Priest Lake
(208) 443-2433
www.gvr.com

The Grandview Resort has been owned by the Benscoter family for over 30 years. It's open year-round, although summer is the high season. Guests can swim in Priest Lake or in the heated pool, fish, go hiking, mountain biking, huckleberry picking, or just relax. Accommodations are in the lodge or in cabins. The restaurant serves steaks, lobster, chicken, and hamburgers, and Saturday features a prime rib dinner. Huckleberry daiquiris are the specialty in the lounge. Complimentary boat dockage is available for guests.

Rooms in the lodge range from $75 to $95 per night. Some have views of the lake. Rustic cottages sleep from 4 to 10 people and cost between $135 and $195 per night, or $825 to $1,395 per week. Bed linens, towels, kitchen utensils, and firewood are provided. Pets cannot be accommodated.

Hidden Creek Ranch
7600 East Blue Lake Rd., Harrison
(208) 689-3209, (800) 446-3833
www.hiddencreek.com

Hidden Creek Ranch is set in an idyllic valley surrounded by 350 square miles of national forest land. During the fall and spring the ranch offers adult-only weeks, and during summer and winter family vacations are offered. The focus throughout the year is on providing a relaxing getaway where guests can leave the hectic pace of modern life behind.

Horseback riding is one of the main attractions at the ranch, and it gets a lot of attention. You get your own horse for the week, and they have horses for every type of rider, from absolute beginners to pros. They offer riding instruction, and teach you how to care for your horse. There are different types of rides and pack trips to choose from during the week.

Other outdoor activities available during the summer include fly-fishing (including instruction), hiking, archery, lake fishing, mountain biking, volleyball, a ropes course, and a climbing tower. During the winter you can choose from snowmobiling, snowshoeing, cross-country skiing, downhill skiing, and snowboarding. In summer and winter, kid's programs include horseback riding, nature awareness, hiking, crafts, roping, drumming, and seasonal outdoor activities.

Accommodations are in the 7,000 square foot lodge or in modern log cabins. Outdoor hot tubs are great for soaking sore muscles after a long day of riding, and the swimming pond is a good place to cool off in the summer. There is also a fitness center and laundry facilities. Rates for the six-night summer programs are $1,969 for adults and $1,615 for children ages 3-11. In the winter, a four night program costs $1,086 for adults and $884 for children. Rates include accommodations, meals, and almost all activities (just a few things, like trap shooting and massages are extra). The ranch can pick you up and drop you off at the Spokane International Airport for $75 per person.

Hill's Resort
4777 West Lakeshore Road, Priest Lake
(208) 443-2551

One of the Inland Northwest's most-loved resorts, Hill's sits on the shores of Priest

Lake and is open all year. Hill's has been chosen by *Better Homes and Gardens* and *Family Circle* magazines as an outstanding family resort, and some families have been coming here since the resort opened in 1946.

Rustic buildings lie along the shores of Priest Lake in a very peaceful and relaxing setting. Accommodations are large and comfortable. Most are lakefront, and sleep from two to ten. Many have fireplaces, which are wonderful in fall, winter, and spring, and many also have fully equipped kitchens. Facilities include tennis courts, mountain bike and cross-country ski trails, swimming beaches, a marina with gas for boats, ski docks, and a laundry room. There are boats, canoes, bikes, and skis for rent. The outstanding restaurant serves such classics as baby back ribs, chops, and shrimp, and is known for huckleberry creations. There is a nice lounge next to the restaurant with a full-service bar, live and recorded music, and a small dance floor.

In the summer, Hill's high season, most accommodations are rented by the week (the exceptions are single bedroom units for two people). During the other seasons, both weekly and nightly rates are available. Rates range from $80 for a two-person unit for one night to deluxe lakefront units with three bedrooms for $2,225 per week. Most weekly rates fall in the $1,000 to $1,500 range. Reservations should be made as far ahead of time as possible.

Red Fir Resort
1147 Red Fir Road, Hope
(208) 264-5287

Red Fir Resort is a quiet place to get away from it all and enjoy the peace and quiet of a Pend Oreille lakefront home. The "cabins" are really homes, and come fully equipped for your stay. The resort has a marina for guests who bring their own boat. Cabin rates range from $85 to $155 per night, and they sleep from four to eight people. Each cabin has a private

Golf is a prime summer attraction for many resort-goers. PHOTO: COURTESY SANDPOINT CHAMBER OF COMMERCE

deck and barbecue grill, and there are laundry facilities for guests. It's a 30-minute drive into Sandpoint for groceries.

Western Pleasure Guest Ranch
1413 Upper Gold Creek, Sandpoint
(208) 263-9066
www.westernpleasureranch.com

Experience the real thing on this third generation cattle ranch north of Sandpoint. Horseback riding is the main activity here, although they are close enough to Sandpoint and Lake Pend Oreille to take advantage of the activities there. With its scenic location at the foot of the Cabinet and Selkirk Mountains, Western Pleasure Ranch offers breathtaking rides, or just a quiet getaway.

During the summer, a three night package including lodging, three meals, and daily rides is $450 per person for adults and $305 per person for children ages six to twelve. A five night package is $700 and $475, respectively. If you have at least four people, you can book an overnight "Cowboy" ride for $130 per person, or just go riding for two hours for $35 per person. There are week long riding camps during the summer for kids ages 10-16 that end with a barbecue dinner and horse show put on by the campers. Riding camps cost $350 per person.

The Coeur d'Alene Resort is a classy yet comfortable destination hotel. PHOTO: COURTESY COEUR D'ALENE RESORT

Camping

Camping is "wildly" popular in the Inland Northwest. On Memorial Day, 4th of July, and Labor Day weekends, you had better have a campground reservation well ahead of time for any but the most remote sites. State parks in both Washington and Idaho, especially those on a lake or river, tend to stay pretty full on the weekends all summer long. South and west of Spokane is dry, desert-like country where you can be fairly certain of sunny summer days. North of Spokane and all of north Idaho are a different story. You may experience the most beautiful, sunny weather you've ever seen, or it may be overcast and raining. This is true throughout the summer, so it's best to come prepared with rain gear and, especially, a rain-proof tent. There's nothing worse than waking up to a soaked-through tent and sleeping bag.

Even when the weather is hot and sunny during the day, the temperature in this part of the country drops considerably at night. You may not notice it if you're staying in a motel, but when you're camping you will. Dress in layers so you can add or remove items of clothing depending on the temperature.

You may encounter mosquitoes when camping in the Inland Northwest, especially if we've had a wet spring. In most areas they aren't too bad, but bringing along mosquito repellent is always a good idea. If you choose to camp in the late fall or early spring you'll avoid most of the mosquitoes, although you'll have to put up with chilly weather in the mornings and evenings. Some camping and hiking areas are closed in the fall for hunting.

Some campgrounds in our area are closed in the winter; I've mentioned it in the individual listings if they are. Some campgrounds cater only to recreational vehicle owners, and some have spaces for both tents and RVs. Campgrounds that have showers have hot showers; our weather is never so warm that you'd want to take a cold shower.

Washington

Washington state parks have a central reservation system for camping between May 15 and September 15. At other times of the year, camping is on a first-come, first-served basis. To make reservations by phone call Reservations Northwest at 1-800-452-5687. The website (www.parks.wa.gov/emailreq.htm) offers information about making reservations by email also. You can make reservations up to 11 months in advance, and the state park system recommends reserving as early as possible.

Other campgrounds listed here are private parks with their own rules and reservations systems.

Deer Park Golf & RV Resort
1201 Country Club Drive, Deer Park
(509) 276-5912, (877) 276-1155
www.deerparkgolf.com

An RV resort that caters mainly to retired golfers, this facility is open from March through November (unless early or late snow forces it to close). The campground is located along the 9th hole of their 18-hole course, and features concrete pads with extra parking spaces for tow rigs. Electrical, cable TV, and phone hookups are available, and there are laundry and shower facilities. The golf course has a driving range, putting and chipping greens, a pro shop, restaurant, and lounge.

Camping fees are $30 per night, $150 per week, or $450 per month. Greens fees for golf range from $16 Monday through Thursday to $21 on the weekends. Seniors get a small discount. Golf lessons are also offered. Deer Park is a small town fifteen miles north of Spokane.

Mount Spokane State Park
26107 North Mt. Spokane Park Drive, Mead
(509) 238-6845
www.parks.wa.gov/mtspokane.htm

Mount Spokane State Park has a small campground with 12 spaces for tents or RVs (no hookups). It is located on Mount Spokane and its primary attraction in the summer is 50 miles of hiking and equestrian trails. The park is open year-round (it is popular for skiing and other snow sports in the winter), but camping is only available from June through September. There are no showers, and pit toilets only.

Riverside State Park
4427 North Aubrey White Parkway, Spokane
(509) 456-3964
www.parks.wa.gov/riversde.htm

This park is right next to Spokane, but its location in the woods along the Spokane River gives it a more remote feel. There are 101 campsites for both tents and RVs, but no hookups. A nature program is offered in the summer, and lots of hiking and mountain biking trails lead away from the campground and along the river. You can fish for trout in the river, but it generally runs swiftly here over a rocky bottom, so don't count on swimming and other water activities near the campground. Below Nine Mile Dam there is a boat launch on Long Lake, and swimming is also available. Riverside State Park has an off-road-vehicle park for motorcycles and ATVs; it is quite a distance from the campground and over a hill, so the noise won't disturb your camping experience. Riverside also manages the adjacent Little Spokane River Natural Area, a natural river corridor that is home to many animals and birds. Canoeing on the Little Spokane is popular from spring through fall.

Campsites at Riverside State Park cost $10 per night, plus a $1 per night "popular destination fee" from April through September. Hot showers are available, and there are both flush and pit toilets. The park is open year-round.

Spokane KOA
3025 Barker Road, Otis Orchards
(509) 924-4722

If easy access and convenience are what you're looking for in a campground, check out the Spokane KOA. It is located in the flat Spokane Valley, surrounded by farms and modern subdivisions. There are level, grassy pull-through sites for RVs (with full hookups) and a separate tent area with shelters, plus a few cabins for rent. A playground and heated pool are on the site, and it is close to the Centennial Trail for walking or biking along the Spokane River. Spokane Transit buses stop near the campground, and the Spokane Valley Mall is only a mile away.

RV sites cost $25 to $29 per night, and tent sites cost $20 to $23 per night. Cabins are $36 to $40. The campground is open year-round.

Yogi Bear's Camp-Resort
7520 South Thomas Mallen Road, Cheney
(509) 747-9415
www.jellystone-spokane.com/

Much more than a campground, Yogi Bear's is a family resort with lots of activities for the whole family. There are tent and RV sites, as well as camping cabins and suites with kitchenettes, air conditioning, and heat. The resort has an indoor pool, a game room, mini golf, playgrounds, basketball and volleyball courts, horseshoes, and a laundry room.

The Idaho Panhandle's wilderness areas are home to a variety of wildlife, including moose.

PHOTO: COURTESY OF THE SANDPOINT CHAMBER OF COMMERCE

Each weekend from spring through fall there are special family activities like pirate's treasure hunts, a '50s sock hop, a game show weekend, and a Hawaiian luau. The holiday weekends all have special activities and packages.

RV rates are about $30 per night, and tent spaces are about $21 per night. Campsites are in a pine forest, with plenty of shade and decent privacy. There are weekly rates also. Camping cabins start at about $60. Families can get an unlimited day pass for $7.50/person, which includes all activities. The resort is open year-round.

Idaho

Idaho state parks do not have a central reservation system. Two north Idaho state parks take reservations: Farragut and Priest Lake. They'll take the reservations by phone, in person, by mail, or by E-mail. You may make your reservation with a Visa or Mastercard, or send a check. You can make reservations up to 11 months in advance, but no later than three days before your arrival. A $6 non-refundable fee is charged for each campsite reservation, in addition to the first night's fee. Specific campsites may not be reserved, and the length of stay is limited to 15 days in a 30 day period. State parks also charge a $3 per day motor vehicle fee for any motor vehicle driving into the park, even if just for the day.

Other campgrounds in Idaho include National Forest Service campgrounds and private facilities. Each has its own reservation system and rules.

Close-up

Camping and Hiking in Bear Country

When you're away from civilization in northeastern Washington and northern Idaho, you're in bear country. North Idaho is habitat for both grizzly and black bears, and it is fairly common to see bears out in the woods (although grizzlies are actually quite rare). It is important to know what to do to avoid a bear encounter, and if you do see one, how to minimize the danger.

Food and odors attract bears, so many safety tips have to do with cooking and storing food. Keep your camp clean, and dispose of all garbage in bear-safe trash containers, which are found in many campgrounds in bear country. Put only sleeping gear and clean clothing in your tent; don't sleep in the clothing you wear while cooking. Cook only with a stove, not over a campfire. Use dehydrated backpacking food and avoid strong-smelling fresh food. Don't bury or burn garbage. Hang all food, garbage, cooking gear, and cosmetics in a tree at least 10 feet above the ground and 4 feet from the trunk of the tree. Some campgrounds have bear-safe devices for storing these items. If you're camping near your vehicle, you can store these things in the trunk. If possible, pitch your tent at least 100 yards uphill from where you are cooking and storing food. Don't let your dog run free; he may find a bear and then lead it back to your camp.

When you're planning to hike in bear country, pay attention to reports of bears in certain areas. Whether you're camping or staying in a lodge or motel, locals will usually know about recent bear sightings. Hikers also let each other know when they see bears. Go out hiking in groups, and make noise by talking or singing to avoid surprising bears. (Experts used to recommend wearing bells, especially in grizzly areas, but recent research has raised questions about the usefulness of this technique. In many cases grizzlies were seen ignoring bells that were well within hearing range). Hike in daylight hours, and stay alert. Don't become so absorbed in your activities that you aren't aware of your surroundings. Look for torn-apart logs, paw prints, and turned-over rocks—these may indicate recent bear activity.

Huckleberries grow on the slopes of many mountains in north Idaho and northeastern Washington. They are popular with both humans and bears, so stay especially alert near berry fields.

If you see a bear, DON'T RUN! All bears can outrun you, and all bears can climb trees. Try to stay calm and don't startle the bear. Detour slowly around it, or wait until it moves away from your route. Stay upwind of the bear so it can tell where you are.

A bear may stand upright when it first detects you. It is probably just using all it's senses to figure out if you are a threat. Most wild bears will move away after they identify you, unless they feel threatened or provoked. If a bear flattens its ears and raises the hair on the back of its neck, it may be ready to charge. Most experts recommend playing dead if a bear charges. Lie flat on your stomach, or on your side in a fetal position. Clasp your hands over the back of your neck to protect your head and neck.

Seeing a bear in the wild can be a thrilling and exciting experience. After all, viewing wildlife is part of the reason you go wilderness camping or hiking in the first place. These warnings aren't meant to scare you away from some of the most beautiful natural areas in the country. However, it is a good idea to know some of the basic rules of bear country etiquette. Come prepared to follow these rules, and your stay should be a safe and pleasant one.

Campers have ample opportunity to enjoy mountain biking and other activities in the Idaho Panhandle.

PHOTO: COURTESY OF THE COEUR D'ALENE RESORT

Beyond Hope Resort
1267 Peninsula Road, Hope
(208) 264-5251, (877) 270-HOPE

On the east shore of Lake Pend Oreille, the Beyond Hope Resort is a full-service RV campground resort. It offers 85 sites with electrical and cable hookups in a nice, grassy area. There are hot showers, laundry facilities, a swimming beach and boat launch, snack bar, and cocktail lounge. Paddle boats are available to rent, and there are volleyball and horseshoe areas. Hiking in the woods or along the lake is popular.

The resort is open from May through October. Rates range from $24 to $26 per day, or $144 to $156 per week. There are discounted rates for stays of a month or more.

Coeur d'Alene KOA
East 10700 Wolf Lodge Bay Road,
Coeur d'Alene
(208) 664-4471
www.koakampgrounds.com

Located on Lake Coeur d'Alene, this KOA campground is close to the city of Coeur d'Alene yet far enough out to enjoy bird-watching and other outdoor activities. It is only a half-mile south of I-90 from Exit 22, but freeway noise is dampened by trees. There are RV and tent areas, and cabins for rent; RV sites have full hookups. Amenities include a heated pool, hot tub, mini golf, a game room, boat rentals, small boat moorage, hiking and biking trails, a playground, laundry room, free modem access, and a store. There are pancake breakfasts, pizza parties, and evening movies offered in the summer.

Nightly rates range from $23 to $29 for an RV campsite, $18 to $21 for a tent site, and $40 to $50 for a cabin. The park is open from April 1 through October 15.

Farragut State Park
Idaho Highway 54, four miles east of
Athol off U.S. 95
(208) 683-2425
www.idahoparks.org/parks/farragut.html

A large (4,000 acres) park on the shores of Lake Pend Oreille, Farragut State Park has miles of forest hiking trails, swimming and fishing areas, and campsites for both tents and RVs. It is close to Coeur d'Alene, and is very popular, but it's big enough to not feel crowded. The scenery in the park and the trails along the lake are beautiful.

During World War II, the Navy had a training center on this site. Almost 300,000 sailors went through basic training here, and Navy reunions are still held at Farragut every fall. There are displays that tell about the park's naval heritage.

Farragut has 90 tent sites and 45 RV sites with electricity and water, plus group sites. There are both pit and flush toilets, and showers. A dump station is available for RVs. Farragut is open all year. Rates range from $7 for a tent site to $16 for an RV site with hookups.

Kit Price Campground
Idaho Panhandle National Forest
(877) 444-6777
www.reserveusa.com

This remote U.S. Forest Service campground is located 32 miles north of Wallace in a wooded area along the Coeur d'Alene River. Fishing, swimming, and hiking are the main activities in this quiet spot. There are no RV hookups and only pit toilets. The Forest Service has banned open fires, including charcoal grills, in this campground, so you'll have to bring a propane or liquid fuel stove to cook.

Campsites cost $12 per night. The campground is open from about May 24 through September 9. Reservations may

Many area lakes offer prime camping and recreation opportunities. PHOTO: COURTESY COEUR D'ALENE CHAMBER OF COMMERCE

be made up to 8 months in advance through the National Recreation Reservation Service, by phone or the website.

Luby Bay Campground
5538 West Lakeshore Road, Priest River
(877) 444-6777
www.reserveusa.com

Luby Bay is a popular National Forest Service campground on Priest Lake, 30 miles north of the town of Priest River. Campsites are located in a pine and birch forest next to the lake. They can be used by both tents and RVs, but there are no hookups for RVs. A waste station is available in the campground. The campground has flush toilets but no showers. A nice sandy swimming beach is next to the camping area, and there is a boat ramp a half-mile north of the campground. Fishing and boating are very popular in the clear blue waters of Priest Lake. A hiking trail goes nine miles along the shoreline from the campground.

Campsites at Luby Bay cost $12 per night. The campground is open from about May 24 through September 9. Reservations may be made up to 8 months in advance through the National Recreation Reservation Service, by phone or the website.

Priest Lake State Park
314 Indian Creek Park Road, Coolin
(208) 443-2200,
(208) 443-2929 (Lionhead Unit)
www.idahoparks.org/parks/priest.html

Priest Lake is known for scenic beauty and clear water. A favorite local getaway, the campground is often full, yet doesn't have a crowded feel. Many people come here in late July and August to pick huckleberries. There are also many good hiking opportunities, and fishing and boating are also popular.

There are campgrounds in three units of the park. The Dichensheet Unit has 11 sites for tents or RVs, none with hookups. It has only pit toilets and no showers or drinking water; it is popular with anglers and is open from May through October.

The Indian Creek Unit has 93 sites for tents or RVs—11 with electric, water, and sewer hookups. This campground also has flush toilets, showers, and a dump station. There is a very nice swimming beach and dock, which is open all year.

The Lionhead Unit has 47 tent or RV spaces with no hookups, and has pit toilets with no showers. It does have a nice swimming area and a boat ramp. It's open from May through October.

The nightly cost for campsites in the park is between $7 and $16. Priest Lake also has rustic 2-room log cabins for $35 per night. They sleep up to six people, and have grills outside for cooking. They're heated for comfort, and are popular with cross-country skiers in the winter.

Round Lake State Park
Two miles west of U.S. 95 on Dufort Road, Sagle
(208) 263-3489
www.idahoparks.org/parks/round.html

Round Lake is a small park popular with families. The shallow lake warms up quickly in the summer, and there is a nice swimming beach. A two-mile trail around the lake winds through stands of cottonwood, Lodgepole pine, birch, alder, spruce, fir, and maple. Fishing is good for trout, bass, perch, bullhead, and crappie. In the winter the park is popular for cross-country skiing, sledding, tobogganing, ice skating, and ice fishing. It is open all year but does not take reservations for campsites.

There are 53 sites for tents or RVs, none with hookups. A dump station is available however, and the campground has showers and flush toilets. Campsites are between $7 and $14.

Springy Point Recreation Area
2376 East Highway 2, Oldtown
(208) 437-3133
www.reserveusa.com

Springy Point is a Corps of Engineers recreation area with 39 tent and RV campsites. It is located on the shores of the Pend Oreille River near Sandpoint. Amenities include flush toilets, hot showers, a dump station, coin laundry, boat ramp, and swimming beach. There are no hookups for RVs.

To get to Springy Point, go south out of Sandpoint on US 95 across the Long Bridge, then turn right (west) onto Lakeshore Drive. Springy Point is three miles down this road. The Recreation Area is open from about May 11 through October 13. Entry gates close at 10 P.M. and open at 7 A.M. Campsites cost $14 per night.

Camping and picnicking in the summer are enjoyable for the whole family. PHOTO: COURTESY COEUR D'ALENE CHAMBER OF COMMERCE

Restaurants

The Inland Northwest is not known for any particular cuisine, but we have a surprising number of good restaurants, where creative chefs use fresh ingredients to come up with delicious and interesting dishes. We also have many of the national chain restaurants and plenty of the usual fast food outlets; if you're craving familiar food, you'll find it here and you won't have to look very hard. The popularity of all-you-can-eat buffets in Spokane is a source of local humor, and the most recent variation on these is the all-you-can-eat Chinese buffets. These restaurants are especially popular with families because the children can see what they're getting ahead of time and if they don't like it they can go back and try something else. There is enough variety for everyone. The prices are reasonable too, for those on a budget.

Many restaurants here don't take reservations, or only take them for groups of six or more. During the week you may not have to wait for a table, but on Friday and Saturday nights, the wait may be 30 minutes to an hour or more. Many restaurant bars have small tables, and you can usually sit in the bar and order dinner. A lot of the restaurant bars are nonsmoking also, so this is sometimes a good option if you don't want to wait for a table in the dining room.

Restaurants in this chapter are arranged from Spokane to Coeur d'Alene, then north to Sandpoint. Unless otherwise noted, they accept at least Visa and Mastercard, and many accept other major credit cards as well. Tipping in restaurants is expected; 15 to 20 percent for good service is the norm.

Price Code

For your convenience, I've created a price code using dollar signs giving you a general idea what you can expect to spend on dinner entrees for two, excluding cocktails, wine, appetizers, desserts, tax, and tip. Lunch always costs less than dinner in the places that serve it, and if you're watching the budget, lunch can be a good time to try the food in some of the more expensive places. Many restaurants have senior citizen discounts and children's selections. Restaurants often have daily specials, usually announced by the server, but they are generally about the same price as an average entrée. Here is the breakdown:

$	$20 or less
$$	$20–$30
$$$	$30–$40
$$$$	$40 and up

Spokane

Bella Union Bistro
9820 North Nevada
(509) 465-8794
$$

Located near the Northpointe shopping area in north Spokane, Bella Union Bistro is a popular restaurant with an eclectic selection that has a little something for everyone. Note: portion sizes are quite large here, and many people split an entrée. Pizzas come with some unusual toppings like smoked chicken and black beans, or smoked salmon, red onion, and capers. Other dinner selections range from steak to grilled ahi to jerk pork chops. At lunch there are tossed-to-order salads, sandwiches, stuffed baked potatoes, and pizza. The kid's menu is a good deal—it includes items like pizza, noodles, and quesadillas. Kids also get a Magna Doodle or Etch-a-Sketch to keep them busy until the food comes. Wine and beer are available. Bella Union Bistro is open every day except Sunday for lunch and dinner.

Café 5-Ten
Lincoln Heights Shopping Center, 2727 South Mount Vernon
(509) 533-0064
$$$

This eatery gets raves from local foodies for its innovative and perfectly executed cuisine. Nightly specials feature the freshest ingredients, and are always a good bet. The menu includes various renditions of fish and seafood, beef, pork, lamb, and pasta. If possible, save room for dessert; the caramel apple pie is mouthwatering. Café 5-Ten is open for lunch and dinner Monday through Saturday, and serves beer, wine, and cocktails. Reservations are recommended.

Clinkerdagger
The Flour Mill, 621 West Mallon
(509) 328-5965
$$$

Clinkerdagger is one of Spokane's nice restaurants, where teens take their date before the prom, and families go for traditional good food. Tables are lined up along the windows overlooking the Spokane River, and the atmosphere is comfortable and elegant. The food is consistently good and non-trendy, with selections like prime rib, steak, chicken, fresh fish, and pasta dishes. The Burnt Cream dessert is famous, and very rich. Cocktails, wine, and beer

The Sawtooth Grill in River Park Square makes some of the best burgers in Spokane. PHOTO: COURTESY THE SAWTOOTH GRILL

are available. Clink's is open Monday through Saturday for lunch and dinner, and Sunday for dinner only. Validated parking is available in a large lot next to the Flour Mill.

David's Pizza
829 East Boone
(509) 483-7460
www.davidspizza.com/
$

Not your traditional pizza chain restaurant, David's pizza is handmade and features unusual toppings like pesto and chicken. They're located in the Gonzaga University area, next to Sonic Burrito. (Although their address is on Boone, they are on the corner of Boone and Hamilton). A build-your-own pizza choice lets you order a plain cheese pizza and add any toppings you like—choices range from traditional sausage, mushroom and olive, to artichoke hearts, spinach, goat cheese, zucchini, and sun-dried tomatoes. The menu also includes hot sandwiches and calzones. There are a few tables to eat-in, or you can get your order to go. They also deliver in the Spokane area.

David's is open daily for lunch and dinner.

The Elk Public House
1931 West Pacific
(509) 363-1973
$

This Browne's Addition pub is a popular meeting place, and has great food to boot. The high ceilings and hard floors reflect noise very well; this isn't the place for an intimate meal and quiet conversation. You can eat at the bar, and there are also plenty of tables in the long, narrow room (although the place is so popular, you may have to wait). The daily specials are usually good, and the house gumbo is excellent. Lunch features salads, sandwiches, and soups, and the dinner menu expands to include unusual pastas, tostadas or tacos, chops, and seafood. There are 18 beers on tap.

Insiders' Tip
Looking for a fun place to eat for the whole family? Everyone loves Chuck E. Cheese, the pizza chain with games, shows, and kid-friendly food. You'll find it at 10007 North Nevada in Spokane.

Although it's a pub, The Elk is non-smoking. It is open daily for lunch and dinner.

Fugazzi
North One Post
(509) 747-9750
$$$$

Fugazzi is a trendy restaurant located on the street level of the Hotel Lusso, a downtown boutique hotel. It's open for lunch and dinner Monday through Saturday, with creative and appetizing selections for every taste. For lunch there are homemade soups and salads, as well as sandwiches, spring rolls, quesadillas, wraps, and vegetarian stir-fry. For dinner you can choose from appetizers like bruschetta, calamari, or salads, followed by ambitious main dishes, including basil seared ahi tuna, grilled top sirloin, pan roasted duck breast, and scallop linguini.

Great Wall
11420 East Sprague
(509) 921-9888
$

One of the largest Chinese buffets in the Spokane area, Great Wall lets everyone in the family stuff themselves for a reasonable price. There are beef, chicken, pork, and seafood dishes with lots of vegetables, rice, egg rolls, fried won tons, soups, and some more exotic selections. Great Wall also has steamed crab legs every day for dinner. Spices, seasonings, and cooking styles draw from Szechuan, Cantonese, Hunan, and Shanghai cuisines. A selection of Japanese sushi is offered at dinner also.

Great Wall is open every day for lunch and dinner. There are discounts for children from 3 to 10 years old, and kids under 3 eat free.

Italian Kitchen Ristorante
113 North Bernard
(509) 363-1210
$$

This busy, noisy eatery has been voted Spokane's best Italian restaurant. It features traditional Italian food, but with a trendy, lighter touch. Fresh pasta and homemade sauces are combined with fine Italian cheeses and imported olive oil in fresh-tasting dishes. The restaurant has a bar and serves cocktails, wine, and micro-brews. It is open daily for dinner. Reservations are suggested.

Luna
5620 South Perry
(509) 448-2383
$$

Luna offers some of Spokane's most creative cuisine, which includes a variety of meat, seafood, and vegetarian dishes. This neighborhood restaurant has an elegant atmosphere, with lovely, marble-topped tables and fine décor. Their signature dish is an outstanding salad with caramelized walnuts, dried cranberries, and Gorgonzola cheese. Luna is open for lunch Monday through Friday, for dinner every day, and for one of the best brunches in Spokane on Saturday and Sunday from 9 A.M. to 2 P.M. The wine list is outstanding. Reservations are recommended.

The Coeur d'Alene Resort offers a choice of dining options, several with world-class views. PHOTO: COURTESY THE COEUR D'ALENE RESORT

Mizuna
214 North Howard
(509) 747-2004
www.mizuna.com
$$

Consistently rated among the top restaurants in Spokane, Mizuna has also been recognized by *Bon Apetit* magazine. A nearly all-vegetarian eatery (a fish selection is offered in the evening), Mizuna does such interesting things with veggies, tofu, and grains that even die-hard meat eaters will enjoy a meal here. Pasta, rice, and potatoes, combined with mushrooms, squash, nuts, herbs, corn, cheeses (there are non-dairy dishes also), and a variety of vegetables make hearty and satisfying meals. Appetizers, salads, and desserts are just as creative. The lunch menu includes salads, soups, and sandwiches. A wine bar (see the Nightlife chapter) offers a relaxing place to try a variety of local and imported wines.

Mizuna is open for lunch and dinner every day. Validated parking is available behind the restaurant. Reservations are recommended.

Niko's
725 West Riverside
(509) 624-7444
www.spokane.net/marketplace/nikosgreek/
$$

A local favorite, Niko's specializes in Greek and Middle Eastern cuisine. Vegetarians will find a good selection here but the specialty is lamb, prepared in a variety of ways, including kebabs, chops, sausages, and curries. There are steak and chicken dishes, and shrimp, scallops, and calamari round out the menu. Outstanding fresh salads are a smart choice for lunch, and the hummus and pita bread made on the premises make a good starter. The extensive wine list has over 700 selections. (Niko's also has a nice wine bar—see the Nightlife chapter for further details). The restaurant is open for lunch Monday through Friday, and for dinner Monday through Saturday.

Patsy Clark's
2208 West Second
(509) 838-8300
$$$

Fine cuisine served in an opulent turn-of-the-century Browne's Addition mansion is what Patsy Clark's is about. At dinner, soft, live piano music in the background is an elegant touch. The most popular dinner entrée is the President's Steak, a New York steak with whisky demiglace that former president George Bush had when he came through Spokane on a whirlwind campaign tour. The menu also features duck, veal, and ahi tuna. A wine steward on staff can help you select the perfect wine to accompany your meal. After dinner, pick up a brochure and take the self-guided tour of the 27-room mansion.

Patsy Clark's is open daily for dinner, and for Sunday brunch. Reservations are recommended.

Pho 5-Star
1801 East Sprague
(509) 535-4677
$

The setting of this small, casual eatery couldn't be more humble—it occupies one end of a busy Asian market and grocery. However, the pho (noodle soup that is Vietnam's national dish) is outstanding, and well worth a trip. The homemade stock is seasoned with the exotic flavors of star anise and ginger, and the fresh rice noodles are added just before serving, so they're not soggy. You can order your pho with beef, chicken, or shrimp, and it is accompanied by fresh, crunchy bean sprouts, basil, hot peppers, and lime wedges. You can add as much as you like. If you like more flavor, bottles of hot sauce and fish sauce are on the table.

The restaurant is open for lunch and dinner every day.

Riverview Thai
The Flour Mill, 621 West Mallon Avenue
(509) 325-8370
$

This is an especially good place to eat on a nice day, when you can sit outside on the deck overlooking the Spokane River. The lunch buffet is a good value and makes a quick meal for those in a hurry. It features rice, a curry dish, and several vegetable and meat dishes. Thai restaurants, like Chinese, are also good places to go with a group and order family style, so each person can try a little of everything. Riverview Thai serves beer and wine, or try the Thai iced coffee or iced tea; it's different but very good.

Rock City Grill
505 West Riverside
(509) 455-4400
$$

Rock City was billed as a "New York style eatery" when it first opened in 1992, and its version of upscale Italian bistro food took Spokane by storm. Since that time national chains have arrived giving Rock City some competition, but it is still one of the area's most popular spots for trendy wood oven pizzas and light pasta dishes. Pizza toppings range from traditional pepperoni to Thai, barbecue chicken, Dungeness crab, and vegetarian. There are excellent salads, and the focaccia bread is really good if you like flatbread—chewy and flavorful. The appetizers are truly appetizing, including steamed clams, oven roasted vegetables, chicken satay, and escargot. You could order a selection of appetizers or a salad and focaccia deluxe (topped with roasted elephant garlic and goat cheese) for an unusual meal.

Rock City is open every day for lunch and dinner. Wine and beer are available, and 13 microbrews are on tap.

Sawtooth Grill
808 West Main Street, River Park Square
(509) 363-1100
$

The Sawtooth Grill is a new Spokane restaurant that has earned a name for delicious, messy burgers. It's located in River Park Square downtown, making it a convenient place to stop for dinner after a day of shopping or before seeing a movie in the theater complex upstairs. It has a comfortable, rustic look and feel, and an attentive waitstaff.

Although burgers aren't the only thing on the menu, they are definitely worth trying. Topped with real cheddar cheese, vine-ripened tomatoes, and Bermuda onions, plus the restaurant's special sauce, they come with a stack of crispy fries. Other choices include salads, chili, clam chowder, fancy hot dogs, chicken burgers, fish and chips, and steak. Wine and beer are available, both with dinner and in the small lounge. The restaurant makes excellent milkshakes and malts, and if you have room, try the signature banana cream pie.

The Sawtooth Grill is open every day for lunch and dinner. They don't take reservations, and do not validate parking in the River Park Square parking garage.

Sonic Burrito
1209 North Hamilton
(509) 484-4158
$

A few years back Spokane suddenly had a slew of burrito restaurants. This was the best of the lot, and this is the one that survived. Located in the Gonzaga University district, Sonic Burrito is popular with students and office workers alike. You can pick a burrito from the menu or "build your own," choosing from various flavored tortillas, regular or low-fat sour cream, chicken or beef, brown rice, two kinds of beans and cheese, and a wide variety of chopped vegetables. When you pick a little of everything, the build-your-own burritos are huge, easily making two meals for smaller appetites. The restaurant also has a variety of drinks and chips, and usually cookies or brownies for dessert. There are tables, or you can get your order to go.

Sonic Burrito is open every day of the week for lunch and dinner.

Steam Plant Grill
159 South Lincoln
(509) 777-3900
$$

If you'd like to see an interesting renovation of one of Spokane's old, brick industrial buildings and enjoy a good meal at the same time, try the Steam Plant Grill. It's located in Steam Plant Square in downtown Spokane, where steam heat was generated until 1986. The renovation kept the industrial tone of the building, giving the Steam Plant Grill restaurant one of Spokane's more unique settings. Dark wood combined with green walls and burgundy trim gives the eatery a warm, cozy feel. On a cold night you can try for a spot by the fireplace.

The Steam Plant specializes in "casual family dining" with salads and soups, sandwiches and wraps, as well as pasta and meat dishes. It is open daily for lunch and dinner. Beers from the Coeur d'Alene brewing company are featured, and the restaurant also has a decent wine list. Before or after your meal you can look in the shops (more are planned), and you can also explore the building and read the numerous wall plaques that tell its history. The Steam Plant Grill is open every day for lunch and dinner. It doesn't have its own parking lot, but validated parking is available in the lot just past the restaurant, north of the railroad viaduct.

Taste of India
3110 North Division
(509) 327-7313
$

Spokane's only Indian restaurant has very good food and attentive service. The lunch buffet is an especially good deal, with rice, flatbread, chicken curry, vegetable dishes, and dal (lentils). The dinner menu features Tandoori chicken, shrimp and fish entrees, curry, and a variety of vegetarian dishes. The tea (chai) is excellent. Taste of India is open Monday through Friday for lunch, and every day for dinner.

Winged Lion
Kempis Hotel, 326 West 6th
(509) 747-7100
$$$$

The Winged Lion is one of Spokane's finest restaurants. Their slogan says it all: "Classically European, exquisitely French, amazingly Spokane." When the restaurant first opened, the owners wanted to bring a new level of dining style to Spokane. They required coats and ties for men and offered a six-course, prix fix menu featuring Provincial French cuisine. They've since relaxed a bit, and now have a standard menu with "First Plates" (appetizers) and "Second Plates" (main courses). They also dropped the coat and tie requirement (although it is a nice restaurant, so you'll feel out of place if you don't dress up). The restaurant was recently named among the Best Restaurants in the World for Wine Lovers by *Wine Spectator Magazine*.

Appetizers range from salads and soups to seafood. The elegant main courses include roast duckling, pan-roasted loin of New Zealand lamb, and beef tenderloin medallions. Desserts are created by the Winged Lion's own pastry chef. The wine selection is one of the largest in Spokane.

The Winged Lion is open for lunch Monday through Friday, and for dinner Monday through Saturday. Their wine cellar is a special room for wine tastings and private parties (for up to 16 people).

Post Falls

White House Grill
620 North Spokane St.
(208) 777-9672
$

This tiny restaurant has gained quite a following in the Spokane/Coeur d'Alene area because of the quality of its food and the friendly personality of chef-owner Raci Erden. Traditional Middle Eastern food, especially lamb, is featured here, and it is generally cooked with a lot of fresh garlic. You can start your dinner with a salad, including one with greens and marinated vegetables. The French onion soup also makes a good first course. Dinners include pastas with shrimp or clams, kebabs, sandwiches on fresh pitas, and chef's specials. The lamb is excellent. For dessert, try the baklava—it's made on the premises.

The White House Grill is open for lunch and dinner Monday through Saturday. Reservations are recommended.

Coeur d'Alene

Beverly's
Coeur d'Alene Resort, Seventh Floor
(208) 765-4000, (800) 688-4142
$$$$

Beverly's is a special occasion restaurant, where perfectly prepared food served in an elegant atmosphere with a view of beautiful Lake Coeur d'Alene combine for a lovely afternoon or evening. Dinner entrees include grilled Atlantic salmon, rack of lamb, prime rib, and sautéed scallops. Upscale appetizers include some ingredients you won't find elsewhere in this area, including foie gras and caviar. New and very popular items are their 99 cent desserts—just a few bites of one of the chef's luscious, sweet creations to finish off a meal.

Beverly's serves cocktails as well as beer and wine. They're open daily for lunch and dinner. Reservations are highly recommended, especially on the weekend.

Capers
315 East Walnut
(208) 664-9036
$$$

This cozy bistro consistently wins accolades for its outstanding Mediterranean-style food. Dinners feature steaks, chops and seafood, like a ribeye with cabernet and shallot sauce topped with caramelized onions and Gorgonzola cheese. Appetizers include dolmades (stuffed grape leaves), bruschetta, fresh mozzarella cheese, and roasted red pepper spread. Delicious breads are made on the premises. Lunch features unusual salads and sandwiches. In the summer you can sit out on the patio. Capers is open Tuesday through Saturday for dinner.

Cedars Floating Restaurant
Blackwell Island
(208) 664-2922
$$

Blackwell Island is located where the Spokane River flows out of Lake Coeur d'Alene. Cedars floats directly on the lake, enhancing the on-the-water experience. The dining room offers a choice of burgers, salad bar, steaks, pasta, and seafood. The fresh seafood specials can be some of the best in the area, featuring both northwest and more exotic selections. Cocktails, wine, and beer are available, and you can wait for a table in the lounge. During the summer it's nice to sit outside on the deck.

Cedars is open daily for dinner. Reservations are recommended.

Crickets
424 Sherman Avenue
(208) 765-1990
$$

Another of Coeur d'Alene's many downtown eateries, Crickets is a good, casual place to bring the whole family. Known as a steak house and oyster bar, Crickets features oysters on the half-shell, oysters Rockefeller, and panfried oysters. The dinner menu also includes rib eye, New York, porterhouse, and sirloin steaks, as well as

In the spring the Spokane River puts on a spectacular show. PHOTO: COURTESY COEUR D'ALENE CHAMBER OF COMMERCE

prime rib, chicken, and seafood. For lunch there are various burgers, sandwiches, and salads.

Crickets serves beer and wine, and is open every day for lunch and dinner.

Hudson's Hamburgers
207 Sherman Avenue
(208) 664-5444
$

Opened in 1907, Hudson's has become a Coeur d'Alene institution. The meat is the star here: burgers are hand formed fresh just before they're grilled. They're topped only with sliced onion and pickles; you can add your own sauce to taste. There are a few tables and stools available in this tiny restaurant but they're nearly always full; on a nice day, get your order to go and find a bench—there are quite a few scattered around the downtown area.

Hudson's is open Monday through Saturday for lunch.

Pasty Depot
601 Northwest Boulevard
(208) 667-2789
$

If you haven't had a chance to try these Cornish meat-filled pies you're missing a real treat. Created in England for miners who couldn't come up out of the mines to eat a nutritious midday meal, pasties (pronounced pas-tees) are handheld pastries filled with meats, or meats and vegetables. You can also order them with gravy and eat them with a fork. The Pasty Depot sells pizza by the slice and soup, as well as deli sandwiches and a daily special. They're open for lunch only, Monday through Friday.

Takara
309 Lakeside Avenue
(208) 765-8014
$$$$

Home of the Inland Northwest's freshest and best sushi, Takara is a comfortable and relaxing place to enjoy an excellent Japanese meal. You can eat in the dining room or ask for one of the intimate and private tatami rooms. The menu features tempura vegetables, meat, and fish, sukiyaki, and teriyaki. Be sure to at least try the excellent sushi—it isn't fishy at all.

Takara is open for lunch Monday through Friday, and for dinner Monday through Saturday. They're also open for dinner on Sunday during June, July, and August. Reservations are suggested.

Tanglewood Bistro
511 Sherman Avenue
(208) 667-8612
$$$

This sophisticated bistro is right on the main drag in downtown Coeur d'Alene, just a couple blocks from the Coeur d'Alene Resort. With an evolving menu that changes as the chef invents new dishes, Tanglewood offers some of Coeur d'Alene's most interesting cuisine. For dinner, main dishes may include such creations as breast of chicken stuffed with feta cheese, spinach and wild mushrooms wrapped in phyllo pastry, or a seared halibut filet with vermouth-spiked pesto cream. Lunches include gourmet burgers, sandwiches, and salads. A children's menu lists such standbys as hamburgers, chicken strips, and spaghetti. Tempting, rich desserts are created on-site by the chef. Wine and beer are available.

Open for lunch and dinner Monday through Saturday all year, Tanglewood is also open on Sundays from May through December.

Sandpoint
Bangkok Cuisine Thai Restaurant
202 North 2nd Avenue
(208) 265-4149
$

You'll find surprisingly good Thai food here, especially Pad Thai, Thailand's national dish. Prices are reasonable too. The restaurant is open daily for lunch and dinner, and they serve beer and wine.

The Beach House
Edgewater Resort, 56 Bridge
(208) 255-4947
$$$

The Beach House offers traditional steak and seafood with views of Lake Pend Oreille and the mountains. In nice weather you can dine outside. The restaurant is located adjacent to the Edgewater Best Western, and is open daily for lunch and dinner. Beer, wine, and cocktails are served.

Ivano's Ristorante Italiano
124 South 2nd
(208) 263-0211
$$

Traditional northern Italian cuisine served with classic wine is Ivano's specialty. Meals begin with antipasti dishes of proscuitto with melon, eggplant parmesan, or Caesar salad, followed by the first course of various pasta dishes, and then the second course of chicken, veal, seafood, and steaks. Ivano's has been voted Sandpoint's best restaurant. They are open for dinner every day. Wine and cocktails are served, and in the summer, you can eat on the deck. Reservations are suggested.

Jalapenos Mexican Restaurant
116 North 1st Avenue
(208) 263-2995
$

Jalapenos offers the most popular Mexican foods, like fajitas, chimichangas, tostadas, and tacos, and they also have some traditional foods you don't find everywhere, like carne asada, chili verde, and carnitas. A children's menu includes cheese enchiladas, tacos, quesadillas, or burritos served with beans or rice and a drink. They have the usual soft drinks, but the specialty is delicious huckleberry lemonade. A selection of bottled and draft beer and house wine are available, as well as several kinds of margaritas. Jalapenos is open seven days a week for lunch and dinner.

Red Martin Vegetarian Café
330 North 1st
(208) 263-0369
$

Heart-healthy and tasty foods are the specialty in this café located next to Coldwater Creek's Cedar Street Bridge in downtown Sandpoint. The have fresh baked breads, soups and sandwiches made with fresh, natural ingredients, salads, and wine and beer. You can eat inside or on the patio overlooking the water. They're open daily for lunch only.

Spud's
102 North 1st
(208) 265-4311
$

This casual eatery offers homemade soups, sandwiches, salads, rotisserie chicken, and steaks, but their signature dish is a fluffy Idaho baked potato that comes with a variety of toppings. Beer and wine are available. Spud's is right on the water and has a nice deck with a view for warm weather dining. They're open daily for lunch and dinner.

Swan's Landing
South end of Long Bridge (Highway 95) at
Lakeshore Drive, Sagle
(208) 265-2000
www.swanslanding.com
$$$

Located just minutes south of Sandpoint, Swan's Landing is a northwest casual eatery overlooking Lake Pend Oreille. The ambitious dinner menu features steaks, chops, seafood, and pasta prepared in unusual combinations with local ingredients. In addition to the upscale choices, there are pizzas, salads, and sandwiches for lighter appetites and wallets. The lunch menu has similar choices, with smaller portions and smaller prices. Swan's also has a popular Sunday brunch, with omelets, eggs benedict, ranchero eggs, and frittatas, as well as salads and sandwiches.

Swan's is open daily for lunch and dinner, and for Sunday brunch from 10 A.M.

to 2 P.M. In the winter you can enjoy specialty drinks by the fire, and in summer dine al fresco on the stone patio next to the water.

Priest Lake

Elkins
404 Elkins Road
(208) 443-2432
www.elkinsresort.com
$$$

This resort restaurant has a beautiful, rustic dining room overlooking Priest Lake. The creative and delicious meals have won a loyal following, and people drive up from Spokane just for dinner. The restaurant is open for breakfast, lunch, and dinner, and is worth a visit for any of these. Breakfasts include frittatas, burritos, eggs Benedict, pancakes, omelets, and other specialties. For lunch you can choose from sandwiches, salads, burgers, pizza, and pasta with chicken, steak, organic greens, sun-dried tomatoes, fresh herbs, portabella mushrooms, and other tasty ingredients. The dining room really shines at dinner, with interesting renditions of salmon, chicken, steak, ribs, and seafood.

Elkins restaurant is open daily, but it is a good idea to call ahead if you have to drive far. Reservations are recommended for dinner.

Silver Valley

Enaville Resort
I-90, Exit 43, 1.5 miles north on
Coeur d'Alene River Road, Enaville
(208) 682-3453
$-$$

Established in 1880 as the Snake Pit, the Enaville Resort has been a bordello, a miner's tavern, and a lumber camp, and is now a restaurant famous for "Rocky Mountain oysters." If these are a little too exotic, try the buffalo burgers, barbecued beef, steaks, or seafood. The Enaville Resort is open for breakfast, lunch, and dinner every day, and serves beer, wine, and cocktails.

Nightlife

Spokane, Coeur d'Alene, and the surrounding areas don't have the glamorous and exciting nightlife of New York or Miami Beach. Ours is more low-key, more casual, and less competitive. There aren't as many options, especially for young adults who are always looking for something new. However, Spokane offers a variety of bars, from quiet, neighborhood hangouts to hopping dance venues. Many places feature live music. Other evening entertainment options listed in other chapters include dances, performances from around the world, poetry readings, hockey games, movies, concerts, and many special events. In smaller towns there aren't as many choices, but there are still things to do in the evening. Many towns have movie theaters and bowling alleys, and just about every place has several bars or lounges where you can sit and talk, shoot pool, watch sports games, or dance. There are several Native American casinos in the area that are open late. The Coeur d'Alene Bingo/Casino operation regularly stages concerts and boxing matches. There are lots of things to do if you look for them.

Smoking is allowed in most bars, although the ventilation is usually very good and few are really smoky. Some restaurant bars and lounges are smoke-free.

Many bars are only open late on Thursday, Friday, and Saturday nights, and some are only open on the weekends. On weeknights the Inland Northwest generally closes up early; even downtown Spokane looks pretty deserted after 10 P.M. during the week.

Bars and lounges serve alcoholic beverages until closing, which is around 2 A.M. on weekends. All nightclubs will be happy to call you a cab after you spend an evening drinking in their establishment. The legal drinking age in Idaho and Washington is 21, and the blood alcohol content necessary for a drunk driving arrest is only .08. The police are vigilant, and are especially suspicious of anyone driving erratically around 2 A.M. when the bars close. It's better to stick to soft drinks, have a designated driver, or call a cab than to take a chance and drive after drinking.

Spokane

Ankeny's
515 West Sprague (in the West Coast Ridpath Hotel)
(509) 838-6311

Ankeny's is a classy lounge next to the restaurant of the same name in the Ridpath Hotel. The view of Spokane is lovely, especially at night. Comfortable tables and chairs are scattered around the room, and the bar is fully stocked. There's live jazz on Friday and Saturday nights. The Ridpath has valet parking (for a fee), or you can park on the street.

Arizona Steakhouse
333 West Spokane Falls Boulevard
(509) 455-8206

The small bar at the Arizona Steakhouse restaurant is a friendly place to meet a friend for a drink. You can choose music from the jukebox or play pool, or just sit and talk. It's right across the street from the Opera House so many people stop in before or after a performance.

Insiders' Tip

Downtown Spokane parking meters only require coins until 6 P.M. Monday through Saturday. At night and on Sundays parking on the street is free—a good deal for night owls.

Insiders' Tip

There are several arterials in Spokane that wind around and become different streets, although you'll feel like you stayed on the same road. The north side Hamilton/Nevada Street arterial is called Hamilton from I-90 to Cleveland Avenue; after that it curves and becomes Nevada Street all the way to its intersection with Hwy. 2, north of town. The north-south Market/Freya/Ray Street arterial is Ray Street on the south side as it crosses 29th Avenue, becomes Thor, then Freya as it crosses I-90 and heads north, then becomes Greene Street as it crosses the Spokane River and goes under a railroad overpass, where it becomes Market Street.

Many restaurant lounges are popular nightspots. PHOTO: COURTESY THE SAWTOOTH GRILL

Bayou Brewing Company
1003 East Trent
(509) 484-4818

The Bayou is a large establishment with a nice pub and a restaurant that serves Cajun food. In the Voodoo Lounge you can listen to live music six nights a week, or enjoy a microbrew with friends. There are pool tables and video games, too. Fat Tuesday's is the Bayou's concert venue, with performances most Saturday nights. Some weeknights are set aside for comedy acts.

Cavallino Lounge
North One Post
(509) 747-9750

The Hotel Lusso's Cavallino Lounge specializes in martinis, today's trendiest drink. In addition to the classic martini, there are variations with orange, lemon, and other flavors (purists would shudder). The smoke-free lounge serves other mixed drinks as well, and a selection of wines and beer.

Dempsey's Brass Rail
909 West First
(509) 747-5362

Dempsey's is known to draw the gay and lesbian crowd, as well as everyone else—and all get along fine. It's a hopping dance club with great music—very popular with all ages (over 21). They serve all types of drinks.

Double Dribble Sports Bar & Grill
8108 North Division
(509) 468-7946

There's always something going on at the Double Dribble. You can play pool, air hockey, or darts, watch all the Sunday and Monday football games on one of the big screen TVs, or play video trivia and golf. On weekends they have a DJ and people come to dance. If you get hungry you can order appetizers like poppers or potato skins, or one of their great burgers or sandwiches.

Europa Pizzeria and Bakery
125 South Wall
(509) 455-4051

This small, smoke-free bar is as intimate as your living room, with antique sofas and chairs arranged to encourage pleasant conversation. They serve a variety of mixed drinks, wine, and beer. The bar is adjacent to the popular Europa Pizzeria restaurant and right across the hall from Suntree Books and Gifts, a great place to browse.

Havana's
908 North Howard
(509) 326-3745

Havana's is on the top floor of the same building the Ram occupies. It is a very popular dance club for twenty-somethings, with a strict dress code (no bandanas, no shorts or Capri pants, guys have to tuck in their shirts, etc.). People get very dressed up to go here. There is a big bar and crowded dance floor, and they sometimes have special events like '70s nights.

Mizuna
214 North Howard
(509) 747-2004
www.mizuna.com

The vegetarian restaurant, Mizuna, has a cozy wine bar that offers wine tasting nightly, by the taste or by the glass, with over 30 selections to try each week. Sit on comfortable couches and share a bottle of wine with friends, or meet other patrons at the bar. On Friday and Saturday nights you'll often hear live acoustic music.

Niko's
725 West Riverside
(509) 624-7444
www.spokane.net/marketplace/nikosgreek/

Spokane's popular Greek restaurant has added a wine bar, where patrons can take a "wine tour" and sample wines from around the world. With over 700 wines in stock, Niko's promises the connoisseur or the novice an interesting experience. The wine list includes varieties from Washington, Oregon, and California, as well as Greece, France, Italy, Spain, and Australia. Patrons can sit at tables or at the bar, where they can chat with the knowledgeable owner. The wine bar is open until midnight on Thursday, Friday, and Saturday.

Outback Jacks
321 West Sprague
(509) 624-4549

This noisy, rowdy bar is popular with the party crowd. The Boomerang Lounge has pool tables, darts, air hockey, foosball, and a jukebox. The Kangaroo Club has dancing nightly and a full-service bar, with crowd pleasers like ladies nights, '80s music nights, wet T-shirt contests, $1 pitchers, and jello shots. They often host live rock bands.

Players & Spectators
12828 East Sprague
(509) 924-5141

This very large night club/amusement center caters to people who want to do more than sit around and talk. They have a popular casino, a very nice bowling alley, pool tables, a basketball/sports court, lots of video games, and restaurant. Kids are allowed in the restaurant, bowling alley, and video game room early in the evening. Live bands (usually Top 40 cover bands) play on the weekends.

The Ram Restaurant and
Big Horn Brewery
908 North Howard
(509) 326-3745

Located right across the street from the Spokane Arena, the Ram is a popular gathering place. The big bar has plenty of room, and patrons can order food from the dining room also. Some nights it's a quiet place, and some nights they have karaoke and dancing.

Rocket Coffee House
24 West Main
(509) 835-3647

Although the Rocket Coffee House is part of Spokane's Rocket Bakery chain, it is a little different from the other shops. This is mainly a place to sit with friends and enjoy a latte, mocha, or other fancy coffee drink. In the evenings they have live music or open mike nights. It's a comfortable, low-key, alcohol-free alternative nightspot.

Steam Plant Grill
159 South Lincoln
(509) 777-3900

The Steam Plant Grill has a very comfortable, smoke-free bar featuring microbrews brewed on-site by the Coeur d'Alene Brewing Company. They also serve wine and mixed drinks, and have a specialty drinks menu. (For more about the restaurant and the Steam Plant building renovation, see the Restaurants chapter.)

The Steam Plant doesn't have its own parking lot, but validated parking is available in the Lincoln Street lot just north of the railroad viaduct.

Thirsty's
21 East Lincoln Road
(509) 777-1010

This dance club is very popular with the under-30 crowd and it gets packed on holiday and event weekends. There's a small bar and big dance floor, and a stage where live bands sometimes perform. On Thursday, Friday, and Saturday nights it's best to get there by 9 P.M.

Stateline

Kelly's
6152 West Seltice Way, Post Falls
(208) 773-5002

Kelly's is a country music dance club, drawing adults of all ages from Spokane and north Idaho. The atmosphere is country casual—you'll see lots of tight jeans and cowboy hats. They're open on Friday and Saturday nights with the Kelly Hughes Band performing country hits. Kelly also brings in many popular guest performers from around the United States. There is a huge dance floor and full service bar. Kelly's is off I-90 in the area called Stateline, which is right on the state line dividing Washington and Idaho.

Fireworks illuminate the city of Coeur d'Alene. PHOTO: COURTESY OF THE COEUR D'ALENE RESORT

Coeur d'Alene

Beachcombers
1414 Northwest Boulevard
(208) 667-3267

This noisy bar has lots of drink specials, happy hour from 4-7 P.M. Monday through Friday, Monday night football nights, and other happenings. Wednesdays are karaoke nights, and Thursdays are open for live jamming by local musicians. On the weekends Beachcombers often hosts a live band.

Capone's Pub & Grill
751 North Fourth
(208) 667-4843

Capone's is a lively, fun sports bar where you can go to meet friends and watch a game. A variety of beers are on tap at the full-service bar. Live blues are featured on Friday and Saturday nights.

Crickets
424 Sherman Avenue
(208) 765-1990

The popular, casual Crickets bar is adjacent to, or part of, Crickets restaurant. You

can't miss it—it's the place with a car on the roof. It's usually packed on the weekends and during special events in Coeur d'Alene. There are a variety of beers on tap as well as wine and mixed drinks. A small stage serves as a venue for live bands.

Tubs Café
313 Coeur d'Alene Lake Drive

This comfortable neighborhood pub is open for breakfast, lunch, and dinner with an interesting menu and great beer on tap. They often host blues bands, which play inside in the winter and outside in the Blues Garden in the summer.

The Wine Cellar
313 Sherman
(208) 664-WINE

The Wine Cellar offers a large selection of wines, and the Bistro menu (with gourmet selections like cassoulet, seafood linguine, paella, and pork chipolata) is served until midnight on the weekends. Live blues and jazz are played nightly.

grant smokes. In the summer you can sit outside. If you arrive before dark you can see the mural, by Sandpoint artists Diana Schuppel and Leif Olson, on the building's west wall that tells the story of beer brewing.

Power House Bar & Grill
120 Lake Street
(208) 265-2449

The Power House Bar is adjacent to the restaurant, which specializes in rotisserie beef and chicken. The full-service bar is open seven days a week and is popular with skiers in the winter. They have a good wine selection, microbrews, and bar drinks. In the summer you'll enjoy great views from the deck.

Silver Valley

Cogswell's Coffee House and Saloon
Corner of Sixth and Bank Streets, Wallace
(208) 752-0382

Cogswell's is located in the historic brick DeLashmutt Building in downtown Wallace. The original tin ceiling is still in place, and a wall humidor which used to hold cigars now houses antiques and collectibles for sale. The beautiful mural behind the polished wood bar was painted in 1980.

Cogswell's offers microbrews on tap, cocktails, and wine, plus espresso and lattes. You can get a Coney Island hot dog or a German sausage to eat, and live music is regularly scheduled. Open mike nights host local talent reading poetry, playing music, singing, or performing comedy routines.

Zany's @ Silver Mountain
610 Bunker Avenue, Kellogg
(208) 784-1144

In addition to great hand-tossed pizza, Zany's has pool tables and a fully stocked bar. There is live music on Friday and Saturday nights. Zany's is a nonsmoking establishment and is popular with the skiers and snowboarders who flock to Kellogg in the winter. It's located upstairs in the half-timbered Silver Mountain Gondola building.

Sandpoint

The Beach House Lounge
Edgewater Resort, 56 Bridge
(208) 255-4947

The Beach House is a comfortable lounge serving beer, wine, and mixed drinks. You can stop in here while waiting for a table in the restaurant, or just to talk and enjoy a drink. In nice weather you can sit outside on the deck. The lounge and restaurant are located adjacent to the Edgewater Best Western.

Eichardt's
218 Cedar Street
(208) 263-4005

This comfortable pub and grill is located downtown on Sandpoint's main shopping street. There are handcrafted beers on tap and a nice wine selection, and the food is very good. A full coffee bar is popular with those who don't wish to imbibe. Upstairs is a game room with a pool table, board games, and darts. Local bands play here on the weekends.

Pend Oreille Brewing Company
220 Cedar Street
(208) 263-SUDS

Sandpoint's microbrewery makes the beer right on the premises. Sample their handcrafted lagers and ales and enjoy a meal in the nonsmoking dining room. The cigar room welcomes aficionados of those fra-

Shopping

Just ten or fifteen years ago, shopping choices in Spokane and the Idaho Panhandle were a little sparse. Coeur d'Alene and Sandpoint were just starting to develop as tourist destinations, and Spokane, while drawing shoppers from around the region, hadn't yet attracted many of the nationwide chains. The situation is very different today—we now have most of the big-name retailers, many national and regional specialty stores, and a plethora of local shops as well.

You can find anything you want in Spokane and north Idaho, and probably many things you didn't know you wanted. If you're looking for something to remember your visit, explore the many little shops in the downtown areas of Coeur d'Alene, Sandpoint, and Wallace. Huckleberries, which grow between 4,500 and 6,000 feet, are found on mountain slopes in both Washington and Idaho; jams, syrups, and candies made with the fruits are a wonderful local souvenir. You'll also see a lot of carved bears and moose, fishing mementoes, and Native American items. In the Silver Valley you'll find gold and silver jewelry, ingots, and mining souvenirs. Many shops carry artwork and crafts by local artists, and there are items to suit every taste and budget.

Most stores in our area are open all year, although many have extended hours in the summer and around the winter holidays. While we traditionally see the most tourist shopping activity in the summer months, north Idaho's reputation as a ski and snowmobile destination has drawn more and more shoppers in the winter also. Spokane is not a seasonal city; it hosts a number of conventions throughout the year, and regularly draws shoppers from as far away as Montana and British Columbia.

If it's food you're looking for, we have selections for every taste, from snacks and pop to organic vegetables and gourmet, imported cheeses. In the summer, farmers markets sell fresh produce and locally made foodstuffs. Several area bakeries produce excellent breads, rolls, bagels, and pastries. And supermarkets abound; the newer ones feature full-service butchers and produce sections that look like old-fashioned markets. For a picnic or a week's stay in a lakeside rental, you'll find everything you need locally.

Here are some of my favorite Inland Northwest stores and shopping areas organized by community, starting with Spokane and ending in the Silver Valley in Idaho. If you enjoy shopping and browsing, you'll like this selection of local shopping spots where you can while away an afternoon or run in and get just what you need.

Spokane

Downtown

Fifteen blocks of downtown Spokane are connected by enclosed, climate-controlled walkways and skywalks, making shopping a pleasurable experience on even the slushiest winter days. River Park Square is the downtown showpiece—an indoor gathering spot with shops, restaurants, and a huge movie theater complex. From River Park Square you can explore downtown by following any of the walkways to more stores and restaurants.

Auntie's Bookstore
402 West Main Street
(509) 838-0206, (888) 802-6657
www.auntiesbooks.com

Spokane's most-loved bookstore, Auntie's is now competing with huge Barnes & Noble, which recently entered the Spokane market. You'll enjoy the warm, friendly atmosphere in Auntie's, where you can sit in comfortable chairs as you browse the big selection of books and magazines. The knowledgeable staff can help you find anything you're looking for, and if they don't have it they can order it. Upstairs you'll find a good selection of used books, both fiction and nonfiction.

Boo Radley's
232 North Howard, across from the
carousel in Riverfront Park
(509) 456-7479

Boo Radley's stocks the most fun and unusual gift items in Spokane. Just about everyone will find something interesting in this store, which has everything from toys to candles to clocks. There are lots of nostalgic things for kids, like Silly Putty and Gumby, plus humorous notecards, mugs, blacklight items, incense, T-shirts, and one-of-a-kind things you won't find anywhere else.

The Children's Corner Bookshop
River Park Square
(509) 624-4820

Find a good book, puzzle, toy, or music CD for the child in your life in this store dedicated to things kids like. Also check the Kidstuff chapter for more about their story-times and special happenings for kids.

Global Folkart
1401 West First
(509) 838-0664

On the fringes of the downtown shopping district, Global Folkart is a nonprofit store selling items from low-income artisans around the world. The prices are reasonable, and you will be supporting a good cause. Typical items include carvings, baskets, handmade jewelry, toys, note cards, and clothing. The store is a project of the Peace & Justice Action League of Spokane.

Joel, Inc.
165 South Post
(509) 624-2354

This classy store carries a little of everything for the home, from kitchen gadgets to furniture. You'll find high-quality glassware and china, candles, cookware, and well-made tables, chairs, and other furniture in Joel, which is a few blocks south of the main shopping area.

Made in Washington
710 West Main, River Park Square
(509) 838-1517

Looking for a souvenir of your trip to Spokane, or a uniquely northwest gift? The Made in Washington store carries huckleberry candies, apple butter, locally made candy and cookies, Washington T-shirts and fleeces, carved bears, fish, and moose, and other northwest items. The store is located on the second floor of River Park Square, the downtown shopping and entertainment complex.

Moose Lake Company
707 West Main
(509) 624-4661

The atmosphere in Moose Lake evokes the rugged northwest, with clothing and gifts for the fisherman, hunter, hiker, and nature-lover. The store carries clothing by Timberland, Woolrich, Patagonia, and Australian Outback, as well as other outdoorsy items.

Suntree Books and Gifts
123 South Wall
(509) 747-1373

An eclectic selection of books, jewelry, knick-knacks, cards, wall hangings, and unusual gift items fill this little store to the brim. The amiable owners, Bob and Darlene Turner, love books and can order anything you don't see in the store. This is a great place to browse while waiting for a table at Europa Pizzeria, right next door.

Other Areas of Spokane
The Flour Mill
621 West Mallon

This remodeled brick building just north of the Spokane River used to be, as the name says, a flour mill. Today it houses a variety of shops and restaurants on multiple levels. As you explore the building, stop in the hallways and look at the historic photos of the mill and of Spokane in her early years. The Copper Colander (327-3523) is packed to the gills with unusual and quality kitchen items. Pots and pans, baking supplies, cookbooks, and kitchen gadgets will tempt any cook. Natural fiber clothing, socks, and handmade jewelry share space with Birkenstock sandals and shoes at Homestead Birkenstock (325-4105), which has a sec-

ond location in Northtown Mall. Wonders of the World (328-6890) is one of those stores that are so filled with interesting things, it takes you awhile to look at it all. Jewelry, artifacts, toys, decorations, and other things from around the world are this store's specialty. (All telephone numbers are area code 509).

Huckleberry's Natural Markets
926 South Monroe
(509) 624-1349

This unique full-size grocery store not only carries all the grocery items you might need at ordinary grocery prices, it specializes in organic vegetables, natural foods, and imported items. Looking for a quick jar of Indian curry sauce for dinner or natural cereal with no added sugar? You'll find it here, along with dairy and frozen items not available in mainstream stores. There is also a large selection of wines and cheeses, and a deli where you can buy meats and prepared foods to go or eat there at one of several small tables. Located on Spokane's educated and hip South Hill.

Insiders' Tip
Bargain hunters will enjoy browsing the many garage sales on weekends throughout the spring, summer, and fall. Look in the Garage Sales listings in the classified section of the *Spokesman-Review* newspaper.

Northtown Mall
4750 North Division
(509) 482-4800

Expanded to two stories in the 1990s, with an additional parking garage added, Northtown just underwent another expansion, which added more parking, a

Nordstrom Rack, Barnes & Noble, and Regal Cinemas. This mall is now quite large and offers several major department stores and specialty stores selling everything from candles to computer games to music boxes to scrapbook supplies. Free strollers and wheelchairs are available at the information booth on the first floor.

Spokane Valley Mall
14700 East Indiana
(509) 926-3700

Twenty minutes east of downtown Spokane on the north side of I-90 (take the Sullivan Road exit), the Spokane Valley Mall has over 120 stores and Regal 12 Cinemas. The Bon Marche, Sears, and JCPenney anchor the light and bright mall, which has a large food court and many specialty shops, including Gap, American Eagle Outfitters, Spencer's, and Hallmark.

White Elephant Surplus Stores
1730 North Division
(509) 328-3100
12614 East Sprague
(509) 924-3006

A Spokane institution, White Elephant isn't fancy but neither are its prices. Specializing in everything for the outdoor sportsperson, the stores are packed with fishing, hunting, and camping equipment. The toy sections have some of the best prices in town on all types of kids toys and games.

REI—Recreational Equipment Inc.
1125 North Monroe
(509) 328-9900

The Spokane branch of this Seattle-based store sports two floors of outdoor equipment and clothing. In the spring and summer you'll find everything you need for camping, backpacking, biking,

Downtown Coeur d'Alene is a great place to while away a Saturday. PHOTO: COURTESY COEUR D'ALENE CHAMBER OF COMMERCE

rock climbing, hiking, canoeing, and kayaking. Fall and winter bring skis, snowboards, snowshoes, and winter camping gear. In addition, the store carries knives, watches, global positioning equipment, books, and maps. If you become a member you get a discount on each purchase and a rebate at the end of the year—a good deal if you buy a lot of outdoor stuff.

Post Falls

Post Falls Prime Outlets
I-90, Exit 2, Pleasant View Road
(208) 773-4555

You can see the stores in this outdoor mall from the freeway—they're on the south side. You won't find the big-name designer clothing stores here that are so popular in some outlet malls, but you will find Black and Decker, Farberware, OshKosh, Fieldcrest Cannon, and Casual Corner—over 40 stores on both sides of the road. The mall also hosts a local artists' co-op gallery, the Riverbend Gallery. See the Arts and Culture chapter for more details. Tip: Be careful crossing the road to get to the stores on the other side. Cars travel pretty fast along Pleasant View Road and drivers aren't always careful to watch for pedestrians.

Coeur d'Alene

Downtown

All Things Irish
315 Sherman Avenue
(208) 667-0131

You don't have to be of Irish heritage to enjoy the attractive Celtic plaques and crosses, Irish tweed caps, and beautiful Irish lace in this shop. This is also the place to buy authentic fisherman's sweaters, hand-knit in the Aron Islands.

Camera Corrall
515 Sherman Avenue
(208) 664-2420

Get your film developed and stock up on photography supplies here. They offer one-hour film processing, and also process slides and will make prints from your digital photos.

Ramblin Rose Boutique
416 Sherman Avenue
(208) 667-1378

If you like off beat international clothing and jewelry, this is the store for you. Beautiful dresses, blouses, jackets, and outfits from Asia and South America can be combined with unusual rings, bracelets and earrings for a stunning outfit. A selection of handbags, scarves, and belts complete the picture.

Coeur d'Alene Plaza
210 Sherman Avenue
(208) 765-4000

The Coeur d'Alene Plaza is a small, upscale shopping mall at the southern end of Sherman Avenue across from the Coeur d'Alene Resort. You'll find a good selection of clothing, arts and crafts, gift items, and knickknacks in this mall which is really just an indoor extension of the downtown shopping area.

Cisco's carries an eclectic selection of northwest and other items, including Native American jewelry, baskets, and pottery; Western saddles, spurs, and chaps; fine art; bear rugs, decoys, and camp blankets; and western-themed furniture. Don Bennett, the amiable owner of Watches by Gosh! will help you find a timepiece to suit your fancy, whether you go for the latest fashion watch by Fossil or Swatch, unique titanium watches by Boccia or Momo Design, or radio-controlled atomic clocks by Junghaus. Are you a fan of Thomas Kinkade's heartwarming light-filled paintings? The Thomas Kinkade Coeur d'Alene Gallery presents the works of this wildly popular, award-winning artist. Looking for that perfect evening dress or a unique outfit? Louie Permelia carries a variety of boutique women's apparel. For the outdoorsy set, Finan McDonald Clothing Company has seasonal outdoor wear and natural fiber clothing, including Scandinavian sweaters from Norway and Iceland, Tommy Bahama sweaters, shirts, and pants, and designer Brighten belts. For rugged outdoor sports you'll find clothing by Columbia, Patagonia, Helly Hansen, and the North Face. CJ's Gourmet Foods carries a selection of those sumptuous north Idaho huckleberry items, like syrup, pancake mix, jam, and chocolates.

Cheryl Burchell Goldsmiths
110 North 4th Street
(208) 676-1645, (888) 711-9938

Cheryl Burchell designs beautiful gold jewelry, including the Heart Like an Awl necklace, a unique Coeur d'Alene design with an awl piercing and ending in the point of a heart. The shop also carries Christian Bauer, Swarovski crystal, Galatea, and Studio 311.

Other Areas of Coeur d'Alene

Fins & Feathers Tackle Shop
and Guide Service
1816 Sherman Avenue
(208) 667-9304

Pick up bait, hooks, and other fishing equipment or arrange for a guided fishing trip at this one-stop shop. They also sell fishing licenses and can advise you where the best fishing spots are. Also see their listing in the Hunting and Fishing chapter.

Northwest Outfitters
402 Canfield (on Highway 95)
(208) 772-1497

This large, modern store stocks all Orvis equipment for the fly-fisher. While you shop you can pick out a fishing book and read it in a comfortable chair by the fireplace, or test various fly rods in the casting pond. The store also sells fishing licenses and can give you up-to-date stream information. They also outfit fishing trips for both beginners and experienced fly fishermen.

Silver Lake Mall
Highway 95 and Hanley
(208) 762-2112

Located on the northern outskirts of Coeur d'Alene, Silver Lake Mall is the city's largest with over 60 retail and food stores. The major anchor stores are JCPenney, Emporium, Gottschalks, and Sears, and the smaller shops include the Book & Game Company (affiliated with Auntie's

Bookstore in Spokane), and Gateway Gardens, a store selling New Age books, crystals, music, and imported clothing.

Wiggett's Marketplace
4th and Lakeside
(208) 664-1524

An antique lover's delight, Wiggett's has four floors of furniture, knickknacks, clothing, and furnishings offered by 75 antique dealers. There's something for every budget and taste.

Sandpoint

Alpine Designs
312 North Fifth
(208) 263-9373
www.alpinedesignsmtb.com

Alpine Designs specializes in mountain bikes, especially for the serious hobbyist and competitive racer. They sell women's versions of several of their top machines, plus road bikes, touring bikes, and BMX bikes. They have a complete bike repair and tune-up shop, and do custom painting. During the winter they sell winter sports equipment like cross-country and downhill skis and boots, winter clothing, accessories, and backcountry provisions.

Art Works Gallery
309 North First
(208) 263-2642

On the main downtown shopping street in Sandpoint, Art Works has fine arts and crafts by regional artists, including original paintings, pottery, glassworks, sculpture, stone, wood, metal, jewelry, basketry, prints, and cards.

Coldwater Creek
Cedar Street Bridge
(208) 263-2265

Coldwater Creek is the mail-giant that sells northwest-style clothing all over the world. They have turned the unique Cedar Street covered bridge in downtown Sandpoint into a Coldwater Creek shopping mall filled with all of their clothing and gift items. An espresso shop and deli is also located inside.

Try Prime Outlets in Post Falls for a variety of good buys. PHOTO: COURTESY COEUR D'ALENE CHAMBER OF COMMERCE

Foster's Crossing
Fifth Street between Cedar and Oak
(208) 263-5911

Foster's Crossing is a mini-mall with 30 local dealers offering antiques, gifts, books, jewelry, and more.

Ground Zero
317 North First
(208) 265-6714

Ground Zero is a board sports specialty shop, carrying snowboards, wakeboards, and skateboards. They also have a selection of appropriate clothing, shoes, and swimwear, and CDs for teens and young adults.

The Incredible Christmas Store
102 Cedar Street
(208) 265-7866

You can't miss this store, with the Christmas decorations year-round. There are handmade and blown-glass ornaments, lights, table decorations, wreaths, and every other type of Christmas item.

Kid Zone
311 North First
(208) 265-1532

Kid Zone carries a good selection of non-violent, educational children's toys, games, books, and cassettes.

Lyman Gallery
100 North First
(800) 607-7748, (208) 263-7748
www.lymangallery.com

The Lyman Gallery specializes in wildlife, landscape, and western art in limited edition fine art prints. They also do custom framing using conservation quality materials.

Pine Street Pawn & Fly Fishing Shop
525 Pine
(208) 263-6022

Get everything you need for fly-fishing here, including rods, reels, line, flies, boots, waders, float tubes, fly tying supplies, and free advice. The pawn shop side has the usual pawned items: jewelry, firearms, electronics, musical instruments, and video games.

The Scandinavian Affair
319 North First
(208) 263-7722

Imports from Norway, Sweden, Denmark, and Finland fill this bright shop, which is quite a change of pace from the northwest-themed stores and galleries nearby. You'll find everything from whimsical signs that say things like "Parking for Swedes Only," to high-quality and expensive silver jewelry and embroidered linens.

Songbird Silverworks
300 North First
(208) 265-4313

This store sells locally made silver and gemstone jewelry, stained glass, stone sculptures, and other handmade items.

Visit the old mining town of Wallace for a unique shopping experience. PHOTO: COURTESY COEUR D'ALENE CHAMBER OF COMMERCE

Kellogg

Bitteroot Mercantile & Antiques
117 McKinley Avenue
(208) 783-5491

Located on the main shopping street in town, Bitteroot Mercantile has a little of everything, including a selection of interesting antiques and gifts, and an art gallery featuring regional artists.

Dave Smith Motors
I-90, Exit 51
(800) 635-8000, (208) 784-1208
www.usautosales.com

Who would think that one of the largest auto dealerships in the country would be located in tiny Kellogg, Idaho? Yet Dave Smith's close to 300 employees sold about 10,000 new and used vehicles in the year 2000, through a combination of Internet sales and fun gimmicks that get customers out to the Silver Valley. They barbecue hamburgers for customers and employees every Saturday, provide passes to ski at Silver Mountain or to see a movie in town for customers waiting for cars, and have a van that will drop service customers off to golf, fly-fish, or take a gold-mine tour while they wait. Customers from all over the United States buy cars, trucks, and SUVs from the dealership, which is known for "no-haggle business," meaning they sell new vehicles at or near invoice price.

Excelsior Cycle
21 Railroad Avenue
(208) 786-3751

Located next to Kellogg's bike trail, Excelsior Cycle is a full-service bike shop offering mountain bike sales and rentals, snowshoe rentals, and information about the many bike trails in the Silver Valley area.

Wallace

Excell Foods
800 Bank Street
(208) 752-1233

This is the only supermarket in Wallace, but it stocks a full line of foodstuffs, ice, cold beverages, bakery, and deli items.

Mining Museum & Gift Shop
509 Bank Street
(208) 556-1592

After you tour the Mining Museum, stop in the gift shop for a unique silver souvenir, or a piece of rock left over from drilling operations.

Needleworks
612 Cedar Street
(208) 556-4204

Owned and operated by Glenda Farley, a refugee from the corporate rat race, Needleworks sells everything for people interested in sewing and quilting. The store carries Bernina sewing machines, fabrics, patterns, and sewing and quilting supplies. They also offer sewing and quilting classes for both beginners and advanced needleworkers.

Silver Capital Arts & Wine Cellar
6th and Bank Street
(208) 556-7081

This eclectic shop has a little of everything, including silver jewelry, minerals and fossils, northwest foods and wine, and a mineral museum. Wine tastings are regularly scheduled; call for dates and more information.

Silver Treasures
506 Bank Street
(208) 660-9044
www.imbris.net/~silvertreasures/

Looking for a special silver souvenir or gift from the Silver Valley? Silver Treasures mints .999 fine silver medallions and buckles using your design or one of theirs.

Attractions

The biggest attraction in the Spokane and north Idaho area is the outdoors—the lakes, mountains, and rivers are what bring people to this area and make them want to stay. The beautiful scenery tends to draw attention away from cities and towns, which sometimes seem like mere entry points to the surrounding nature. However, there's a lot to see and do in town, too, as many tourists and convention goers have discovered as they explore our downtown areas, discover interesting shops and a wide variety of restaurants, and enjoy our historical sites, city parks, and trails.

You may have heard that north Idaho is a haven for white supremacists and other intolerant people. We need to dispel that rumor right now. Like many other areas of the country, we do have white supremacist groups here. But the community does not support them; in fact, the whole Inland Northwest is home to a strong "movement against hate." There is an initiative in Idaho to change the state's motto to "Idaho: The Human Rights State" in response to the bad (and, locals feel, undeserved) press the state has received in recent years. People in the uncrowded West tend to live and let live, but our communities have really pulled together to counter the message of hate spread by these small groups of mainly outsiders.

I encourage you to come to eastern Washington and north Idaho and see for yourself. Ours are warm and welcoming communities that need more diversity to grow stronger. Twenty years ago this area, especially rural Washington and Idaho, had a resource-based economy; mining and forestry were king. Today, we have shifted to high-tech industry and tourism, and we are welcoming new people with new ideas. Our mining towns are celebrating their histories with museums and other attractions, while lumber towns are creating new jobs in forest restoration and management. Our forest roads have become ATV and snowmobile trails. Tiny Kellogg, in the Silver Valley, has the one of the country's largest Internet auto sales companies, Dave Smith Motors. We're changing, and we want people to know about it.

If you're accustomed to prices in major metropolitan areas, you may be pleasantly surprised by the cost of things here. We aren't one of the cheapest areas of the country, but our prices are still reasonable. Many activities are free and when they aren't, admission prices are usually well under $10. There are often discounts for families, children, and seniors; don't hesitate to ask.

In addition to this chapter, be sure to read the chapters on Recreation, the Arts, Shopping, Lakes, Kidstuff, Winter Sports, and Hunting and Fishing for more things to do in and around the Inland Northwest.

Spokane Area

Cat Tales Zoological Park
17020 N. Newport Highway, Mead
(509) 238-4126
www.cattales.org/

What began as a large cat rescue operation out of the home of Mike and Debbie Wyche has turned into an educational center and zoo school that hosts thousands of school kids and adults annually. While zoos may not be high on the list of politically correct places these days, this zoo does a lot of good work, and it strives to educate the public about conservation and environmental protection.

With 40 big cats on the premises, this is an interesting place to see and learn all about them. Cat Tales has adopted many large cats kept as pets (!) until the owners could no longer care for them, and they also breed endangered species. A big hit with children is the Children's Petting Zoo, with pygmy goats, chicks, geese, ducks, and bunnies. Cat Tales also hosts a school of zookeeping, with students from all over the country.

Cat Tales is located in Mead, which is just north of Spokane. Take Division Street north in Spokane to the intersection of Hwy. 395 and Hwy. 2. Turn right on Hwy. 2 for about six miles to the Carney Road exit.

Cathedral of St. John the Evangelist
127 E. 12th Avenue, Spokane
(509) 838-4277
(509) 747-4403
www.stjohns-cathedral.org/

The gothic tower of the Cathedral of St. John on Spokane's south hill is visible from most parts of the city. The Episcopal church was designed by Harold Whitehouse, a congregation member, in 1925. Exterior stone used in the cathedral originated in the Tacoma area, while the sandstone in the nave came from Idaho. The cathedral contains three separate chapels, commemorating the three parishes that were combined to form the cathedral parish.

In addition to worship services and tours, the cathedral hosts a variety of educational activities, seminars, concerts, and special movie showings for the whole community. Guided tours are available after worship services on Sunday, and between noon and 3 P.M. on Monday, Tuesday, Thursday, and Saturday.

Fairchild Heritage Museum & Airpark
100 E. Bong Street,
Fairchild Air Force Base
(509) 247-2100

For military buffs, this museum is a fun place to learn more about military history and air power. The museum itself is housed in old World War II Women's Air Corps barracks. Its exhibits cover the history of flight, beginning with balloon flight during the Civil War. Memorabilia

from local military installations is displayed, including Fort George Wright, the former Army post.

In addition to the barracks buildings, the park houses a B-52 cockpit simulator and historical library in nearby stationary railroad cars. The simulator was originally used for pilot training during the years that Fairchild was under Strategic Air Command (SAC). Today, instead of bombers, the base houses refueling planes and its mission is mid-air refueling of aircraft around the country and world.

Outside, set among green, manicured lawns are displays of various military planes, from the B-52 bomber to the F-105 fighter and C-47 cargo plane. There are eight aircraft total.

The museum is open from 10 A.M. to 2 P.M. Monday, Wednesday, Friday, and Saturday. If you don't have a military ID card, you'll have to stop at the gate and get a free pass to enter the base.

John A. Finch Arboretum
3404 West Woodland Boulevard, Spokane
(509) 625-6655

Located west of downtown Spokane, the 65-acre arboretum's lawns and trees are visible from the freeway. It is a peaceful garden with over 2,000 labeled ornamental trees, flowers, and shrubs. Maple trees put on a great show of color in the fall, while in the spring, lilacs fill the garden with lavender and violet.

The arboretum features both native, inland northwest trees and shrubs, and plants from around the world that grow well in our climate. There are a variety of landscapes, including a native pine forest and rhododendron glen. The arboretum is open from dawn to dusk all year.

Fort Spokane
Washington Highway 25 at Lake Roosevelt

Established as Camp Spokane in the fall of 1880, Fort Spokane was the last of the frontier army outposts in the northwest. At that time, the fort was located at the confluence of the Spokane and Colum-

Native American powwows are held throughout the summer and fall. PHOTO: COURTESY COEUR D'ALENE CHAMBER OF COMMERCE

bia Rivers, although today it overlooks Lake Roosevelt, the body of water created by Grand Coulee Dam. Camp Spokane became Fort Spokane in 1882, when construction of a permanent post began. By 1894, over 45 structures had been built.

The fort, like most forts in the frontier west, was established to protect white settlers and keep an eye on the nearby Indian reservations. Most of the Indians sent to these reserves originally lived elsewhere, and tensions were high in the area. In addition, the Northern Pacific Railroad had come and was advertising the region's farming potential. Preventing clashes between the unhappy, resettled Indians and the land-hungry settlers was of primary concern.

Despite these early fears, relations between settlers and Indians were mostly peaceful, and soldiers at the fort saw little action. Troops hunted and fished, played baseball, and lived a relatively easy soldier's life. When the Spanish-American War broke out in 1898, the entire garrison was moved to Fort George Wright in Spokane.

In the following years, the fort was used as headquarters of the Colville Indian Agency, as an Indian boarding school, and as a hospital. In 1960 the National Park Service took it over and began restoration efforts.

Today you can see four of the remaining original buildings; the Guardhouse serves as the visitor center, which is open daily from mid-May through early September. On Sunday mornings during the summer, park rangers in period costumes give tours. Fort Spokane is part of the Lake Roosevelt National Recreation Area. Down the hill near the lake, the Park Service operates a campground and swimming beach in the summer months.

Green Bluff
Day-Mt. Spokane Road and
Green Bluff Road
(509) 238-4709
www.greenbluffgrowers.com

This farming community northeast of Spokane is locally famous for its late-summer and fall harvest festivals, although most farms sell produce from spring through late fall. In July, cherries are featured; you can pick your own or buy them already picked, plus enjoy live entertainment and a fun run called the Cherry Picker's Trot. August features pick-your-own peaches, while September and October are the time for apples, pumpkins, and other seasonal produce.

Because Green Bluff is so close to Spokane, it's a popular outing for city dwelling families. Especially on fall weekends, each grower's parking area gets packed with cars as people go from farm to farm sampling the wares. There are craft and food booths, straw mazes, pumpkin patches, farm animals, and lots of fresh apples, corn, grapes, and other products. Earlier in the summer you can pick strawberries, raspberries, and apricots. The grower's association produces a map and schedule of activities.

Manito Park
S. Grand at 18th Avenue, Spokane
(509) 625-6622

The city of Spokane has a lot of parks, but Manito (pronounced MAN-it-oh) Park is the city's showcase. Beginning at about 17th and Grand on the South Hill, Manito Park extends as far south as 25th, and as far west as Bernard. It is a hilly park, with roads leading to main attractions, as well as many paved and unpaved paths.

Manito owes its timeless beauty and design to the Olmstead Brothers, who also created Central Park in New York City. Originally called Montrose Park, its name was changed in 1903 to "Manito," which means "Spirit of Nature" in the Native American Algonquin language. The Olmstead Brothers were retained in 1907, and they created much of what is seen in the park today.

Manito Park is endowed with formal gardens, large grassy areas, a conservatory, and a duck pond. Located at the north end of the park, the duck pond area is a nice place to picnic, feed the ducks, and enjoy a game of Frisbee or football on nearby lawns. Following the road or paths further south, you'll come upon the Gaiser Conservatory overlooking Duncan Garden, a favorite place for weddings in the summer. The conservatory, designed and built by John Duncan in 1913, houses tropical plants and seasonal floral displays. The formal plantings surrounding the perfectly manicured lawns and walkways of Duncan Garden are perfect for a leisurely stroll.

Further west, Rose Hill showcases over 150 varieties of roses. It is an All American Rose Selections test garden where older rose plants are used to breed modern hybrids. The Nishinomiya Japanese Garden is a symbol of the friendship between Spokane and her sister city in Japan, Nishinomiya. Nagao Sakurai, a famous Japanese landscape architect, began designing the garden in 1967, and it was dedicated by both cities in 1974. The ponds, bridges, and traditional Japanese plantings provide a tranquil look at another culture.

All attractions in Manito Park are free. It is open until dusk every day.

Northwest Museum of Arts & Culture
2316 West First Avenue, Spokane
(509) 456-3931
www.northwestmuseum.org

The Northwest Museum of Arts & Culture, formerly known as the Cheney

Cowles Museum, is closed as this book goes to press for a major expansion that will more than double its size. As a regional museum serving all of eastern Washington and northern Idaho, it will be heartily welcomed back when it reopens in the late fall of 2001.

The Northwest Museum has its roots in historical displays arranged by the Eastern Washington State Historical Society in one of Spokane's historic homes, the A.B. Campbell House. In 1958, the museum moved into a new building next door to the house, dedicated to the memory of Major Cheney Cowles. The home was restored, and became part of the museum. In 1991, Spokane's Museum of American Cultures closed, and the Cheney Cowles Museum inherited its collections.

In 1999, work was started to expand the museum and make it a gathering place for learning, research, community meetings, local and touring exhibits, and entertainment. It will focus on regional history, visual arts, and American Indian and other cultures of the region.

Future operating hours and admission prices were not available at press time. You can check the museum's website or call them for more information.

Riverfront Park

Back in the early 70s, Spokane's riverfront, right next to downtown, was a run-down eyesore. Then the city decided to hold a World's Fair, Expo '74, on the riverfront and Havermale Island, and began a massive clean-up effort that transformed the city. Expo was a huge success, and Spokane won accolades for being the smallest city to ever host a World's Fair. The Expo site is today's Riverfront Park.

The park draws people all year—it's the site of outdoor concerts, 4th of July activities, an annual food fair, miniature boat races, Indian powwows, and myriad other festivities. The celebrated Centennial Trail runs through the park, providing a path

Running with the permanent runners (by sculptor David Govedare) in Spokane's Riverfront Park.
PHOTO: ELLIE EMMANUEL

for walkers, in-line skaters, bicyclists, and runners. Bridges from both sides of the river lead to Havermale Island, and paths connect everything.

The Spokane Opera House and adjacent Convention Center sit on the south side of the river. To the west, be sure to ride on the hand-carved 1909 Looff Carousel, a National Historic Landmark. If you sit on the outer row of horses you can try to grab plastic rings as you go by, and toss them in the clown's mouth. Grab a brass ring, and your next ride is free. Outside the carousel you can catch a ride on the park tour train, and nearby, kids will enjoy the huge Radio Flyer wagon, which doubles as a slide. Further west you can take a gondola ride over Spokane Falls, especially dramatic in spring and early summer.

On Havermale Island, the Pavilion amusement park features rides for young

Accessible, paved trails run throughout Riverfront Park. PHOTO: COURTESY SPOKANE CHAMBER OF COMMERCE

and old; it also has a skating rink in winter and a miniature golf course in summer. The IMAX Theater next door features a giant screen and stereo sound. Just outside the theater you can buy passes for all the park attractions; it's a better deal than buying individual tickets.

In the spring when the river is high, walk across the bridges on the north side of the island and marvel at the raging river. There are several parking lots north of the river, and side streets where you can park for free; walking bridges make it easy to get to the park.

Steptoe Butte State Park
East of Washington Highway 195 on
Hume Road

About 45 miles south of Spokane sits one of our area's most interesting geological and historical landmarks. Named after Lieutenant Colonel Edward J. Steptoe, who led troops to defeat in the area in 1858, the butte is a remnant of ancient, Precambrian rock surrounded by layers of younger basalt lava. Geologists have since adopted the term "steptoe" to refer to landforms of older rock protruding out of newer formations.

At 3,612 feet, Steptoe Butte is the highest point in the rolling Palouse landscape. A winding, four-mile road leads to the top, where on a clear day you can see past the miles of wheat fields to the Bitterroot Mountains in Idaho and the Blue Mountains in southern Washington. Outstanding photographs are possible, especially early and late in the day when the light creates interesting shadows. A day-use picnic area at the base is a nice place to relax. To get to the park, follow signs from the town of Steptoe, off Hwy. 195.

Turnbull National Wildlife Refuge
26010 South Smith Road, Cheney
(509) 235-4723
www.r1.fws.gov/turnbull/turnbull.html

What was once an old farm has been restored into a natural habitat for waterfowl, deer, elk, coyotes, beaver, muskrats, and other small animals. As many as 50,000 ducks, geese, and other migratory birds stop here in the fall. Many species also nest here in the myriad lakes, ponds, marshes, trees, and brush. But what makes this a gem for casual visitors is its accessibility. There is a five-mile, self-guided auto tour route through the refuge so everyone can enjoy watching the wildlife. Hiking trails run through the park, and various observation points and boardwalks are built over the marshes to give observers a better view. The entry fee of $3 per car is only charged March through October.

For families with younger children, a great way to see the refuge is via bicycle. The five-mile route is just the right length, and kids love hopping off their bikes to explore things along the way. People touring by car generally drive very slowly, so it's pretty safe. It's also fun to cross-country ski through the refuge in the winter.

Turnbull is a bird watcher's paradise, with its quality breeding and nesting habitat. Spring and fall migrations are the best time to see as many as 200 species of birds. An excellent list of birds seen here can be found at the U.S. Geological Survey's Northern Prairie Wildlife Research Center web site: www.npwrc.usgs.gov/resource/othrdata/chekbird/r1/turnbull.htm

Coeur d'Alene/Post Falls Area
Coeur d'Alene City Park and Boardwalk

The City Park in Coeur d'Alene is right next to downtown and the Coeur d'Alene Resort, making a convenient core with everything in walking distance. The Idaho Centennial Trail runs right through the park, which also has lawns and tennis courts, plus, of course, the beach. In summer this is THE place to be. This beach has lifeguards in summer and can get extremely crowded on weekends and holidays.

The public boat dock lies right next to City Park, where you can take a boat, float plane, or helicopter tour of the lake, rent bicycle boats, or parasail. Just east of the public dock is the world's longest floating boardwalk, which circles the marina. It makes a nice three-quarters of a mile stroll, and has benches to sit and look at the lake. To the east of the boardwalk you can see Tubbs Hill, a 120-acre natural park. Part of the homestead of Tony Tubbs, Coeur d'Alene's first Justice of the Peace, the hill was threatened with development in the 1960s, so the community raised the money to purchase the hill for open space. It was a good investment. There are several trails covering the hill, but the most popular is the two-mile perimeter trail.

The town's showpiece is the 18-story Coeur d'Alene Resort (see the Guest Ranches and Resorts chapter), which overlooks the lake. Its 300 rooms, marina, spa, and restaurants are outstanding, and the Coeur d'Alene Resort Golf Course (see the Recreation chapter) was named America's most beautiful resort golf course by *Golf Digest* magazine.

Museum of North Idaho/Fort Sherman Museum
115 Northwest Boulevard, Coeur d'Alene
(208) 664-3448

You can walk to the interesting little Museum of North Idaho from City Park— it's right next door. Artifacts depict life before and after United States exploration and settlement, as well as area logging and fire fighting. A twenty minute video tells the history of the Coeur d'Alene region.

General William Tecumseh Sherman came west in 1877 and established an army fort where City Park and North Idaho College are now. Pioneers settled around the fort and a sawmill was established. A sternwheel steamer was built which was used as a patrol and supply boat on the lake. When gold, silver, and lead were discovered in the Coeur d'Alene district in 1883, the Army used the boat to take miners from Fort Sherman to the headwaters of the lake. The fort was abandoned in 1900, when all the troops were sent to fight in the Spanish American War.

Most of the remaining buildings of Fort Sherman are on the campus of North Idaho College, located a few blocks north-

west of the Museum of North Idaho. The Powderhouse Museum houses artifacts and information about the fort. You can also see the Officers' Quarters, built in 1878, and Barracks Co. A.

The Museum of North Idaho is open Tuesday through Saturday, 11 A.M. to 5 P.M., April through October. It's closed July 4. The Fort Sherman Museum is open Tuesday through Saturday from 1 P.M. to 4:45 P.M., May through September. It's closed on holidays. Admission is $1.50 for adults and $.50 for kids ages 6 to 16. Children under 6 are free.

Treaty Rock Historic Site
Junction of 7th and Compton Streets, Post Falls
(208) 773-0539 or 773-8147

This is one of those sites many local people drive by all the time but never stop to see. It's not hard to find; signs direct you from I-90 in Post Falls straight to the parking lot. Well worth a stop, this historic rock commemorates the spot where Coeur d'Alene chief Andrew Seltice transferred land to Frederick Post, founder of Post Falls. A wheelchair-accessible path leads around the hill to the site. You'll see red figures of a man on horseback and a coyote leading a family group, and the incised letters of Frederick Post's name.

The land exchange happened in 1871, when Post arrived from Illinois and wanted to establish a sawmill. He paid Chief Seltice $500 for the 298 acres along the Spokane River where he built a combination saw and grist mill. Future developers saw the falls' potential for water power, and Post was able to sell the land and most of the water power rights in 1900 for $25,000. By 1903, a high-voltage transmission line was supplying power from Post Falls to mines in the Silver Valley. Treaty Rock is open daily from dawn to dusk.

North of Coeur d'Alene
Silverwood Theme Park
26225 North Highway 95, Athol
(208) 683-3400
www.silverwood4fun.com

If you have kids, you won't want to miss

the northwest's largest theme park (it's pretty fun for grown-ups too!). There are all kinds of rides, from the heart-stopping Tremors roller coaster to the old-time train ride around the park and through the woods (where the train is stopped by "train robbers"). In summer, the water rides have long lines. In addition to rides there is an old-fashioned Main Street with shops and a restaurant, carnival games, magic and ice shows, and lots of snacks and quick foods like hamburgers and hot dogs. The scale of the park is just right—large enough to make it a fun, all-day outing, yet small enough to be manageable.

Silverwood is open daily from June through August, and weekends and holidays the rest of the year. The admission price of $23.99 ($15.99 for ages 3-7 and over 64) covers all rides and shows, so you can enjoy your favorites as many times as you like.

Test your bravery on "Tremors," one of Silverwood's thrilling rides. PHOTO: COURTESY COEUR D'ALENE CHAMBER OF COMMERCE

Silver Valley

Big Creek Sunshine Mine Memorial
Exit 54 off of I-90, four miles west of Kellogg

Make a stop at this sobering monument to see how mining, for years the main source of jobs in the Silver Valley, also brought tragedy to many area families. On May 2, 1972, a fire broke out in the Sunshine Mine just south of here. Ninety-one miners lost their lives in the mine that day, and there are many tales of bravery and heroism as miners and rescuers worked to save those who were trapped deep in the earth.

Northern Pacific Depot Railroad Museum
219 Sixth Street, Wallace
(208) 752-0111

Railroads played an important part in the history of the Silver Valley, and this museum tells all about it. Located in a restored railroad station, the museum takes you back in time to the railroad's heyday. Photos and railroading relics tell the history of the chateau-style depot, which was built in 1901 and operated until 1980. The depot was listed on the National Register of Historic Places in 1976.

The museum is open from about 9 A.M. to 5 P.M. daily during the summer, and closes for the winter on October 15. Admission is $2, or $1.50 for ages 60 and older, and $1 for ages 6-16.

Oasis Bordello Museum
605 Cedar Street, Wallace
(208) 753-0801

Providing an authentic glimpse into the Coeur d'Alene mining district's bawdy and none-too-distant past, the Bordello Museum is a quirky and interesting place to visit. The Bi-Metallic Building, home of the museum, started out as a hotel and saloon. It eventually became the Oasis Rooms, one of many brothels serving the silver mining camps where men outnumbered women nearly 200 to one. At one time there were five such brothels along Wallace's main street.

The bordello tour shows the upstairs rooms almost exactly as they were the day they were abandoned, in 1988. You feel as if you've stepped into a time warp, with the shag carpet, furnishings, and colors of an earlier time. Tour hostess Michelle Mayfield has lived in Wallace all her life, and she has gathered information from the townsfolk, from police officers to hairdressers, who used to interact with the bordello. It makes for a fascinating tour.

The museum and gift shop are open every day. It is $5 for the guided tour, which includes the second floor rooms as well as other areas of interest, including a basement still.

Old Mission State Park
I-90, Exit 39, Cataldo
(208) 682-3814

Sitting on a hill just south of I-90, the Mission of the Sacred Heart is the oldest standing building in Idaho and a registered National Landmark. It was built from 1850 to 1853 by members of the Coeur d'Alene tribe under the direction of Jesuit Father Antonio Ravalli. Designed by Fr. Ravalli in Greek Revival style, it was built with simple tools and local materials. Structural beams were secured with wooden pegs instead of nails, and the walls were made of straw and grass daubed with river mud. The carved statues on either side of the altar, and the altar itself, were carved by Fr. Ravalli.

The Coeur d'Alenes had to leave the mission in 1877 because their reservation land didn't extend that far. The building

> **Insiders' Tip**
> The Cataldo Mission east of Coeur d'Alene is the oldest standing building in Idaho and was built in 1848 without the use of nails.

fell into disrepair, but it has since gone through two major restorations. It became a state park in 1975. Each year the Coeur d'Alenes return to the Cataldo Mission, as it's also known, on the Feast of the Assumption, August 15th. Following a celebration of the Mass there is a feast of traditional foods and a pageant commemorating the arrival of the missionaries called The Coming of the Black Robes. The park also hosts an annual Mountain Man Rendezvous in August (see the Annual Events and Festivals chapter).

The Mission is easily reached by taking Cataldo Exit 39 off of I-90, about 25 miles east of Coeur d'Alene. There is plenty of parking and a nice picnic area on the grounds. Touring the Mission and grounds does require walking, some of it uphill. An interpretive center tells about Catholic missionaries and their impact on the Northwest. The park is open daily from 8 A.M. to 6 P.M., June 1 through Labor Day, and 9 A.M. to 5 P.M. the rest of the year.

Sierra Silver Mine Tour
420 Fifth Street, Wallace
(208) 752-5151

Don't miss a mine tour while you're in the Silver Valley; after all, that's what the valley is all about. This tour begins in downtown Wallace, where visitors board a trolley that takes them to the mine entrance. On the way, the driver will point out some of Wallace's interesting sites. After donning hard hats, visitors are led into the mine's main drift by an experienced local miner. When I went on the tour, the miner told stories of mining life in the area and showed the group how some of the equipment operated. Displays and exhibits inside the mine show how silver, lead, and zinc were mined here.

This tour does require walking over uneven ground in fairly dark, narrow spaces. Children under 4 are not allowed. Tours operate May through September, and take just over an hour.

Silver Mountain Gondola
610 Bunker Avenue, Kellogg
(208) 783-1111
www.silvermt.com

For something a little different, don't miss the world's longest single-stage gondola at Silver Mountain. Departing from the Base Village in Kellogg, the enclosed, eight-person gondola cars take riders on a 19-minute ride up the mountain. At the end of the ride is the Mountain Haus, with U.S. Forest Service interpretive center, a food court, and marvelous views of northern Idaho. During the summer, music groups perform in an open-air amphitheater on the mountain, and mountain biking and hiking are popular activities (take the gondola up and hike or ride down!). In the winter, Silver Mountain is a popular ski area. Sightseers can ride the gondola in either season.

In the summer (July 1st to the first part of September), the Silver Mountain gondola only operates on weekends. The cost is $9.95 per adult and $7.95 per child for a round-trip ride. An all-day mountain bike pass is $10.95. Winter weekend lift rates are $30 for adults and $23 for children, but on weekdays everyone rides for $23. There are family and group rates also. To reach the Base Village, take exit 49 off of I-90 in Kellogg.

Wallace's Wild Past

In the late 1800s Idaho's Silver Valley grew into one of the largest mining districts in the country. Mining was a dangerous job, and Silver Valley mine workers led the country in organizing to demand better pay and working conditions. Labor disputes culminated in an uprising of valley miners and dynamiting of a Bunker Hill mine concentrator. The entire male population of Gem, Burke, and Murray were arrested in that incident, and union workers were banned from the mines for many years. Fires, floods, and avalanches also took their toll, but in spite of it all, the mines prospered.

The valley was somewhat isolated, with a frontier mentality that was more tolerant of drinking, gambling, and prostitution than more sedate, farming areas. Miners came to the Silver Valley to make money, not to raise families, and the businesses that followed them catered to their interests. There were 28 saloons in Wallace, one teacher, and one preacher. Brothels were another prominent and accepted business in these wild parts. In 1884 an Irish immigrant calling herself Molly b'Damm established a thriving brothel business with a row of cabins in Murray. She also came to be loved in the Silver Valley for her tireless work fighting a smallpox epidemic in 1886. When she died in 1888, every shop in town closed for her funeral.

In 1910, a huge forest fire broke out that almost destroyed the town of Wallace. Only a few buildings survived, including the Bi Metallic, a brick hotel and saloon built in 1895. As Wallace rebuilt, the Bi Metallic Saloon/Hotel became the Oasis Rooms, a brothel, one of five along the town's main street. The brothels operated profitably for many years but eventually closed down in the other Silver Valley mining towns; for some reason they stayed open in Wallace, giving it a "reputation." For years the brothels operated openly, advertising with neon signs, until in 1973 a Boise *Statesman* article charged that a politician was going easy on crime in north Idaho in exchange for a campaign contribution. Wallace's brothels were hurriedly closed, but not without controversy. At halftime during a University of Idaho football game, students unfurled a 40-foot banner saying GIVE WALLACE BACK ITS HOUSES.

The brothels did open again, but tried to be inconspicuous. It wasn't that people didn't know about them, but they wouldn't acknowledge their existence. The working women did contribute to the town, however—they even bought band uniforms for the local school.

In January 1988, the Oasis Rooms, the only brothel left open, got wind of an imminent raid by law enforcement agents. The women, who were mostly from out-of-town, dropped everything and left. The place was shut down and sealed; all the food, dirty dishes, clothing, and make-up stayed where they were until the present owners, Michelle and Jack Mayfield, bought the building and turned it into a museum.

Today the Oasis Bordello Museum pays tribute to Wallace's bawdy past. The Mayfields talked to local maids, hairdressers, bouncers, and police officers who had dealings with the Oasis Rooms, and they kept the upstairs pretty much the same as it was when it closed. They give interesting tours with lots of insider information and in the summer, they dress up in turn-of-the-century costumes and pose for tourist photos. Some people in Wallace didn't want this part of the past kept alive, but it has become a major tourist attraction and adds to the town's quirkiness.

Kidstuff

Kids the world over say "there's nothing to do!" but around here, there are plenty of things to keep kids entertained. We don't have one big major attraction, like the beach, but we have four distinct seasons, plenty of lakes, rivers, and mountains, and many organized activities geared toward kids and families. Both Spokane and the Idaho Panhandle are very family-oriented; people settle down here and several generations often live within visiting distance. Many things are on a smaller scale here and less crowded than in a larger city, making them more accessible and more fun.

When traveling with children, keep their ages and attention spans in mind when planning activities. Younger children will probably enjoy just going to a park with play equipment, feeding the ducks, or swimming in the summer and sledding and building snowmen in the winter. Older kids may enjoy more structured activities like laser tag, bowling, an Imax movie, fishing, or skiing. In any case, you'll find plenty of activities for kids of all ages in the Inland Northwest.

Keep safety in mind when doing anything with children here, especially if it's not something they're used to doing. If you're from a small town, keep an eye on kids when you're in Spokane; we have some big city problems and small-town kids may not be streetwise. If you're visiting from a big city and are planning on spending time outdoors, especially in wilderness areas, remember that there are predatory animals out there, like cougars, which sometimes attack small children. When boating with children, make sure everyone is wearing a lifevest. If you're out sledding or skiing with children in the winter, make sure you take them to an area appropriate for their ages—some sledding hills are popular with older teens and young adults who are too rowdy and go too fast for smaller children. Usually a nearby section of the hill will be available. Being safety-conscious doesn't mean you can't have fun—you can. Just try to have fun and be safe at the same time!

In this chapter I've listed some of the best attractions and activities for kids in Spokane and the Idaho Panhandle. Some are listed in other chapters too, but here I've tried to point out why they'd be interesting for children specifically. This list is not exhaustive—after all, you can do just about anything with kids except go to bars and nightclubs or go gambling. However, you'll have no problem finding the more mundane activities on your own. Keep reading for an Insiders' view of the best of the Inland Northwest for kids.

Children's Museum of Spokane
110 North Post Street, Spokane
(509) 624-5437
www.childrensmuseum.net

Located downtown just up the street from the new River Park Square, the Children's Museum is a place kids will love. Kids will learn without realizing it as they explore all the hands-on exhibits in the Fort Spokane Construction Zone, including a bed of wet sand used to illustrate erosion, and an area where kids can build a fort or learn about earthmoving equipment. Upstairs is a re-created Greek village where children can dress up in Greek country clothing and role-play in the market, restaurant, cottage, and kitchen. In the Children's Garden, children under 4 can crawl and climb, touch different textures, and dress up in animal costumes. The museum also has a parent resource room with information on child rearing, and special events and programs throughout the month.

The Spokane Children's Museum is open Tuesday through Saturday from 10 A.M. to 5 P.M. Admission is $3.75 per person; children one year old and under are free.

Cat Tales Zoological Park
17020 N. Newport Highway, Mead
(509) 238-4126
www.cattales.org/

This zoo and educational center strives to educate the public about conservation and environmental protection. In addition to seeing and learning about the big cats,

kids will enjoy the petting zoo, with pygmy goats, bunnies, chicks, and ducks. Kids and adults (12 and over) may enjoy hand feeding the lions and tigers (you don't get in the cage with them). The zoo is open Tuesday through Sunday from 10 A.M. to 6 P.M. in the summer (May through September), and Wednesday through Sunday from 10 A.M. to 4 P.M. in the winter. Admission is $6 for adults, $5 for students and seniors, and $4 for children 12 and under. See the Attractions chapter for more details.

Amusement Centers

Amusement parks and recreation centers are always popular with kids. From bowling alleys to all-inclusive theme parks, the Inland Northwest has a variety of entertainment centers for the whole family. They range in price from a few dollars to almost $20, but some have summer passes and other deals to help make them more affordable. We don't have any of the huge, Disney-type amusement parks here; ours are smaller and easier to get around.

Kids Play Indoor Fun Park
233 East Lyons Avenue, Spokane
(509) 484-2102
www.kidsplay.com

Rated the best place to have a kids party by area residents, Kids Play provides enough excitement to wear out even the most energetic kids. A giant 3-level playground where kids can climb, crawl, slide, swing, bounce, play in plastic balls, and drive small electric cars, Kids Play is a great value, especially on rainy or snowy days when the young ones are going stir crazy inside. A snack bar offers standard favorites like pizza, corn dogs, pop, and ice cream. Admission is $5.95 for children and $3.95 for toddlers, who can play in a separate toddler area.

LaserQuest
202 West 2nd Avenue, Spokane
(509) 624-7700

The first LaserQuest center opened in 1989 in England, and since then it has become popular around the world. It is an action adventure game played in a darkened, 12,000 square foot, three-level, fog-filled maze. Kids love it, but people of all ages

are welcome and can have fun. Hours of operation change with school holidays and summer vacation, but generally LaserQuest is open in the evenings on weeknights and from about noon until midnight on Saturday.

Lilac Lanes
1112 East Magnesium, Spokane
(509) 467-5228

Lilac Lanes just moved into their new, modern facility a few years ago, and it's a popular family bowling center. All lanes have pop-up bumpers for small children, and they'll enjoy bowling more without constant gutter balls. They usually have open lanes mornings, afternoons, and early evenings; after 6 P.M. is when all the bowling leagues take over. You'll pay $2 per game and $2 for shoe rental.

R & S. Alley
120 South Division, Sandpoint
(208) 263-4233

This small-town style bowling alley has 16 lanes, a video arcade, pool tables, and foosball. It may not be as big and exciting

The Big Red Wagon is a kids' favorite. PHOTO: COURTESY OF SPOKANE PARKS AND RECREATION DEPT.

as the bowling alleys in larger cities, but for kids sometimes smaller is better.

Silverwood Theme Park
26225 North Highway 95, Athol
(208) 683-3400
www.silverwood4fun.com

Families can have a great time at Silverwood because there's such a variety of things to do: rides and arcade games for the kids, shops, old-time movies and shows, a train ride through the wilderness, and an aviation museum. Only 15 minutes north of Coeur d'Alene on Hwy. 95, Silverwood makes a fun day-outing. See the Attractions chapter for more information.

Triple Play
Corner of Highway 95 and Orchard Avenue,
Hayden Lake
(208) 762-PLAY
www.3play.com

This big, new family amusement center just a few miles north of Coeur d'Alene provides a smoke-free venue for all kinds of fun activity. There's a kid's soft play gym, a rock climbing wall, virtual golf, 20 lanes of bowling (including laser and blacklight bowling at night), miniature golf, laser tag, and an arcade. As if that wasn't enough, they're also working on batting cages, a golf driving range and an indoor soccer arena. All this exercise will make you hungry, so a pizzeria and grill are on the premises to help get rid of hunger pangs.

Wild Walls Climbing Gym
202 West 2nd Avenue, Spokane
(509) 455-9596

Whether your kids are already into climbing or they've never even visited a climbing gym, they'll enjoy Wild Walls. Once kids discover how safe and easy it is, they love scrambling up different areas of the wall. Parents will be pleased to note that the gym emphasizes safety; it also offers lessons, birthday parties, youth programs, and competitions. All new climbers are required to take a safety and climbing lesson. A two-hour climbing lesson, including all necessary gear, is $45 for ages 10 to 14 and $30 for ages 14 and up. Private lessons are available for children under 10, but they must be accompanied by parents, during lessons or when climbing. For kids who already know how to climb, a single visit pass is $13 for ages 10 and older, or $10 for under age 10.

Wild Waters
2119 North Government Way, Coeur d'Alene
(208) 667-6491

Coeur d'Alene's waterslide park is easy to find—just take the Hwy. 95 exit off of I-90 and you'll see it right in front of you. (However the entrance is around the block, on Government Way). With a variety of slides, hot pools, an indoor video arcade, gift shop, and lawns for lying in the sun and watching the action, this is a popular place on hot summer days. Admission is $15.99 for people 48 inches and over, $12.99 for under 48 inches. The senior rate is $5.99 and kids under 3 are free. A twilight rate starts at 3 P.M. and costs $9.99.

Wonderland Family Fun Center
10515 North Division, Spokane
(509) 468-4FUN

There's enough here to keep a family busy for several hours. First, play a round of indoor or outdoor miniature golf, then hit the arcade games. The go-karts and bumper cars are fun, and some will enjoy trying out the batting cages. When you get hungry, order a pizza and pop at the restaurant.

Parks and Recreation

City parks and recreation departments offer many opportunities to keep kids occupied. Lessons, sports, arts and crafts, and after-school programs are just a few of the activities offered by city parks departments in the Inland Northwest. While most structured programs are geared toward residents or long-term visitors, one-day passes or memberships are usually available to use parks and recreation facilities. In addition to lessons and structured activities, city parks are a venue to keep in mind for a fun day with kids.

Spokane

Riverfront Park
507 North Howard
(509) 625-6600
www.spokaneriverfrontpark.com

You can always take the kids to Riverfront Park—you'll find lots to do any time of the year. In the summer there is a small amusement park and arcade in the Pavilion area, with carnival rides and miniature golf. An excursion train offers tours of the park (leaving from the area next to the carousel), and you can rent all types of bikes and in-line skates from Quinn's, also near the carousel. The gondola provides a thrilling ride over the falls, and you can see an IMAX movie or ride the historic Looff Carousel any time of the year. Riverfront Park is the site of Spokane's 4th of July celebration, with entertainment and activities all day and fireworks after dark (hint: get here early to reserve a spot).

Spokane Parks and Recreation Department
808 West Spokane Falls Boulevard, 7th Floor
(509) 625-6200
www.spokanecity.org/parks

You'll find interesting and fun classes for just about any child in the Parks Department's seasonal offerings. Topics range from tumbling, bowling, and Spanish to swimming and ballet. In the summer the Supervised Parks and Playgrounds Program offers free, supervised sports, crafts, and other activities in most city parks from 9 A.M. to 4:30 P.M. on weekdays—an exceptional deal. There are also youth sports leagues in summer, and swim lessons at city pools. Recreational swimming

Swimming classes and summer—they go together. PHOTO: COURTESY SPOKANE PARKS AND RECREATION DEPT.

is free at city pools (open from the middle of June through the end of August) for kids under 18.

Spokane Skate Board Park
Corner of Fourth Avenue and McClellan
(509) 625-6625

Skate boarders waited a long time for this outdoor park, located just south of downtown under the freeway. Riders take turns doing gravity-defying stunts on the concrete half pipe and pyramid structures. The park is free; bring your own skateboard.

Spokane Youth Sports
2202 East Sprague
(509) 536-1800
www.sysa.com

Getting kids involved in sports is the mission of Spokane Youth Sports, which organizes baseball, football, soccer, softball, basketball, and skiing teams, camps, and special events for children 4 and up in the Spokane area. SYSA also operates an indoor sports center and a soccer field that are available to rent for birthday parties or other events. It's a great deal when you consider how clean your house will stay.

Coeur d'Alene

Coeur d'Alene City Park
Sherman Avenue and Northwest Boulevard

On summer weekends you'll have lots of company at this popular 15-acre park, as area families settle into a grassy spot with blankets and picnic supplies. The sandy beach and cool water will keep the kids busy for hours, and there's a nice playground, too. Volleyball and basketball facilities are available for sports lovers. If you forgot the picnic lunch you can walk up Sherman Avenue to Hudson's (see the Restaurants chapter) for one of their famous fresh burgers.

Coeur d'Alene Skatepark
Mullan Avenue and Lincoln Way

Skateboarders in Coeur d'Alene used to damage park benches and run into pedestrians because they didn't have a special place to practice their sport. Supporters of a skating area raised the money to create this model park, which is now widely supported by the community. The comfortably large park has plenty of room so skaters aren't running into each other; there's also a hockey rink and grassy area for relaxing.

Sandpoint

Sandpoint Recreation Department
1123 Lake Street
(208) 263-3613

The Afternoon Academy offers after-school classes in basketry, computers, orienteering, and other interesting subjects. Youth sports leagues get kids started in all the major team sports, and an agreement with Schweitzer Ski Area gives local kids a break on certain ski times and lessons.

Sandpoint City Beach
(208) 263-3158

Less hectic than Coeur d'Alene's City Park, Sandpoint's beach is a nice place to spend a summer day. Enjoy walking on the sandy beach or on the walking paths, play in the water in the roped-off swimming area, or take the kids to the playground. There are covered picnic tables and barbecues, and a refreshment stand for cold drinks and munchies. You can play also play tennis or volleyball, and rent boats from the nearby marina. To get there, go north on First Avenue to Bridge Street and turn right—it leads right to the beach.

Winter Fun

When winter comes its time to think of new activities—either indoors where it's warm and dry, or outside in the snow and ice. Many people save indoor things, like museums and bowling, for the winter months because they want to spend the summer outdoors. Others look forward to winter for playing in the snow, skiing, and ice-skating. You can do things indoors all year, so those types of activities are listed above. In this section you'll find ideas for taking advantage of the winter weather outdoors.

The easiest thing to do when it snows is take the kids outside to build a snowman or snow forts for snowball fights. Sledding is a fun and inexpensive activity too—most hardware and discount department stores sell sleds in all different prices, and there are lots of places to find good sledding hills.

Sledding

Manito Park
S. Grand at 18th Avenue, Spokane
(509) 625-6622

Drive south on Grand Blvd. to 18th Avenue, where you'll see a parking area and sledding hills to the right. There are a variety of hills here for all ages; just try to stay in the open areas away from the trees. For more information about Manito Park, see the Attractions chapter.

Downriver Golf Course
3225 North Columbia Circle, Spokane
(509) 327-5269

Many of the city golf courses groom trails for cross-country skiing but not all have good sledding hills. At Downriver, you'll find the sledding hill right next to the parking lot, making it easily accessible.

Round Lake State Park
Off of Highway 95, Sagle
(208) 263-3489
www.idahoparks.org/parks/round.html

Round Lake has a very popular, long sledding hill with a 1,000-foot run down to the lake. It's also a beautiful place for cross-country skiing, and ice fishing is available when the lake freezes. To get there, drive 10 miles south of Sandpoint on Hwy. 95, then west two miles on Dufort Road.

Ice-Skating

Ice-skating is another fun winter activity. You can enjoy it at several indoor rinks year-round, but winter is the season for outdoor skating. Here are some of the top places.

Round Lake State Park
Off of Highway 95, Sagle
(208) 263-3489
www.idahoparks.org/parks/round.html

Unlike some of our mammoth lakes, Round Lake is small enough to (usually) freeze over and makes a great skating rink. On winter weekends park staff often have a bonfire blazing. Kids who like to skate fast are in luck here—a separate speed

Insiders' Tip

When you visit the Inland Northwest, don't just see the cities. Our mountains, rivers, and lakes are beautiful and unique; to really get a feel for this rugged place, rent a car or take a bus tour and see some of the countryside.

skating rink is available. See directions above under Sledding.

Riverfront Park Ice Palace
Riverfront Park, downtown Spokane
(509) 625-6687

The Pavilion area in Riverfront Park hosts rides and miniature golf in summer, ice-skating in winter. Non-skaters can sit in the bleachers and watch (dress warmly—it's outdoors) while skaters glide around the rink. It's open from November through early March, Monday-Thursday noon to 8 P.M., Friday and Saturday from noon to 5 P.M. and 7 P.M. to 10 P.M., and Sunday from noon to 5 P.M. Lessons are offered as well as family nights and other special events. It costs $4.50 for adults and teens plus $2 for skate rental, but the best deal may be a Winter Day Pass to Riverfront Park which includes skate admission, skate rental, one IMAX movie, and unlimited carousel rides.

Eagles Ice-A-Rena
6321 North Addison, Spokane
(509) 486-9295

Eagles is an indoor rink offering public skating year-round. Spectators have a comfortable, warm place to sit, and a snack bar offers all the usual foods for hungry skaters. Skating lessons, including figure skating and hockey lessons, are available, and the rink hosts adult and youth hockey leagues. Call for public skate times and more information.

Kids of all ages enjoy riding Spokane's historic Looff carousel. PHOTO: COURTESY SPOKANE CONVENTION & VISITORS BUREAU

Ice World USA
21510 East Mission Avenue,
Liberty Lake
(509) 927-9030

Practice arena of the Spokane Chiefs ice hockey team, Ice World offers a state-of-the-art facility with very good quality equipment rentals, skating, hockey, and figure skating lessons. Public skating is on Saturdays from 2:30 to 4 P.M. and Wednesdays from 11 A.M. to 1 P.M. It costs $5 with skate rental, and $3 without.

Skiing

49° North
Chewelah Peak Mountain Resort
3311 Flowery Trail Road, Chewelah
(509) 935-6649
www.ski49n.com/index2.html

Many people with children enjoy the low-key atmosphere of 49° North, which wins top ratings from local families year after year. The resort offers complimentary lessons, day care, rentals, and a restaurant. See the Winter Sports chapter for more information.

Lookout Pass
I-90 east of Wallace
(208) 744-1301
www.skilookout.com/

Thousands of local kids have learned to ski and snowboard at Lookout Pass's free Saturday Ski School, and the outstanding snowboard runs are well-known. Prices are low compared to other ski areas. See the Winter Sports chapter for more info.

Silver Mountain Gondola
610 Bunker Avenue, Kellogg
(208) 783-1111
www.silvermt.com

All the ski areas have children's programs and you'll be comfortable bringing the kids to any of them. However, only at Sil-ver Mountain do you get to take a 20-minute gondola ride just to get to the ski area. The excitement may be lost on small children, but older kids will appreciate the views as they're carried up the mountain. See the Attractions chapter for more details.

Rentals

REI Recreation Equipment, Inc.
1125 North Monroe, Spokane
(509) 328-9900

You can rent downhill and cross-country skis, snowshoes, and other outdoor equipment from this popular northwest outdoors store. Look upstairs for good quality (and stylish) outdoor clothing for the whole family.

Read a Book!

Spokane Public Library
906 West Main, Spokane
(509) 444-5300
www.splnet.spokpl.lib.wa.us/spl.html

Spokane's new public library is worth visiting just for the view of the Spokane River and the falls, but kids will probably be more interested in the books and videos. The library has a large children's section, and a separate area for teens also. Both residents and nonresidents may read or play games (the library has a selection of kids games) and take part in the programs like Storytimes and Summer Reading. Internet access is available on a first-come, first-served, reservation basis for periods of one hour (call 444-5336 to reserve Internet time at the downtown library). Library cards are free to city residents, and nonresidents may purchase a library card for $10 per quarter or $40 per year.

The downtown library is open on Monday and Tuesday from noon to 8 P.M., and Wednesday through Friday from 10 A.M. to 6 P.M. It is closed Saturday and Sunday. All of the branch locations are open the same hours, except they are open on Saturday from 10 A.M. to 6 P.M.

Children's Corner Bookshop
714 West Main, Skywalk Level of River Park Square, Spokane
(509) 624-4820

Skip the giant, nationwide book warehouses (we have several) and discover a small bookstore dedicated just to children. The Children's Corner is a magical place for the readers in your family, and nonreaders will enjoy the puzzles, games, puppets, and audio books. During the summer the store hosts a storytime hour, when one of the employees dresses up in costume and tells stories to children ages 6 to 10.

Coeur d'Alene Public Library
201 East Harrison Avenue, Coeur d'Alene
(208) 769-2315
www.dmi.net/cdalibrary/

The friendly Coeur d'Alene library has popular kids programs for all ages—from infants to preteens. They also offer a homework tutor after school. Library cards are available to almost anyone: Any resident of the five northern counties of Idaho is eligible for a card; Idaho residents who have current library cards from their home libraries are eligible for a card; and

Monday-Thursday from 10 A.M. to 8 P.M., Friday and Saturday from 10 A.M. to 6 P.M., and Sunday from noon to 6 P.M.

Sandpoint Library
1407 Cedar Street, Sandpoint
(208) 263-6930
www.ebcl.lib.id.us/ebcl/

One of three libraries in the East Bonner County Free Library District, the new Sandpoint Library was just finished in April, 2000. It's open from 10 A.M. to 8 P.M., Monday-Thursday and from 10 A.M. to 5 P.M. on Friday and Saturday. Special programs include Storytime for pre-schoolers, a summer reading program, and a homeschool program with crafts, stories and library skill instruction for homeschool kids.

out-of-state residents may get a card for a $20 deposit (you'll get $15 back when all items are returned). The library is open

See a Movie

The Garland Theater
924 West Garland Avenue, Spokane
(509) 327-1050

When was the last time you went to a move at an old-time, neighborhood theater? That's what the Garland is, and it's located right in the Garland shopping district. Second-run movies are only $1,

and a bottomless bucket of popcorn is $3. The Garland is very popular with families so arrive early. If the line stretches down the street, don't despair, moviegoers get in line before the theater opens, and the theater is large. There's free parking in the back.

Annual Events

The seasons determine our annual events, from winter snow festivals to summer arts and crafts fairs. You'll find a wide variety of events in this chapter, with something for every interest. In the summer, classic car enthusiasts have several celebrations, and each town has at least one art festival, with live entertainment and lots of food. In the winter, there are cross-country ski races, snowmobile festivals, holiday lighting shows, and other winter activities. Take a look through this chapter and find the events that interest you. If you're planning a visit, they'll give you something to look forward to on your trip; if you're a resident, this chapter will probably give you some new things to plan for throughout the year. Most events do not have entry fees; if there is a charge, it is noted in each individual listing.

January

Polar Bear Plunge
Sanders Beach, Coeur d'Alene
(877) 782-9232

A New Years Day tradition in Coeur d'Alene is going to the beach and plunging into the icy-cold waters of the lake. The faint-of-heart only make it part way, but some diehards go all the way in and swim around. Most wear beach shoes or waterproof sandals, as the "beach" may be snow instead of sand, and will definitely be cold. Each year the news media comes out to cover the event, so you could be on TV or in the paper.

Northwest Game Fish Show
Spokane Fair and Expo Center
404 North Havana, Spokane
(509) 624-2928

Anglers can prepare for spring looking at all the boats and fishing equipment on exhibit in this big show. There are seminars and tackle demonstrations, a casting pond, and drawings for fishing trips and equipment. There is a $5 entry fee.

Sandpoint Winter Carnival
Sandpoint Chamber of Commerce
(800) 800-2106

Held the third weekend in January (it's a long weekend, starting on Thursday), the festival has something for everyone. The Taste of Sandpoint food fair lets local restaurants show off their best creations. There's also a parade, broom hockey, the Mr. and Mrs. Winter Carnival contest, ice sculpting, a chili cook-off, and a fudge contest.

Deer Park Winter Festival
Deer Park, WA
(509) 276-2340

The small community of Deer Park, north of Spokane, holds its winter festival the third weekend in January. It features snowshoe baseball, hayrides, ice sculptures, and other snow and ice activities.

Spokane National Boat Show
Spokane Fair and Expo Center
404 North Havana, Spokane
(509) 991-1002

For over 46 years the Spokane Yacht Club has sponsored this show, bringing boat and boating accessory vendors from around the northwest to Spokane.

Experienced boaters can learn about the latest technology and drool over the newest watercraft, and beginners can learn what they need to know to buy their first boat. There are racing boat films and racing boats on display, and the virtual fishing will interest the kids. Admission is $5.

February

Langlauf
Mt. Spokane Nordic Center
Mount Spokane State Park
(509) 922-6080
www.pegasusmedia.com/langlauf.htm

This 10 kilometer cross-country ski race is held on the first weekend in February, with a Junior Langlauf for skiers 10 and under and a freestyle race for skaters on Saturday, and the main event on Sunday. The race has a mass start with four start zones. Elite skiers (the fastest) start first, then fast skiers, then sport skiers (those who are experienced and rarely need to stop), then beginners, children, and people who are just out to enjoy the scenery. Times under two hours are recorded.

Because people of all ages enjoy the sport, there are time handicaps for each five years of age over 65. Winners get trophies, and in each age class winners get Langlauf pile vests and a medal. Second through fifth place in each age group receive ribbons. There are also great door prizes given out during the awards ceremony, like skis, boots, and ski trips.

A Langlauf tradition is the awards for Woolies and Woodies. Those who dress in old-time, wool cross-country ski wear are eligible for the Woolies awards for best costumes. The Woodies awards go to the top male and female finishers on wooden skis, if they're dressed in Woolies style.

Area restaurants provide tasty food for a continental breakfast and hot lunch for all participants.

The Junior Langlauf is free, but children must be registered. The entry fee for the freestyle and traditional Langlauf races is $15, or $25 on the day of the race.

To get to Mount Spokane State Park from Spokane, take Hwy. 2 north to Hwy. 206, turn right, and take Hwy. 206 about 15 miles to the Park entrance.

Sno-Fest Snowmobile Rodeo
Wallace
(208) 556-4271

Held in January or February, this is north Idaho's largest snowmobile festival. Wallace is a center for snowmobiling, and allows the vehicles on city streets. This festival features drag races, an obstacle course run, a torchlight parade through historic downtown Wallace, and a wild west party. There are hundreds of miles of snowmobile trails in the mountains surrounding Wallace; see the Winter Sports chapter for more information.

Lionel Hampton Jazz Festival
Kibbie Dome, University of Idaho Campus
Moscow, Idaho
(208) 885-6765, (800) 325-7328
www.jazz.uidaho.edu/

Held during the last full week in February, this high-quality concert series brings top jazz musicians to the small university town of Moscow, Idaho. During each day of the festival, junior high, high school, and college students compete in vocal and instrumental jazz contests. Evenings feature concerts by these same students, plus professional musicians like Lionel Hampton, Hank Jones, Nancy Wilson, and Paquito D'Rivera. Ticket prices range from $18 to $25.

Moscow is about 85 miles south of Coeur d'Alene, and sometimes the weather and roads are bad in late February. Idaho Hwy. 95 leads south from Coeur d'Alene to Moscow, but it is a very curvy road through mountainous country. The road south from Spokane, Washington Hwy. 195, is much straighter and wider, and it will take you to Pullman, home of Washington State University. From there it's just ten miles across the border to Moscow.

March

St. Paddy's Day Parade
Downtown Spokane
(509) 880-2785

On St. Patrick's Day (March 17) or the Saturday closest to it, Spokane celebrates with a green parade from noon to 1 P.M. Many local restaurants serve Irish food and green beer.

Traditional Kosher Dinner
Temple Beth Shalom
1322 East 30th Avenue, Spokane
(509) 774-3304

For sixty years, Temple Beth Shalom has been putting on this very popular dinner and day of Jewish music, dance, and theater. It goes from 11 A.M. to 7 P.M., and is usually held on a Sunday in mid-March. Tickets are $12 for ages 12 and up, and $6 for kids under 12.

April

Junior Bloomsday
Joe Albi Stadium, 4918 West Everett, Spokane
(509) 328-7307

Held in mid-April, Junior Bloomsday is a two-mile race just for children 12 and under. Sort of an offshoot of the much larger Bloomsday race, which is for all ages, Junior Bloomsday has a closed and monitored course, so kids run or walk it by themselves. Parents have to watch from the bleachers. The entry fee is $5, or $10 if you wait until about ten days before the race to enter.

May

Bloomsday
1610 West Riverside, Spokane
(509) 838-1579
www.bloomsday.org

Spokane, Washington is the site of one of the largest, timed road races in the world: Bloomsday. Each May, over 50,000 runners, walkers, and people in wheelchairs turn out for the 12-kilometer race. Finishers and volunteers get T-shirts; quite a few locals have T-shirts for all 25 years the race has been held. Actually, it isn't really a "race" for many participants, it's an event, and you'll see people walking and talking with their friends, pushing kids in strollers and grandmas in wheelchairs, and generally having a good time.

Starting positions are based on your estimated finishing time, and those at the very front are professional athletes who have to qualify for top seeding—the prize for first place is $7,000. Elite wheelchairs start first, and they finish the grueling, hilly course in an amazingly short time. Next come the elite runners, and they aren't far behind. Everyone else follows in stages. Along the way are water stations and vendors handing out goodies and souvenirs.

Begun in the mid-70s, when "fun runs" became popular, Bloomsday was a success from the very beginning. It attracted 1,000 runners the first year, and 5,000 the next. In 1996, a record 61,298 people participated in the event. It's very

Fourth of July is a day of fun family activities, like these sack races for kids in Sandpoint. PHOTO: COURTESY SANDPOINT CHAMBER OF COMMERCE/DUANE D. DAVIS, PHOTOGRAPHER

well organized, and a dedicated group of volunteers each year ensures that everything runs smoothly. Every finisher's time is listed in the *Spokesman-Review* newspaper on the Tuesday following the race.

Bloomsday is a local inspiration. Every spring, people get out and start running and walking, preparing for Bloomsday. Bloomsday clinics are sponsored by local organizations, getting people into a regular exercise routine to prepare for the event. There is a "Fit for Bloomsday" program for local elementary school students.

Bloomsday is held the first Sunday in May. The entry fee is $10 (or $25 for late entrants, about a month or less before the race). Entry forms are available in grocery stores, sporting goods stores, fitness centers, and other places around Spokane in the spring, and you can also register online at the Bloomsday website. The race starts at 9 A.M., and be warned that the weather can range from hot to cold and rainy.

Lost in the '50s
Sandpoint
(208) 263-9321

On Armed Forces weekend in mid-May, Sandpoint holds its Lost in the '50s weekend, with a classic car rally showing more than 400 vehicles, and a '50s-style dance. If you still have a poodle skirt and bobby socks, this is for you.

Lilac Festival
3021 South Regal, Spokane
(509) 535-4554
www.spolilacfest.com

Spokane's Lilac Festival showcases the area's fragrant lilacs, which bloom in the spring and are found all over town. It celebrates the accomplishments of residents, encourages kids to get involved, and salutes the military forces in the area.

The third Saturday in May (Armed Forces Day) is when Spokane's Lilac Festival's Armed Forces Torchlight Parade is held in downtown Spokane. Despite

Spokane's size, this is a real, hometown parade, with high school marching bands, floats created by local organizations, fancy cars, and horses. Each high school in the city holds a competition to select a Lilac Princess, and from these the Lilac Queen is selected. She and her princesses preside over the Lilac Parade, and attend other parades and events throughout the region.

As part of the festival, a Junior Lilac Parade is also held, giving elementary and junior high students a chance to partici-

pate in a smaller parade. There is also a golf tournament, variety show, luncheons and dinners, and a biathlon.

Fred Murphy Days
Sherman Avenue, Coeur d'Alene
(208) 664-4808

This salute to Coeur d'Alene's colorful tugboat skipper is held the last Saturday in May. The parade down Sherman Avenue begins at 11 A.M. There are arts and crafts booths, food vendors, and more in this springtime celebration.

June

Artfest
Northwest Museum of Arts and Culture
2316 West First Avenue, Spokane
(509) 456-3931

This is Spokane's big summer art festival, held on the grounds of the Northwest Museum of Arts and Culture in historic Browne's Addition. The museum sponsors the show, along with the Spokane Art School. Many of the area's top artists have exhibits and booths here, and there is a Make It Art area for hands-on participation. Evening concerts feature a variety of jazz, dance, and world music. Parking is difficult in Browne's Addition, and the festival often contracts with nearby parking lots for additional free parking, with a shuttle bus to bring festival-goers back and forth. This information can usually be found in the local newspapers, or call the number listed above.

Timberfest
Sandpoint
(208) 263-0887

Held the second weekend in June, this festival celebrates north Idaho's timber heritage, and features the Idaho State Timber Sport Competition. The competition includes axe throwing, different kinds of wood chopping and sawing, log truck loading and driving, lumber grading, a loggers team relay race, and a tug-o-war.

There are both professional and amateur classes; some professionals come from as far away as Wisconsin. There are exhibits and food booths for the whole family, and a youth division for teens 13 and up with contests in pole climbing, cross-cut sawing, and other timber-industry activities.

Car d'Alene Classic Car Show
Downtown Coeur d'Alene
(208) 667-4040

Held in mid-June, this popular event brings classic car enthusiasts from around the region to show off their beautifully restored automobiles and to admire the efforts of others. There's also a Friday night car cruise, '50s dinner and dance, a collector car auction, and swap meet.

Hoopfest
601 West Riverside, Suite 206, Spokane
(509) 624-2414, (888) 880-HOOP
www.hoopfest.org

Everyone's crazy about basketball in this hugely popular 3-on-3 street basketball tournament that keeps growing each year; in fact it has become the largest 3-on-3 tournament in the world. Held on the last weekend in June, Hoopfest turns downtown Spokane streets into a complex of basketball courts, vendors, street performers, kid's contests, and food. Teams are grouped by age (the youngest are in third grade) and height, and some are very competitive. There are also lots of teams comprised of a few friends or relatives out to have a good time. The elite division has included professional and college basketball players.

In 1999 the tournament hosted 5,231 teams, and over 100,000 people came downtown each day to watch. Each team is comprised of four people: three players and an alternate. Entry forms come out in March, and it's best to enter early (you can also enter online via their website). Hoopfest is a nonprofit corporation; all proceeds are donated to local charities.

Bridge the Years
Old Mission Park, Cataldo, Idaho
(208) 682-3814

This non-competitive bicycle ride from the Old Mission to the historic Enaville Resort (approximately 5 miles) is held annually on the summer solstice (around June 20).

July

4th of July Celebration
Sandpoint

Sandpoint's Fourth begins with a Kiddie Parade in the morning, followed by the official Fourth of July parade. At dusk, the fireworks show over the lake is spectacular.

4th of July Festival
Coeur d'Alene
(877) 782-9232

This is one of the most popular Independence Day celebrations around, drawing huge crowds to downtown Coeur d'Alene. It includes a grand parade, live music, barbecue, and, the best part, fireworks over Lake Coeur d'Alene. Many people take boats out on the lake to watch the fireworks overhead, and the Coeur d'Alene Resort offers fireworks cruises (call way ahead for reservations, 800-688-5253 or 208-765-4000).

> ## Insiders' Tip
> Don't forget your camera and binoculars when going for a cruise on Lake Coeur d'Alene. There are beautiful views and birds and wildlife to see.

Historic Skills Fair
Old Mission State Park
Cataldo, Idaho
(208) 682-3814

You'll see demonstrations of spinning, quilting, candle-making, Indian crafts, and black powder shooting at this fair celebrating historic crafts and skills. Participants dress in period costume, and there are traditional food and music. It's held on the grounds of the historic mission, which lends a period ambiance.

Coeur d'Alene Wooden Boat Festival
Lake Coeur d'Alene
(877) 782-9232

With so many lakes in the Inland Northwest, boating is a very popular activity in the summer. This celebration, which usually takes place on a weekend in mid-July, attracts people who love boats, especially the finely crafted wooden kind. Although the boats are the center of attention, there are also arts and craft booths, the Art by the Lake show, food vendors, and a fireworks show.

River City Rod Run
Coeur d'Alene Greyhound Park, Post Falls
(208) 777-1712

In mid-July this hot-rod celebration brings car enthusiasts to Post Falls for three days of fun and entertainment. The show features a vendor's alley, a spectacular fireworks show, Miss Hot Rod, a burnout contest, tricycle races, and well-known entertainers.

July-amsh
Greyhound Park, Post Falls
(800) 523-2464

The annual Coeur d'Alene Tribal encampment and powwow is one of the Northwest's largest powwows, and it gets bigger every year, with over 30,000 attendees in 1999. It is a celebration, social gathering, and friendly dance competition for Native Americans from around the country. There is a grand entrance ceremony, dance contests, drumming, food (especially popular are frybread and Indian tacos), and crafts. The $3 parking fee includes admission.

August

Art on the Green
Coeur d'Alene
(208) 667-9346
www.artonthegreen.org

A three-day celebration of the arts held on the North Idaho College campus the first weekend in August. There are hundreds of booths selling pottery, jewelry, textiles, paintings, photography, and other crafts, as well as live music and food. For more information, see the listing in the Arts and Culture chapter.

A Taste of the Coeur d'Alene's/Downtown
Street Fair
Coeur d'Alene
(208) 664-4808
(208) 667-4040

This food and crafts festival is often held the same weekend as Art on the Green to make Coeur d'Alene one big party town. You can walk from the NIC campus to City Park for these activities, which also extend down Sherman Avenue into downtown. Local restaurants have booths in the park selling some of their most popular and famous dishes, and there are craft and other vendors, strolling performers, live music, and lots of people.

Royal Fireworks Festival and Concert
Riverfront Park, Spokane
(509) 455-6865

Held the last weekend in July, this festival features baroque entertainment and arts exhibits like live chess games, landscape painting, wood carving, needlework, Maypole dances, children's games, King of the Log and Soak-a-Bloke for teens, baroque magic shows, jugglers, storytellers, and sword fighting demonstrations. On Sunday night at about 10 P.M., the fireworks show is timed to coincide with the final two movements of Handel's Musick for the Royal Fireworks.

The Festival at Sandpoint
Sandpoint
(888) 265-4554

Held in August, the Festival at Sandpoint is a celebration of music, bringing world-class performers to north Idaho for outdoor concerts every summer. For more information, see the Arts and Culture chapter.

Coeur d'Alene Indian Feast of the
Assumption
Old Mission State Park
Cataldo, Idaho
(208) 682-3814

Every August 15, the Coeur d'Alene Indians make a pilgrimage to the Cataldo Mission for the Feast of the Assumption. It commemorates their participation in the mission's construction 150 years ago. The celebration begins with a Mass, followed by dancing, drumming, and traditional foods. The public is welcome.

Arts and Crafts Fair
Pend Oreille Arts Council
Sandpoint City Beach
(208) 263-6139

Held on the second weekend in August, this juried art show and sale draws artists from around the country, and attracts

Celebrating autumn colors at the Fall Foliage Festival in Spokane. PHOTO: COURTESY SPOKANE PARKS AND RECRE-
ATION DEPARTMENT

visitors from all around the region. For more information, see the Arts and Culture chapter.

North Idaho Fair and Rodeo
Kootenai County Fairgrounds
4056 North Government Way,
Coeur d'Alene
(208) 765-4969
www.northidahofair.com

Usually held around the fourth weekend in August, the five-day North Idaho Fair celebrates the summer's harvest and the area's western traditions. There are home and garden exhibits, 4-H farm animals, arts and crafts, horse shows, carnival rides, and food. Top cowboys, including many national finalists, compete in the rodeo.

To get to the Kootenai County Fairgrounds, head north on Government Way out of Coeur d'Alene. Admission to the fair is $5.50 for ages 13 and older, $2 for ages 6 to 12, and free for ages 5 and under.

September

Apple Festival
Green Bluff, WA
www.greenbluffgrowers.com

The orchards in Green Bluff (northeast of Spokane) celebrate fall with the Apple Festival, held on weekends from late September through the end of October. This has become a favorite outing for Spokane families, where kids can pick their own apples and pumpkins, and see farm animals up close. There are pony rides, corn and hay mazes, fresh pressed cider, apple butter cooking in huge kettles, craft booths, live entertainment, and lots of fall harvest produce for sale. On the last weekend in September, the Apple Pickers' Volkswalk is held. It is a free, noncompetitive 10-kilometer walk through apple orchards and along country lanes. Call (509) 489-3198 for more information.

Fall Foliage Festival
Finch Arboretum
3404 West Woodland Boulevard, Spokane
(509) 624-4832

With different activities planned throughout the fall, the Foliage Festival celebrates the changing colors of autumn. Finch Arboretum lies right next to I-90, occupying 65 acres along Garden Springs Creek. It has over 2,000 labeled trees and shrubs, and many turn colors in the fall.

Pig Out in the Park
Riverfront Park, Spokane
(509) 625-6685

You get a chance to sample the fare of a variety of Spokane restaurants in this food festival held in Riverfront Park on Labor Day weekend. The festival usually runs from Thursday through Monday, and can get so crowded you can hardly find a place to sit. It's fun to bring the family—everyone can have the food that appeals most to them, and the variety is wonderful. You'll find everything from barbecued chicken and ribs to huge chimichangas to Caribbean cuisine to pizza to gourmet salads. There are tempting desserts too, including huge, fried elephant ears and the most delicious ice cream bars. There is live entertainment throughout the day, with headliners in the evening. A variety of other vendors set up booths nearby.

Spokane Interstate Fair
Spokane Fair and Expo Center
404 North Havana, Spokane
(509) 477-1766
www.spokanecounty.org/fair/
Welcome.htm

The Spokane Interstate Fair begins the Friday after Labor Day and lasts for 10 days. You can easily spend an entire day or more looking at all the exhibits, trying

---

Insiders' Tip

Canada is only 90 miles from Spokane and Coeur d'Alene, and many Canadians visit our cities for shopping and entertainment. When the Canadian dollar is strong, you'll see many businesses advertising "Canadian at Par" to try to lure Canadians with an advantageous exchange rate.

the carnival rides and games, and attending the concerts and other shows. See prize horses, pigs, cows, sheep, rabbits, and chickens of every variety, huge pumpkins and zucchini, lovely homemade linens and lace, and other typical state fair exhibits. A wide selection of food is available to suit every taste, and vendors fill endless rows of stalls with everything from freestanding fireplaces to bicycles. A Pee Wee Rodeo gives kids a chance to compete in events like barrel racing, goat tail tying, and pole bending. The official P.R.C.A. Rodeo draws top competitors. Other entertainment runs the gamut from country music to monster truck races. Admission to the fair is $7 for adults, $5 for students ages 12 to 17 and seniors over 64, and $3 for children ages 6 to 11. Kids under 6 get in free.

November

Fantasy in Lights Lighting Ceremony
The Coeur d'Alene Resort
(208) 765-4000, (800) 688-5253
www.cdaresort.com

The day after Thanksgiving is the first day of the Fantasy in Lights celebration, and it is marked by a parade in downtown Coeur d'Alene and a lighting ceremony with fireworks. The lights and fireworks make a beautiful sight on a winter night. See the entry in December for more information about the Fantasy in Lights event.

December

Yuletide Lighting Festival
Wallace
(208) 753-7151

The first weekend in December is a great time to travel up into the mountains to Wallace for the Yuletide Lighting Festival. You can walk around the historic downtown and see the seasonal lighting displays as you browse in the many interesting shops. The festival also includes a gingerbread contest and raffle.

Fantasy in Lights
The Coeur d'Alene Resort
(208) 765-4000, (800) 688-5253
www.cdaresort.com

The Coeur d'Alene Resort claims this is the largest on the water holiday light show in America, and it is impressive. It features 150 computer-controlled static and animated displays on the floating boardwalk and resort grounds.

If you stay in the resort, you can request a room overlooking the boardwalk for a front-row seat, or you can take a Fantasy in Lights lake cruise. The boats have large, heated rooms with plenty of windows, but it's fun to go out on the deck to have a really clear view. After going around the boardwalk so you can see all the displays (which include an animated Santa going over a ski jump), the boat heads across the lake to the "North Pole," where the Claus family sits in a well-lit boathouse and greet all the kids on the cruise. There are more lighting displays on shore. It really is fun for kids of all ages.

The lights go on the day after Thanksgiving and are turned off after the New Year's celebration. It is best to make reservations for the cruise ahead of time. It gets dark between 4:30 and 5 P.M. in December so cruises start early.

Arts and Culture

The rugged mountainous country of north Idaho and northeastern Washington appeals to quite a few artists and writers, who find inspiration in the spectacular scenery and varied climate. Local Native American history and culture inspires some artists, while others are drawn by the wildlife or sporting images. Some local artists work during the cold and snowy winters, and spend manic summers traveling to shows and galleries around the region.

North Idaho has two towns that have built a reputation as "arts" communities: Coeur d'Alene and Sandpoint. For a town of only 5,000 people, Sandpoint, especially, hosts an amazing number of arts events and musical performances. The Pend Oreille Arts Council is very active in the community, bringing the arts into the schools and organizing many events throughout the year. If the arts are an important part of your life or vacation, check out what Sandpoint has to offer.

Spokane also has a good variety of cultural offerings; of course, it's a bigger city and is able to draw some of the top performers traveling around the country. It also has many galleries and a good collection of public art. In 1981, the city mandated that 1% of certain capital construction costs be used to purchase artwork for public spaces and buildings. Sculptures adorn Riverfront Park and other places, and libraries, fire stations, and other government buildings all have unique artwork.

This chapter is an introduction to some of the best cultural offerings in the Inland Northwest, but it is by no means exhaustive. It is designed to give tourists and short-term visitors plenty of ideas for activities during their stay, and provide a starting point for residents new and old to begin exploring the arts in this area.

A note to people from large cities: Attending performances like the opera or the symphony is an occasion for some in our area to dress in evening clothes or at least nice suits and dresses, as they would in many cities. However, here in the Inland Northwest, a lack of formal wear in the wardrobe doesn't stop people from attending these highbrow performances; a man in a tux may be seated next to someone in jeans and a sweater. (I've never seen anyone wearing shorts though.) If you want to attend a music or theater performance in our area, feel free to wear your formal attire—you'll fit right in. Or just put on a pair of slacks and a clean shirt—that will do also. As the Spokane Symphony brochure says, "We want your evening out to be as fun as possible, so dress up or dress down . . . as long as you dress comfortably."

Organizations and Venues

Coeur d'Alene

Citizen's Council for the Arts
P.O. Box 901, Coeur d'Alene, Idaho 83816
(208) 667-9346

The Citizen's Council is a nonprofit organization that exists to promote the arts in the Coeur d'Alene area. It sponsors the Art on the Green festival, the Corner Gallery, and other programs, and is always looking for volunteers.

Coeur d'Alene Cultural Center
414 Mullan Avenue
(208) 765-8196

The Cultural Center is located in a historic brick building at the edge of City Park. The building once served as a switching station for Coeur d'Alene's electric train system. Today, the Center provides cultural and scientific activities for the whole family, including gallery and garden tours, classes, workshops, and performances. Classes are offered for kids and adults in graphic arts, dance, science, crafts, and performing arts. The Center is also a venue for photography and art exhibitions.

Sandpoint

Panida Theater
300 North First Avenue
(208) 263-9191
www.panida.org/

Built in 1927 with sumptuous styling and attention to detail, the Panida was a north Idaho showpiece. By 1984 it was vacant and crumbling, until a handful of local citizens got the whole town involved in saving it. Just about everybody contributed what they could, and today the Panida is again a showpiece, with a busy schedule of concerts, plays, old and new films, and musical productions.

Pend Oreille Arts Council
P.O. Box 1694
(208) 263-6139

For more than 22 years the Pend Oreille Arts Council has arranged visual and performing arts programs in Bonner County. Each year they sponsor It's Happening in Sandpoint, with a variety of musical, dance, and theater performances from around the world. Recent performances have included James Kline, classical guitarist; the Roots of Brazil dance, music, and theater performance; M-Pact, hailed as one of the best a capella groups in the world; and a performance of the Strauss operetta, Die Fledermaus. Performances are generally scheduled during the fall, winter and spring in the Panida Theatre. During the summer, the Council sponsors the annual Arts and Crafts Fair.

Classes

Spokane

Corbin Art Center
507 West 7th
(509) 625-6677

Part of the Spokane Parks and Recreation Department, the Corbin Art Center offers affordable classes and workshops for adults, teens, and children. One day workshops range from about $10 to $35, while classes lasting six to seven weeks generally cost between $45 and $65. Classes are offered in topics such as art history, drawing, painting, stained glass, papermaking, calligraphy, and fiber arts. There are all kinds of classes and workshops for kids from pre-schoolers through the early teens. The Corbin Art Center is housed in the historic D.C. Corbin house, built in 1898. It is listed on the Spokane Register of Historic Places and is in the Marycliff/Cliff Park National Register Historic District.

Spokane Art School
920 North Howard
(509) 328-0950

The Spokane Art School offers classes for young and old, beginners and accomplished artists. Professional artists teach studio techniques appropriate to the age and level of the students. Classes and workshops are reasonably priced, generally from $20 to $30 for workshops and $70 to $100 for classes, which generally last for nine weeks. Classes are offered in subjects such as ceramics, jewelry, photography, drawing and painting, and design. There are introductory classes for small children to experience art with their parents, and drawing, painting, ceramics, and other media classes for kids in elementary school. An interesting birthday party idea for some children might be one of the Art School's Art Parties, where a group of chil-

Art on the Green in Coeur d'Alene is one of the summer's most popular events. PHOTO: COURTESY COEUR D'ALENE CHAMBER OF COMMERCE

dren get to take part in a class structured around the birthday child's interests.

Coeur d'Alene

Coeur d'Alene Cultural Center
414 Mullan Avenue
(208) 765-8196

The Cultural Center offers classes for both kids and adults in graphic arts, dance, science, crafts, and performing arts.

Hands-On Art Studio
6680 North Government Way
(208) 664-0683

The Hands-On Art Studio offers classes for kids and adults. Learn to make items like pottery, fused glass ornaments, linoleum block prints, and painted floor cloths.

Museums

Jundt Art Museum
202 East Cataldo, Spokane
(509) 328-4220, ext. 3211

This Gonzaga University museum, located in a new brick building overlooking the Spokane River, has been a welcome addition to Spokane's cultural offerings. It holds works by regional, national, and interna-

tional artists, including major pieces of glass art by Dale Chihuly and Auguste Rodin bronze sculptures. Collection pieces are rotated from storage vaults to the exhibition areas. There is also space for traveling exhibits. The museum is open Monday through Friday from 10 A.M. to 4 P.M., and Saturday from noon to 4 P.M. (It is often closed on school holidays, so it's best to call ahead). Admission is free. Although the address is officially on Cataldo, the museum is really located at the southeast corner of Desmet Avenue and Pearl Street.

Performances

Spokane

Interplayers
174 South Howard
(509) 455-PLAY
www.interplayers.com

The Spokane area's only full-season professional theater troupe, Interplayers offers a mix of recent hits and theater classics. Founded over 20 years ago, Interplayers performs from September through May. Recent performances have included recent award winners like Art and Sideman, as well as classics like Arsenic and Old Lace. Tickets range from $14 to $18, depending on day of the week and seating. You can purchase tickets online, through the Interplayers Web site, or by phone. Save by purchasing a subscription for the entire season. Senior citizens receive discounted rates on subscriptions. The theater is located downtown on South Howard, between Second Avenue and the railroad overpass. Parking on the street in that area is mostly free, and subscribers may purchase a parking permit for all the plays for $10.

Silver Spurs International Folk Dancers
1426 East 19th
(509) 533-9955

Silver Spurs is a popular non-profit dance troupe for kids ages 9-18. They perform

Budding actors ham it up in community drama classes. PHOTO: COURTESY SPOKANE PARKS AND RECREATION DEPT.

traditional folk dances from all areas of the United States, as well as international cultures. They often perform at fairs and festivals around the Inland Northwest, but have also performed abroad.

Spokane Children's Theatre
315 West Mission, Suite 23
(509) 328-4886

Children enjoy these fun performances created just for them and featuring many young local actors. Shows are generally scheduled for February, April, June, October, and November, and are held either in the Spokane Civic Theatre or The Met. Recent performances have included *Annie*, *Pinocchio*, and *Babes in Toyland*. Tickets are only $5 or $6, and a season ticket to all four shows is $12.

Spokane Civic Theatre
1020 North Howard
(509) 325-2507, (800) 446-9576
www.spokanecivictheatre.com

The Spokane Civic Theatre, incorporated in 1947, is one of the oldest civic theaters in the country. It's also one of the few community theaters to own its own building and land, which is located across from the Spokane Arena and houses two playing areas, the Main Stage and Firth Chew Studio Theatre. They operate a theater school for children and adults, and bring live performances to nontraditional venues like community centers, elementary schools, and civic organizations. Over 2,000 volunteers contribute countless hours each year. The main theater season runs from October through mid-June, with performances ranging from Shakespeare to modern, award-winning plays. Tickets are $14 for plays and $17 for musicals; seniors and students receive discounts. The Firth Chew Studio Theatre is a venue for smaller, experimental productions. Tickets are $8.

Spokane Symphony
Ticket Office: 601 West Riverside, Bank of America Skywalk
(509) 624-1200

From September through May, the Spokane Symphony, with Fabio Mechetti

conducting, performs a wide variety of classical, pops, broadway, and musical tributes. Their main venue is the Spokane Opera House, but they also perform at The Met Theater, the Masonic Temple, and in Coeur d'Alene at North Idaho College. Tickets range from $11 to $35. The symphony also does SymFunnies Family Concerts, which are educational concerts that help get the kids interested in classical music. Before each SymFunnies concert, children can try different instruments, try conducting, and tour backstage. Tickets for these Sunday afternoon performances are $6 for children and $9 for adults.

Silver Valley

Silver Mountain Concert Series
610 Bunker Avenue, Kellogg
(208) 783-1111, (800) 325-SEAT for tickets
www.silvermt.com

During July and August, Silver Mountain's mountaintop outdoor amphitheater is a popular venue for concerts under the stars. Performances tend to alternate between country and rock, with recent shows by Pat Benatar and Kenny Chesney. Tickets are $23 or $29, which includes a roundtrip ride up the mountain on the gondola.

Sixth Street Melodrama
212 Sixth Street, Wallace
(208) 752-8871, (877) SIXTHST

Wallace's popular melodrama theater started its 17th season in 2000. During July and August, one-hour melodramas that reflect the area's mining history encourage audience participation. They run Tuesday through Saturday, and tickets cost less than $10. Fall through spring bring a variety of plays and musicals, with ticket prices from $5 to $15. There are discounts for students, seniors, and groups, and the theater is wheelchair accessible.

Sandpoint

The Festival at Sandpoint
Memorial Field
(888) 265-4554

The Festival at Sandpoint is a celebration of music, bringing world-class performers to north Idaho every summer. The August concert series features classical, jazz, blues, folk, and popular music, drawing over 20,000 people each year. The concerts are held under the stars on a beautiful outdoor stage set up in Memorial Field, next to Lake Pend Oreille.

Unicorn Theatre Players
Sandpoint
(208) 263-9191

Providing community theater productions in and around Sandpoint, the Unicorn Theatre Players are a dedicated bunch who perform everything from musicals to dramas throughout the year. Always looking for more volunteers to act, direct, make costumes, work on lighting and other technical problems, or anything else, they seek to give anyone interested in the theater a chance to learn and participate.

Arts and Crafts Fairs

Spokane

Annual Juried Fine Arts and
Crafts Christmas Sale
Corbin Art Center
507 West 7th Avenue
(509) 625-6677

The year 2000 marked the 25th anniversary of this popular show. You'll find beautiful, creative, handcrafted items by some of our area's top artists at this juried show and sale. It's held in the beautiful, old D.C. Corbin House, home of the Corbin Art Center. It is free to the public, and is usually held the first weekend in December.

Artfest
Northwest Museum of Arts & Culture
2316 West First Avenue
(509) 456-3931
www.northwestmuseum.org

Artfest is an annual juried arts and crafts fair and family event. It lasts three days and is held on the grounds of the Northwest Museum of Arts & Culture in historic Browne's Addition. There are art demonstrations, children's workshops, and lots of great music. It's held the first weekend in June. Also see the listing in the Annual Events chapter.

Inland Craft Warnings
15205 North Shady Slope Road
(509) 466-2973

This is an annual arts and crafts show and sale that is judged in April and held the last full weekend in October, just in time to get an early start on Christmas shopping.

Coeur d'Alene

Art on the Green
North Idaho College
(208) 667-9346
www.artonthegreen.org/

One of the Inland Northwest's finest arts and crafts shows, Art on the Green is held in August on the beautiful North Idaho College campus, which is close to downtown and adjacent to Lake Coeur d'Alene. Artists and craftspeople fill hundreds of booths selling everything from paintings to photos to jewelry to pottery. There are many interesting and unusual items. One area is set aside for adult's and children's hands-on art projects, with materials and instruction provided. An outdoor stage hosts music and dance performances throughout the day and evening, and there is food and drink for sale to hungry fairgoers. You can park on the grounds of North Idaho College (with more than

50,000 attendees during the three-day weekend, it can get pretty crowded), or a free shuttle bus operates between downtown Coeur d'Alene and the festival.

Sandpoint

Arts and Crafts Fair
Pend Oreille Arts Council
Sandpoint City Beach
(208) 263-6139

What started as a small, local craft festival in the '70s has grown into a major juried arts exhibition. Held on a mid-August weekend each year, the fair draws artists from around the country, and attracts visitors from all around the region. There is a wide variety of arts and crafts to look at and buy, with something for every budget and taste. In addition, entertainment by regional musicians is scheduled throughout the weekend, and the children's hands-on art booth keeps kids interested.

Art Galleries

Spokane

Art @ Work
123 North Post
(509) 458-3580

This large gallery, which is affiliated with the Northwest Museum of Arts and Culture, is currently located on the street level of a former downtown department store, but it may move to another downtown location. It's worth finding for the large and varied selection of works by more than 90 local and regional artists. All artwork is for sale or rent, but it's interesting to just go in and look. Hours are Monday through Thursday and Saturday from 10 A.M. to 3 P.M., and Fridays from noon to 7 P.M. On the first Friday of the month from 7 to 8 P.M. the gallery holds Friday Night Salons, where local artists meet the public and share personal insight into their art.

Chase Gallery
808 West Spokane Falls Blvd.
(509) 625-6050

The Chase Gallery features monthly exhibits of local and regional artists. It is located in the lower level of city hall, adjacent to the council chambers. It is free and open to the public during the building's normal hours, Monday through Friday, 8 A.M. to 5:50 P.M., and also through the city council's evening meetings on Mondays.

Lorinda Knight Gallery
523 West Sprague
(509) 838-3740

This gallery shows the work of over 25 local and regional artists in a bright, light-filled space. It displays mostly contemporary sculpture, paintings, photography, ceramics, and mixed media works, and also does one-person shows. The gallery is open Tuesday through Saturday from 11 A.M. to 6 P.M.

Pottery Place Plus
621 West Mallon
(509) 327-6920

Located inside the Flour Mill (see the Shopping chapter for more information about this building), Pottery Place Plus is a cooperative of potters and craftspeople. All work is produced by local artists, who also staff the shop. There are both functional and decorative items in a variety of media, including pottery and stoneware, glass, porcelain, and metal.

Post Falls

Riverbend Art Gallery
4069 Riverbend Avenue
Post Falls Prime Outlets
(208) 773-8716

A nonprofit artists co-op with twenty members, the Riverbend Gallery displays the work of artists from Post Falls, Coeur d'Alene, Hayden Lake, and Spokane. It's staffed by the artists, and is easily accessible (right in the Post Falls Outlet Mall; take I-90, exit 2, in Idaho).

Coeur d'Alene

J. Clizer Studio
512 Sherman Avenue
(208) 664-5213

You can watch art being created in this working artist's studio open to the public. It features humorous original art, posters, small prints, and T-shirts.

The Art Spirit Gallery
908 Sherman Avenue
(208) 765-6006

This gallery, located in one of Coeur d'Alene's gracious, older homes, carries works by many nationally famous regional artists. There are changing monthly shows as well.

The Corner Gallery
North Idaho College, Boswell Hall
1000 West Garden Avenue
(208) 667-9346

Sponsored by the Citizen's Council for the Arts, this gallery holds touring exhibits from around the country. It's open Monday through Friday from 10 A.M. to 4 P.M., and is closed during July and August.

Sandpoint

Art Works Gallery
309 North First
(208) 263-2642

You'll find the amazing creations of Hope, Idaho, watercolor painter Barbara Janusz here, as well as those of other watercolor painters, mixed media artists, and sculptors.

Lyman Gallery
301 North First
(208) 263-7748, (800) 607-7748
www.lymangallery.com

The beautiful wilderness paintings of the late Stephen Lyman, who was a Sandpoint resident, are on display here, as well as Northwest photography by Ross Hall and works by Bev Doolittle, Carl Brenders, and Terry Redlin.

Olivetree Gallery
323 North First
(208) 255-7449

The watercolors of Sandpoint artist Robert Lindemann are shown in this small gallery, which also carries the work of other local and national artists.

POAC Gallery
Old Power House Building
120 Lake Street

The Pend Oreille Arts Council sponsors this gallery and exhibition space. Monthly shows by local artists and a permanent display of Ross Hall photographs of the old Northwest are featured.

Selkirk Fine Art Gallery
212 North First
(208) 263-8041

Watercolors of fish by nationally known artist Eileen Klatt are on display in this gallery. Even if you think you don't like fish, you'll catch some of the artist's enthusiasm when you see her beautifully rendered and colorful paintings.

Hunting and Fishing

The romantic image of the West is a land of endless forests filled with deer and elk and bear, lakes and streams filled with fish, cattle ranches and mining towns, and a population of rugged, self-sufficient people. In many parts of the West this image is far from reality—some western cities rival New York in cosmopolitan sophistication. But in much of northeast Washington and north Idaho the Western romance is still there. We have mountainous backcountry that's as untamed as it was in the early 1800s. Over two-thirds of Idaho is owned and managed by the federal government, and in some north Idaho counties the percentage is even higher. Boundary County, for example, next to the Canadian border, is 73 percent public land. The vast Idaho Panhandle National Forest comprises over three million acres in Idaho's five northern counties. North of Spokane in Washington, the Colville National Forest covers almost a million acres.

All this public land plus the myriad lakes, rivers, and streams in our area make this a hunting and fishing paradise. It's not like some places, where hunting means paying a landowner to hunt on a private game reserve. You do have to get permission to hunt or fish on private land here, but there is a lot of public land available where all you need is a license.

The weekend corresponding with National Fishing Week (usually around the second weekend in June) is a "Free Fishing Weekend" in Washington, and the Saturday of that weekend is a "Free Fishing Day" in Idaho. Anyone, resident or nonresident, of any age, may fish any waters open for fishing on these days in Washington and Idaho, without a license. All other regulations must be followed.

Licensing and Regulations

Washington

The Washington Department of Fish and Wildlife is responsible for regulating hunting and fishing in the state of Washington. You can get all the details about hunting and fishing licenses and seasons from their yearly hunting and fishing pamphlets on their excellent Web site. Don't hesitate to contact them if you have any additional questions about what is and isn't legal, or about their fish and game management policies.

Washington State Department of Fish and Wildlife
Spokane Office
8702 North Division Street
(509) 456-4082

Fishing Hotline:
(360) 902-2500 (this is a local Seattle number, long-distance from Spokane)

New in 2000 and 2001 is the Washington Interactive Licensing Database (WILD) that's making it easier to buy a hunting or fishing license. License sellers all have access to the database, and when the system is completed you'll also be able to order your license by phone by dialing a toll-free number, or purchase it on the

Internet with a credit card. By the time this book goes to press these processes should be in place; call the WDFW License Division (360) 902-2434 or visit the WDFW Web site at www.wa.gov/wdfw/ for more information.

Those age 16 and older must have an access stewardship decal to use identified WDFW lands and access facilities to hunt or fish. These decals are free when you buy your license.

Idaho

The Idaho Department of Fish and Game regulates fishing and hunting in Idaho.

Offices are open Monday through Friday from 8 A.M. to 5 P.M. Their Web site is a good reference for all the detailed rules and regulations regarding hunting and fishing in the state. The Department also publishes annual booklets of rules and regulations for hunting and fishing in Idaho; pick them up at stores that carry equipment for these sports.

Department of Fish and Game
Panhandle Region
2750 Kathleen Avenue, Coeur d'Alene
(208) 769-1414
www2.state.id.us/fishgame/

Fishing

Washington

Declines in certain wild salmon, steelhead, and trout species have caused the state to restrict fishing for them in some waters. However, the state's fish hatchery system in 1999 grew 118 million salmon, 14 million trout and kokanee, and seven million steelhead for harvest. Hatcheries also reared and released almost 600,000 warm water fish, including crappie, channel catfish, bluegill, largemouth bass, and tiger muskie.

Catch record cards are free with your fishing license and are required when fishing for salmon, sturgeon, and steelhead. You must record any of these fish you catch on the catch record card and turn it in the following year by April 30th. This helps the Department of Fish and Wildlife manage these species. The annual catch limit on sturgeon is 10 fish, and the limit on steelhead is 30 fish.

Statewide rules state that lakes, ponds, and reservoirs are open to fishing for game fish year-round. Rivers, streams, and beaver ponds are open to fishing for game fish from June 1 through October 31. The individual rules for each body of water and type of fish are very complex and are subject to change each year; to make sure

you know what you can fish for and when, pick up a free *Fishing in Washington* pamphlet from any fishing supply store, or find it online at www.wa.gov/wdfw/.

To find out more about fishing in any of the Washington State Parks, call (800) 233-0321. Before fishing on Indian reservations, contact the tribe for necessary permits and rules: Colville Confederated Tribes, (509) 634-4711; Spokane Tribe, (509) 258-4581.

A Washington State fishing license is required for both residents and nonresidents over the age of 14. A resident is defined as a person who has lived in Washington at least ninety days and who doesn't hold a resident license from another state. You must be carrying your license while you fish.

Freshwater fishing licenses are $20 for resident adults ages 16 to 69, $40 for nonresidents ages 16 and up, and $5 for residents age 70 and up. A two-day license is $6 for everyone.

Where to Fish

Spokane County has a plethora of small lakes suitable for fishing. Locals all have their favorite spots, but any of these lakes may be productive if the fish are biting.

North Idaho rivers and streams lure anglers from all over the world. PHOTO: COURTESY OF THE COEUR D'ALENE RESORT

Badger Lake, 12 miles south of Cheney on the Cheney-Plaza Road, has been planted with rainbow trout and has fishing resorts and public access. Fishing season runs from the last Saturday in April through September.

Bear Lake, 20 miles north of Spokane, is part of the Spokane County parks system, so there is a $2 per person charge to get in. However, it holds brown trout, bluegill, largemouth bass, smallmouth bass, crappie, and rainbow trout. Since this is a county park, picnic and restroom facilities are available.

Chapman Lake, also accessed from the Cheney-Plaza Road, is a quiet place to enjoy a day of fishing and swimming. With a 5 mph speed limit on the lake, you won't find jet skis and fast boats here. The only access to the lake is through Chapman Lake Resort, which charges $2 to launch a boat, and rents fishing boats for $5. Fishing here is good for largemouth and smallmouth bass, as well as rainbow trout and kokanee.

North of Spokane near Chattaroy, Eloika Lake is open year-round and has several resorts and public access south of Gray's Landing. Spring and fall are the best times to catch crappie and largemouth bass, and you can fish right from the dock. Eloika Lake is popular with ice anglers in winter.

Liberty Lake is east of Spokane near the Idaho border. Access is easy via I-90. There is a county park with a swimming beach, and a public boat ramp nearby. The lake is planted with rainbow and brown trout, and it also holds a variety of warm water fish.

Located off of I-90 west of Spokane, Silver Lake holds bluegill, crappie, perch, bass, and pike. It is also stocked with several kinds of trout, and provides good access for everyone from shore anglers to float tubers.

Idaho

The Idaho Panhandle has almost 140 lakes and outstanding river and stream fishing. Priest Lake is famous for trophy cutthroat and rainbow trout, and big mackinaw. The St. Joe, the world's highest navigable river, offers premier cutthroat trout fishing. Many Idaho record fish have been taken from the region, including rainbow trout, bull trout, kokanee, northern pike, and tiger muskie.

The Idaho Department of Fish and Game's hatcheries rear and stock nearly 23 million fish each year. The Cabinet Gorge Hatchery in Bonner County east of Sandpoint is a kokanee fry production plant. Kokanee has struggled in Lake Pend Oreille in recent years, giving the hatchery increased importance. A hatchery in the Silver Valley supports rainbow trout fishing in the Coeur d'Alene and St. Joe Rivers, and near Clark Fork, a hatchery supplies cutthroat eggs and rears several game fish species, including brook trout, golden trout, and Arctic grayling.

Fishing licenses cost $23.50 for adult Idaho residents, and $12.50 for juniors ages 14 to 17. Children under 14 don't need a license to fish in Idaho. For nonresidents, a fishing license is $74.50, or $38 for juniors. Nonresidents may also purchase a one-day fishing license for $10.50, plus $4 per day for additional days.

Where to Fish

Trout

Almost every species of trout are found in Idaho waters. Rainbow trout are found almost everywhere. The kamloops variety, which grows to giant size, is found in Lake Pend Oreille. The upper St. Joe River is an excellent place for fly-fishers to catch cutthroat trout. Above Prospector Creek it is catch-and-release only. Cutthroat is also found in the Coeur d'Alene River and its tributaries, the Clark Fork River, Priest River and its tributaries, and Kootenai River. Mackinaw, or lake trout, are found in Lake Pend Oreille and Priest Lake. Many smaller lakes and mountain streams hold brook trout. Fernan Lake, which is right next to Coeur d'Alene (just drive east on Sherman Avenue and follow the signs to Fernan), provides a quick and easy fishing experience close to town. Several species of trout are caught here, as well as warm-water fish. Ice anglers can catch perch here in the winter.

Warm Water Fish

Most north Idaho lakes are havens for warm-water species. The chain lakes along the Coeur d'Alene River are popular for northern pike and largemouth bass. The Idaho state record northern pike, at 38 pounds and 9 ounces, was caught in Lake Coeur d'Alene in 1992. Hayden Lake, just north of Coeur d'Alene, holds crappie, perch, and bullhead, as well as both large and smallmouth bass. Hybrid tiger muskies, which cannot reproduce, were recently introduced to Idaho lakes as an experiment to help control roughage fish like carp and suckers. They've become popular with anglers and can be found in Hayden, Coeur d'Alene, and other north Idaho lakes. Huge Lake Pend Oreille is home to largemouth bass and crappie, and the Pend Oreille River has bass, perch, crappie, and bullhead. Perch is a popular target of ice fishermen—see the Close-up on ice fishing for more about this popular species.

Salmon

Landlocked chinooks and kokanee are found in many north Idaho lakes, especially Coeur d'Alene and Pend Oreille. The kokanee population has had trouble in recent years because of dams and predators, including the chinook, so they are sometimes made off limits.

Charter Fishing on Lake Pend Oreille

If you want to catch the really big fish and don't have access to a boat or gear, try one of these Coast Guard certified licensed charter operations with fully equipped boats, all fishing equipment, and knowledgeable guides. They know where the fish are.

There are many fine lakes in the Inland Northwest where kids can enjoy a day of fishing.
PHOTO: ELLIE EMMANUEL

Diamond Charters
P.O. Box 153, Hope
(208) 265-2565

Pend Oreille Charters
P.O. Box 905, Sandpoint
(208) 265-6781

Seagull Charters
P.O. Box 208, Kootenai
(208) 263-2770

Winter Fishing

Winter is no deterrent in these parts for the avid fisherman. The big lakes like Coeur d'Alene, Pend Oreille, and Priest in Idaho, and Roosevelt in Washington, offer deep-water fishing for salmon, mackinaw, and rainbows. (Some lakes are usually closed to fishing in the winter though; check locally for current conditions).

When the weather gets really cold, smaller lakes freeze over and are safe for ice fishing. In Eastern Washington the best ice fishing lakes include Fourth of July, Williams, Hog Canyon, and Hatch Lakes for trout, and Sprague and Long Lakes for mixed species. North Idaho's best ice fishing lakes include Fernan and Hayden for large northern pike, Hauser, Round, and Cocolalla for mixed species. Spirit Lake is so popular for kokanee that the ice fishing season is sometimes closed early.

Some rivers and streams stay open in the winter and may offer good fishing during the cold weather for hardy anglers. Fly fishing for trout in the Spokane River and Rocky Ford Creek can be productive in cold weather, and the waters aren't crowded. Another winter catch in area streams is whitefish, which are found in deeper, slower moving rivers and streams like the Coeur d'Alene and St. Joe in Idaho and the Little Spokane in Washington.

Ice Fishing

Great fishing in spectacular surroundings is one of the big draws of the Inland Northwest. Anglers who want to make it a year-round sport will eventually try ice fishing, which can be fun and rewarding with a minimum of special equipment. Local fishing stores will carry what you need, including an ice auger to drill a hole in the ice (a hand-operated one will work just fine), some kind of slotted ladle to keep your hole free of ice, and an ice fishing top or short jigging rod. The most common species caught under the ice are perch and trout, and bluegill and crappie are other possibilities. They go for a variety of bait, such as worms, maggots, and cut bait. Put everything in a bucket, which can serve as a seat while you're fishing.

Once you locate a spot, use your auger to drill a hole. Make it no wider than 10 inches, for the safety of other anglers who may step through it when it has a thin film of ice on it later. Try fishing at different levels; perch usually like deep water and are often found close to the bottom, while trout may be a little further up. If you don't get any strikes after a few attempts, move to a different spot.

Safety tip: The Inland Northwest doesn't always have the prolonged cold necessary to put a solid sheet of ice on lakes. Before venturing very far out on frozen lakes, drill a test hole to make sure the ice is thick enough. One person needs three to four inches of clear solid ice for safety, and a snowmobile or ATV needs at least five inches.

Fernan Lake, near Coeur d'Alene, hosts a lone ice fisherman on a gray January day. PHOTO: ELLIE EMMANUEL

Hunting

Washington

Everyone born after January 1, 1972 must show proof when purchasing a license that they have completed a hunter education class or that they are not first-time license holders. Licenses may be purchased from any of over 700 sporting goods stores throughout Washington, or through the WILD program (see pages 109–110).

People of all ages must have a valid hunting license and any required tags, permits, or stamps to hunt wildlife in Washington. Big game licenses range from $20 to $66 for residents, allowing them to hunt various combinations of bear, cougar, deer, and elk. Nonresidents pay from $200 to $660 for the same licenses, while youth under 16 pay from $10 to $33. Small game licenses allow people to hunt for wild animals and wild birds, other than big game. The cost for residents is $30, for nonresidents, $150, and for youth under 16, $15. Nonresidents can also purchase a 3-day small game permit for $50. There are additional charges to kill a second bear or cougar in a season, and permits to hunt for goats, moose, bighorn sheep, additional buck deer, and additional bull elk are divvied up by random drawing or raffle. A migratory bird stamp added to a small game license is $6 (residents and nonresidents), or free for youth under 16.

Hunter orange clothing is required in all areas open to modern firearm deer and elk hunting. A minimum of 400 square inches must be worn above the waist—an orange hat will not suffice.

Small game seasons are generally from early September to the middle of March. The season for black bear in eastern Washington is from August through October, and for cougar from August through the middle of March. Deer seasons are from September through December, with certain dates for different types of deer, hunters over 65 and youth, disabled hunters, and graduates of Advanced Hunter Education programs. Elk seasons also run from September through mid-December.

Idaho

Hunters must carry a license to hunt in Idaho, and all hunters must be at least 12 years old. A hunting license for an adult resident is $11.50, and for juniors ages 12 to 17, it's $6.50. There are combination hunting and fishing licenses for $16, but seniors over 65 who have lived in Idaho for five years, and disabled people, only pay $4.50. Resident tags for deer are $18, for elk they're $28.50, for bear or mountain lion, $10.50, and for turkey, $18. There are reduced prices for juniors, seniors, and disabled hunters.

Nonresidents pay quite a bit more to hunt in Idaho. A hunting license is $128.50, or $73.50 for small game only. Nonresident deer, bear, and mountain lion tags are $235, and an elk tag is $338.50.

Idaho also requires everyone born after January 1, 1975 to complete a state-approved hunter education course before they can buy a hunting license.

Suppliers

Washington

The General Store
2424 North Division, Spokane
(509) 444-8000
www.generalstoreofspokane.com

The General Store is one of Spokane's most popular sporting goods stores. It carries a little of everything, from guns and hunting supplies to fishing tackle to camping stoves and lanterns, tents, archery equipment, boats and motors, clothing, boots and shoes, kitchen supplies, toys, and gifts.

Silver Bow Fly Shop
1003 East Trent, Suite 140 at Riverwalk,
Spokane
(509) 483-1772, (800) 732-7815
www.silverbowflyshop.com

Everything for the fly fisher, including tackle and accessories, can be found in this comprehensive store. They carry Sage, Winston, St. Croix, and Scott rods, reels by Ross, Pate, Bauer, and Redington, as well as flies and fly tying material. There are books and videos about fly fishing, and they arrange fly fishing expeditions both locally and worldwide.

White's Outdoor
4002 East Ferry (west of the Spokane
Interstate Fairgrounds), Spokane
(509) 535-1875
www.whitesoutdoor.com

This big (over 7,000 square feet) store carries a huge variety of fishing tackle for every type of angler. They have demo rods and reels, and hold free fishing seminars. There is a large selection of outdoor and travel wear, as well as shoes and boots.

Idaho

Black Sheep Sporting Goods and Toys
308 Seale Avenue, Coeur d'Alene
(208) 667-7831

This big outdoor store carries everything for the hunter or angler, including fishing equipment, guns and ammunition, and camping gear. There is also a discount toy section.

Fins & Feathers Tackle Shop and Guide
Service
1816 Sherman Avenue, Coeur d'Alene
(208) 667-9304

You can buy all your fishing supplies at Fins & Feathers, including bait, hooks, rods, reels, and other equipment. Owner Jeff Smith is a fishing guide who takes anglers to productive spots in local lakes and streams. The store sells fishing licenses and can tell you what's biting and where. Also see their listing in the Shopping chapter.

Tom's Sportco
22424 North 4th, Coeur d'Alene
(208) 667-2726

This store advertises savings of 30-70% on all hunting, fishing, and camping equipment. They sell fishing and hunting licenses and carry a selection of outdoor wear for both summer and winter.

Tri-State Outfitters
6275 Sunshine Street, Coeur d'Alene
(208) 772-0613

Tri-State Outfitters sells fishing and hunting licenses, as well as every type of outdoor clothing and gear. It's located on the east side of Hwy. 95, north of I-90.

Winter Sports

As a year-round travel destination, the Inland Northwest has much to offer during its snowy winter season. Some Insiders can't wait for winter so they can go skiing, snowboarding, snowshoeing, and snowmobiling. Others stay inside and wait for spring. If you don't like winter there are a lot of activities you can do inside to keep from getting too lethargic—mall walking, working out at fitness clubs, playing basketball and volleyball, or swimming in indoor pools. But the people who really take maximum advantage of this area are the ones who enjoy some winter sports, too.

Although we have some very classy resorts, our prices here are still relatively low because we haven't been "discovered" yet. You'll be pleasantly surprised if you're used to prices in places like Aspen, Sun Valley, and Whistler. And some of the smaller areas frequented by locals have especially good deals—places like Lookout Mountain and 49 Degrees North. But don't just take my word for it here, continue reading until you find a place that sounds interesting, then go check it out!

If you're into winter sports you're probably accustomed to winter dangers, but I'll detail some precautions anyway. Our winter days up here in the north are very short—in midwinter it doesn't get light until after 7 A.M. and gets dark about 4:30 P.M. Keep an eye on your watch if you're out exploring the woods on snowshoes or cross-country skis, and don't get caught out after dark. Stay on marked ski and snowmobile trails; every year people get lost when they go off the trails, and in the backcountry avalanches are a real danger. Be extremely careful when driving, and carry extra warm clothes, a blanket, a flashlight with extra batteries, flares or emergency warning lights, sand or something else for emergency traction, and matches. Carrying a cell phone is always a good idea. Most of the roads in this area stay open all winter so there usually isn't a problem getting where you need to go.

Skiing and Snowboarding

Skiing inspires a passionate love of winter that few other sports do. That's why so many skiers live around here. Insiders know our ski areas don't have to take a backseat to the more famous places. After all, who wants to pay $100 for a lift ticket when you can pay under $40 and enjoy great skiing and snowboarding at all levels of ability? We think we've got the advantage, and when you read the listings on the following pages, you'll see why.

Snowboarders have been the renegades on the ski slopes, but as their numbers grew, most ski resorts added separate snowboard areas. Snowboarding is especially popular here with young people, who will mound up some snow and create fun jumps in local parks when they can't get to the slopes. All of the ski areas listed here have areas for snowboarders.

Spokane Area

49° North
Chewelah Peak Mountain Resort
3311 Flowery Trail Road, Chewelah
(509) 935-6649
www.ski49n.com/index2.html

One of the West's best-kept ski and snowboard secrets, 49° North is an Insider favorite for its friendly people, smaller crowds, and lower prices. Continually voted the region's best family resort, it offers dry powder and great skiing in the Colville National Forest. From the top of Chewelah Peak, you can see the entire Pend Oreille River Valley and several mountain ranges.

The ski and snowboard school at 49° North specializes in introducing fearful beginners to the joys of skiing or boarding packages for everyone from small children to adults make it easy to get started in these exciting sports. The 49°er Club provides day care and ski or snowboard lesson packages for kids 5 to 12. Holiday camps offer group lessons and fun for teenagers. On weekends and holidays, the resort offers a complimentary 1-hour group lesson in the morning in alpine skiing, snowboarding, and telemark skiing with the purchase of a lift ticket. In addition, the lodge offers rentals, equipment repair, a retail ski shop, and grill.

49° North is open from 9 A.M. to 4 P.M. Friday through Tuesday, and seven days a week during the winter holidays. Lift tickets on weekends and holidays cost $32 for ages 18 to 64, and $22-$24 for everyone else. Midweek prices are cheaper at $25 for ages 18 to 64 and $20-$22 for other ages. Kids 6 and under ski free.

Mt. Spokane Ski and Snowboard Park
End of Mt. Spokane Park Drive
(509) 238-2220
www.mtspokane.com

Spokane's closest ski and snowboard area has a vertical rise of 2,000 feet, four double chairs, one beginner lift, 30 trails, a terrain park for snowboarders, sledding and tubing hills, restaurant, day care, ski schools,

and good night skiing. Its big advantage is that it's close, but you do have to drive up some windy mountain roads to get here.

Mt. Spokane's SnoPlay Daycare provides a fun atmosphere for kids too young to ski, or for kids who's parents want to take a quick run down some more advanced slopes. Kids get snacks, games, and indoor/outdoor activities. They also offer a combined day care and ski lesson package for children under 10. Reservations for day care are strongly recommended, call (509) 238-2220, ext. 229.

Lift tickets for ages 21 to 61 cost $29 on weekends and holidays, and $22 Wednesday through Friday. Young adults, seniors, military members, and college students pay $26, juniors pay $23, and seniors over 70 pay $10 on weekends; weekday prices are correspondingly less. Kids 6 and under ski free. The best deal is night skiing from 4 P.M. to 9:30 P.M., which only costs $15 for a lift ticket, and $5 for seniors over 70.

North Idaho

Lookout Pass
I-90 east of Wallace
(208) 744-1301
www.skilookout.com/

You'll see this ski area from I-90 as you're traveling east of Wallace, Idaho. It's open 9 A.M. to 4 P.M. from the first snowfall in November until early April every Thursday through Sunday, plus holidays, and daily from December 14 through January 1. Lookout Pass gets lots of snow (average 387 inches per year) and has 180 acres open for skiing with 16 runs and two terrain parks. There are runs for each skill level, and snowboarders love the natural half-pipe run, with huge banks, mounds, and launches. Lookout Pass has operated a free 10-week Saturday Ski School for 50 years, and has taught over 35,000 kids to ski. It operates free buses to the school on Saturday mornings from pickup points in the Silver Valley. There's also a snowboarding school, a day lodge, and complete rental shop. Lift tickets cost $20 per day for adults ages 19 to 61, $15 for ages

7 to 18 and over 61, and children 6 and under are free. There are specials on Thursdays and Fridays.

Silver Mountain
610 Bunker Avenue, Kellogg
(208) 783-1111
www.silvermt.com

Silver Mountain is Kellogg's answer to mine closures. Since mining jobs were disappearing and people didn't want to leave their Bitterroot Mountain town, they developed a ski mountain and had a Swiss company, Von Roll Tramways, build a European-style gondola to take skiers up the mountain. The gondola opened in 1990, and the ski resort has been growing ever since.

One of Silver Mountain's attractions is its accessibility. I-90 leads directly to Kellogg, which has a big, free parking area next to the gondola office. The 8-passenger gondolas will take you and your equipment up to the ski area. Lift tickets, purchased at the bottom of the mountain, include the gondola ride. Weekend lift prices are $30 for adults, $25 for college students and seniors, $23 for ages 7 to 17, and free for 6 and under. Midweek prices are a bargain at $23 for everyone (6 and under still free). Special night skiing deals begin at 3 P.M. on Friday and Saturday during January and February.

Silver Mountain features runs for all ski and snowboard skill levels, including special beginner slopes for those just learning. The Mountain Haus Grille in the lodge offers burgers, pizza, salads, and sandwiches, plus fresh fruit, candy, and cookies for a quick pickup. On sunny days you can enjoy drinks or a barbecue out on the deck. There's also a food outlet out by the chair lifts for hungry skiers who can't stop long enough to go to the lodge.

Schweitzer
10,000 Schweitzer Mountain Road,
Sandpoint
(208) 263-9555
www.schweitzer.com

With 2,500 acres of terrain for downhill, cross-country, and snowboarding, and drop-dead views of Lake Pend Oreille, Schweitzer appeals to everyone from families to young snowboarders. Plus only at Schweitzer can you ride Stella, the new five-person chairlift leading to 150 recently opened acres of new terrain. Full-day lift tickets are $37 for adults, $27 for juniors, and $32 for seniors. If you don't mind night skiing you'll pay just $10 from 3 P.M. to 9 P.M. Kids 6 and under ski free at any time.

You can learn to ski or snowboard at Schweitzer with the EZ 1-2-3 program, which includes two lessons and three days of rentals for $70. There are also private lessons available, and you can get personalized instruction for a group of three or less for $35. There are ski lessons and camps for kids too.

Schweitzer operates a shuttle that allows you to park at the bottom of the mountain and ride up.

Cross-country skiing

Downhill skiing's slower and much cheaper cousin, cross-country has many aficionados in the Inland Northwest. It's easier to learn, safer, more accessible, and you don't have to save all year to afford the equipment you need. It's great exercise, and almost anyone can do it, even older people who've never skied before. Need I say more?

All the ski areas listed above have cross-country ski areas. Schweitzer offers a beginning cross-country package for $32 that includes instruction and equipment rental.

Washington State operates a Sno-Park program to provide cleared parking areas for winter recreation. There are several of these on Mount Spokane, providing access to over 24 miles of groomed trails. A Sno-Park permit is required when parking in a Sno-Park; these cost $8 per day or $20 per season per vehicle. Idaho's similar program is the Idaho Park-n-Ski lots. Washington and Idaho accept each other's permits for parking. To find out which vendors are selling the permits call (208) 334-4199 in Idaho or (800) 233-0321 in Washington.

When the snow is deep enough in Spokane, city golf courses groom trails for cross-country skiers. This is a fun and easy way to enjoy cross-country. Many golf courses become snowy wonderlands in the winter, with lots of trees and rolling terrain to make the routes interesting. Be sure to stay away from the marked greens to avoid damaging the more fragile grass underneath.

The northwest's largest cross-country ski race, the Langlauf, is held the first Saturday in February on the Nordic trails of Mt. Spokane; it is a fun event for the whole family. The Alp Horn Society plays giant Tyrolian-style horns, and the Woolies and Woodies awards go to the ten skiers dressed in the most old-fashioned skiwear. A Junior Langlauf for skiers 10 and under is held earlier in the day. Call (509) 458-8880 for more information.

Snowshoeing

Just starting to get really popular, snowshoeing is easier even than cross-country skiing, especially with the modern, smaller snowshoes. Too boring to be of interest to most young adventure-seekers, snowshoes appeal to the energetic but more sedate types who want to explore the woods and see some of nature instead of whizzing by it.

Snowshoeing is easy to learn and you don't need to go to a special area—all you need is snow. You can rent snowshoes for about $10 a day at Mountain Gear, 2002 North Division, Spokane.

Snowmobiling

Because our forests have been both logged and used for recreation for many years, there is an extensive network of roads running through them, and these make perfect snowmobile trails. Idaho's Silver Valley has teamed up with northwestern Montana to create what they call Silver Country, with over 1,000 miles of trails. Other areas of Idaho and northeast Washington also have extensive snowmobile areas. If this is a sport you enjoy or you think you'd enjoy, you can try it out in the Inland Northwest.

Hidden Creek Ranch
7600 Blue Lake Road, Harrison, Idaho
(208) 689-3209
www.hiddencreek.com
Ride miles of groomed trails or ride into unbroken snow in Hidden Creek's beautiful valley. When snow conditions are good you can ride right from their lodge. Snow-shoeing and cross-country skiing are excellent here, too. Hidden Creek trails connect with hundreds of miles of trails through the mountains so you can get your fill of winter fun. The ranch offers full day and extended weekend snow-mobile tours, which include a packed lunch for the trail, snowmobile and one tank of gas, clothing, and guide service. Prices start at $175 per day.

Silver Country
Wallace, Idaho
(800) 643-2386
Starting out in Wallace, the town that lets you ride your snowmobile right through the streets, you'll be taken on a full-day's exploration of the mountains. A full-day ride, including the snowmobile, gas, clothing and helmet, lunches, and guide costs $179 per person.

Lakes

Inland Northwest Insiders know that natural lakes are what set our part of the country apart from other mountainous rural areas. Ask most people what they're doing on a summer weekend and they'll probably say, "Going to the lake." It doesn't matter which lake; there are many to choose from. Going to the lake here is the equivalent of going to the shore back east, or going to the beach in California.

Most of our lakes warm up nicely in the summer, becoming recreational playgrounds on hot days. Even Lake Pend Oreille, so big and deep it has hosted a submarine base, warms up enough at the edges to provide comfortable swimming areas. In winter, some lakes freeze over for ice fishing, ice-skating, and even snowmobiling.

Most northern Washington and Idaho lakes were formed by glacial activity over thousands of years. During the peak glacial period, the 4,000-foot thick Cordilleran ice sheet covered the mountains of British Columbia and extended south almost as far as Coeur d'Alene. As the glaciers retreated, they ground out lake basins in some places and their debris blocked river flow in others. Priest Lake lies in a glacial-scoured basin, and so does Lake Pend Oreille. Lake Coeur d'Alene was formed when glacial debris blocked the northward flow of the St. Joe River.

The Spokane area lakes were formed somewhat differently. Part of what's known as the channeled scablands, this area was gouged and channeled by the great floods from ancient Lake Missoula.

Today, some of our lakeshores are crowded with summer homes while others are more natural. Just about every lake has at least one public beach and picnic area. Some are known for swimming and water sports, while others provide excellent fishing. In this chapter, I'll introduce you to the wonders of Inland Northwest lakes; look in the Accommodations and Guest Ranches and Resorts chapters for information about places to stay on or near our beautiful waters.

Washington

Liberty Lake

The closest lake to Spokane, Liberty Lake is a small, local lake with a beautiful mountain backdrop to the south. Much of the lakeshore is privately owned, but there is a county park on the eastern side. It's a good park for families, with a small, roped-off beach and grassy picnic areas. The park also has a campground. Children enjoy just playing in the warm water, but boating and fishing are also possible. To reach Liberty Lake County Park, take I-90 east from Spokane and turn off at Liberty Lake, exit 296. Turn east on Mis-sion Avenue and go about a mile to a small sign directing you left to the park.

Lake Roosevelt

Created by the Grand Coulee Dam on the Columbia River, Lake Roosevelt is unlike any other lake listed in this chapter. Not only is it not a natural lake, but its dry landscape has more in common with Arizona or Nevada than with the green, forested land just a few miles to the east.

Named for President Franklin D. Roosevelt, the lake is 130 miles long and is especially popular for houseboating, water skiing, and fishing. The weather at Lake Roosevelt is a little more predictable than the weather in north Idaho—it's more likely to be warm on the summer day you decide to go there. There are camping ($10 per night per site May through September, $5 the rest of the year) and picnicking areas around the lake, which is now part of the Lake Roosevelt National Recreation Area. The National Park Service maintains several boat launch facilities ($6 per day). To reach the park and several of its campgrounds, take Hwy. 2 west from Spokane to Davenport. In Davenport, take Hwy. 25 north. Along this highway there are turn-offs to several campgrounds, including Porcupine Bay and Two Rivers. The Fort Spokane Visitor's Center, just before Two Rivers campground, has park information and maps.

Lakes West of Spokane

To the west of Spokane are more than a dozen small recreation lakes, offering low-key fishing, swimming, and boating. Many have nearby campgrounds and some offer family resorts and boat rentals. Fish Lake, on the Cheney-Spokane Road, is a county park offering fishing, swimming, and camping. To reach Fish Lake, take the Pullman Hwy. (exit 279) off of I-90 west of Spokane and go south for about three miles. Take the Cheney-Spokane Road exit to the right and follow that road about 12 miles to Fish Lake.

Williams Lake, southwest of Cheney, has a boat launch, swimming area, and a resort. Williams Lake can be reached from Spokane by going west on I-90 to exit 270 and traveling south about six miles to Cheney. On the southwest side of Cheney take the Turnbull Wildlife Refuge turnoff onto Cheney-Plaza Road. Travel 11 miles to Williams Lake Road and turn right. The lake is three more miles.

Clear Lake, north of Cheney, is a sandy, relatively shallow lake with low-key resorts, swimming and fishing, and canoe rentals. Clear Lake is easily accessible off of I-90 west of Spokane. Take exit 264 and turn right twice onto Clear Lake Road. Clear Lake is three miles down this road.

It shouldn't be hard to find a nice lake to spend the day—just pick one and go take a look. None are very far.

Idaho

Priest Lake

About 75 miles north of Coeur d'Alene, Priest Lake is the insiders' choice for summer recreation. While other large panhandle lakes have become civilized resort areas, Priest Lake retains its pristine, wilderness feel. Much of the shoreline is publicly owned and managed for timber production or recreation. Numerous campgrounds and resorts are scattered around the lake, far enough apart to enhance the feeling of isolation. Priest Lake is actually two lakes: the Upper Lake is only 3.5 miles long and is connected to the Lower Lake by a 2-mile long slow moving river known as the Thoroughfare.

During the summer the shallow waters along the shore of the lake sometimes equal the air temperature, about 75 degrees. On the east side of the lake, Priest Lake State Park has sandy swimming beaches, day-use picnic areas, and public boat docks. On the west side, the U.S. Forest Service Priest Lake Ranger District maintains picnic facilities and swimming areas at Luby Bay and Reeder Bay Campgrounds. In winter, this area gets about four feet of snow—enough for excellent cross-country skiing, snowshoeing and

Lake Pend Oreille offers spectacular scenery and unlimited recreation. PHOTO: COURTESY COEUR D'ALENE CHAMBER OF COMMERCE

snowmobiling. The mountains around the lake boast over 400 miles of groomed snowmobile trails; maps are available at most area businesses. Dog sledding is also becoming increasingly popular.

Spring and fall are the prime fishing seasons. Idaho's record Mackinaw trout (57.5 lbs.) was caught here, as well as the U.S. record kokanee salmon (6.5 lbs.). Fishermen also catch Dolly Varden, rainbow, and cutthroat trout. The history of these fish in Priest Lake illustrates what happens when humans tamper too much with nature. Mackinaw trout were introduced to the lake in the 1920s and displaced native bull trout and other species. Kokanee salmon were introduced in 1942 as food for the Mackinaw trout, and then mysis shrimp, a Canadian crustacean, were introduced as food for the kokanee. Unfortunately the shrimp competed for food with the kokanee, which all but wiped out the Mackinaw and kokanee populations. Restoration efforts have been quite successful and the lake provides great fishing once again. (See the chapter on Hunting and Fishing for more details.)

All kinds of recreational boating can be enjoyed on Lower Priest Lake. However, the Thoroughfare connecting the lakes is a no-wake zone, and motorized craft may not tow skiers or wake boarders in Upper Priest Lake. That leaves the upper lake peaceful and calm for canoes and kayaks. More than a dozen boat launches are located around Lower Priest Lake, and most resorts and marinas have gas available as well as boat rentals and other boating services.

To get to Priest Lake from Spokane, take Hwy. 2 north to Priest River, and State Route 57 north to Priest Lake. From Coeur d'Alene, take Hwy. 95 north to Sandpoint, Hwy. 2 east to Priest River, and State Route 57 north to Priest Lake.

Lake Pend Oreille

The "mammoth of the north," Lake Pend Oreille is nearly 43 miles long and six miles wide—it is twice the size of Lake Coeur d'Alene. At 1,225 feet, it is one of the deepest lakes in the United States. It lies along a geologic fault, and was probably eroded by glaciers to its present great depth.

David Thompson, famous explorer and geographer, came through this area in 1809 while mapping land for the North West Company. He established the first trading post in the northwest, Kullyspell House, near present-day Hope,

Looking for excitement? Try parasailing on Lake Coeur d'Alene. PHOTO: COURTESY COEUR D'ALENE CHAMBER OF COMMERCE

The Pend Oreille Paddler

You've heard of Nessie, Scotland's legendary Loch Ness monster? Well, there are reports of a monster in Lake Pend Oreille too, although nobody knows if it's a monster, a really big fish, or the Navy trying to hide its submarine testing activities.

Many Idaho lakes have legendary Indian tales of strange serpents or very large fish. However, the Pend Oreille Paddler story started in more recent times. In 1944 the first water monster sighting was reported in the Farragut Naval Training Station base newspaper. After World War II, the base closed but the Navy kept open a secret submarine testing station at Bayview, and unexplained sightings continued. In 1977, the Paddler got its nickname when a local teenager claimed to have been attacked by a lake monster on the beach, and a photo of the monster appeared in the paper. Mysteriously, it looked just like a huge papier-mache catfish that had appeared earlier in a school play.

Although no sturgeon has ever been caught in Lake Pend Oreille, some think the prehistoric-looking fish, which can grow up to 12 feet in length, could be living undisturbed in the huge lake and could be responsible for some of the sightings. Others think the Navy might be taking advantage of a gullible public and releasing "monster" sightings to cover up their secret submarine operations. Local people are especially suspicious of the Navy's insistence that the lake is much shallower than scientists say it is—perhaps to hide the true capabilities of the submarines they test in the lake.

Whatever lies beneath the waters of Pend Oreille, it doesn't stop thousands of people from enjoying the lake each summer. The lake is big enough to hide a monster—or a Navy sub—and still provide great boating, swimming, and fishing for the rest of us.

on the shores of Lake Pend Oreille. Settlers followed, then the railroad, and then lumber mills, which provided the economic base for the area. In World War II the U.S. Navy established a training and submarine testing base at the southern end of Lake Pend Oreille. Although the base was shut down and has been turned into Farragut State Park, the Navy still tests submarines in the lake.

Pend Oreille has a more rugged beauty than other panhandle lakes. In some places it has an almost fjord-like quality, with forested mountains descending steeply to the lake shore. There are unlimited boating opportunities, with many secluded coves and landmarks to explore all around the lake. Fishing is great in the lake, with catchable species including kamloops trout, whitefish, kokanee salmon, cutthroat and brown trout, bull trout, mackinaw, bass, crappie, and perch. The world record rainbow trout (37 lbs.) was taken from this lake in 1947.

To see the lake up close, rent a kayak or take a kayak tour with Full Spectrum Tours in Sandpoint. Everyone from kids to seniors can enjoy this easy and fun activity, and you'll discover birds and wildlife you'd never see otherwise. Full Spectrum Tours is located at 405 N. 4th Avenue, or you can call (208) 263-5975.

Lake Pend Oreille is located north of Lake Coeur d'Alene. Take Hwy. 95 north from Coeur d'Alene to Athol, where you'll see a turn-off to the right to Farragut State Park. If you continue north on 95 you'll come to the Long Bridge, which crosses the lake and leads into Sandpoint. From Sandpoint you can take a scenic drive down the east side of the lake on State Route 200 to the small towns of Hope and Clark Fork.

Lake Coeur d'Alene

Coeur d'Alene is a gem in the Gem State, its inviting, sparkling blue water surrounded by upscale homes, beaches, resorts, and forested hills. On a clear, sunny day it will take your breath away. On a hot day, the water draws you: people are boating, swimming, fishing, sunning by the lake, and you want to be there, too.

The Salish-speaking Schitsu'-Umsh people lived on the shores of Lake Coeur d'Alene for thousands of years before the explorers arrived in the nineteenth century. Renamed Coeur d'Alene by French fur traders, the native people have retained their interest in the lake and its surrounding land. In the 1990s, the Coeur d'Alene Tribe filed lawsuits against the Silver Valley mining companies that allowed deadly mining wastes to flow down the Coeur d'Alene River into the lake for a hundred years. They are working with the federal government to restore the river and lake, a difficult task because the heavy minerals settled into the sediment at the lake bottom.

Coeur d'Alene is the most accessible of the Idaho Panhandle lakes. Only a half-hour from the city of Spokane, the lake is easy to reach and central to most attractions in the area. The city of Coeur d'Alene provides amenities like a beach, public dock, and walking paths along the lake. Accessible boat cruises show visitors the lake from the water, and seaplanes take them up for a bird's-eye view. You can drive part or all the way around the lake, and if you really like it, you can buy a house on or near the lake and still be close enough to a city to find a job.

Wolf Lodge Bay, near the mouth of the Coeur d'Alene River just off of I-90, has become a favorite wintering area for bald eagles. They arrive in November and leave in February—January provides the best viewing. Nearby, the 3.3 mile Mineral Ridge Trail leads up to incredible views of Beauty Bay and the lake. Hiking trails abound in the wilderness areas near the lake.

Real Estate

Spokane and the Idaho Panhandle used to be quiet, out-of-the-way places, merrily going about their own business without trying to keep up with the rest of the country. Good blue-collar jobs were available, the communities were stable, and residents didn't want anything to change. But change came anyway; in north Idaho logging and mining gave way to tourism, and in Spokane, consumer and business services provided different types of jobs. Then people from California and other states discovered the Inland Northwest's lower prices, recreational amenities, good schools, and friendly communities. From 1990 to 1995 the population of Spokane County grew 11 percent. The median sales price of a home in this area went up 12 percent per year. Our real estate market had been depressed before and this boom just brought us in line with most other places in the west. However, it was quite a shock to some homeowners when they found out just how much their houses had appreciated. Since that time our real estate market has been relatively stable. The average price of a home in Spokane County is $116,000. It is about the same in Coeur d'Alene and Sandpoint, but lower in the Silver Valley and some rural areas.

The one factor that makes the difference in the price of a home in the Inland Northwest is water. Waterfront property is the most desirable, and with all the lakes and rivers there is quite a bit available. Keep in mind that some lakes and rivers tend to flood in the spring so look carefully at homes close to the water. Large waterfront homes close to town list from $300,000 to more than $1 million, while remote, hard-to-reach places may be available for $120,000 or less.

As you start to look for real estate in the Inland Northwest you'll find there's something for almost every budget and taste. There are still quite a few small, older homes listed for about $55,000 and up. New-style 3-bedroom, 2-bath homes with a two-car garage list for about $115,000 and up, although there are some developments in Post Falls and Airway Heights selling new homes for under $100,000. Homes with more amenities or land can be found from $130,000 and up. Beautiful waterfront homes or ranches with horse setups may approach $1 million or even more.

Reality Check

The cost of real estate in the Inland Northwest is still quite low compared to many parts of the country, especially for people who love skiing and the outdoors. Other ski areas, in Colorado for example, have seen real estate appreciate into the stratosphere. People from the west coast also find our real estate surprisingly affordable. Many vacationers come here to ski or sightsee and start taking a look at real estate. They think, "I could buy a beautiful home up here for what I'm paying for a hovel back home," they purchase what for us would be a luxury home, and make the move. They forget to check a few things, like the unemployment rate and the average income. When they look for jobs, they're surprised at the low pay—the average per capita income in this area is about $20,000 per year. The unemployment rate averages between 5 and 8 percent, and many people who move here with good education and experience take lower-skill jobs in order to be able to stay in the area.

Spokane

Spokane and the surrounding area are divided into distinct neighborhoods. The south hill is the entire area of the city south of downtown—so called because it's on a hill. The residential area closest to downtown and the freeway—the lower south hill—has many rental and low-income properties. From about 12th Avenue all the way south to Hangman Valley is, in large part, one of the most desirable areas of the city to live. There are many large, older homes and many small bungalows to choose from. Homes around Manito Park are especially sought-after. The schools in this area are known to be good, with strong family support.

The northeast part of Spokane (north of Sprague and east of Division) is a lower-income area with corresponding lower home prices. Many new immigrants settle in this area, and it is one of the most diverse parts of Spokane. Hillyard is an old railroad community along Market Street near Olympic; it's known for antique and junk shops.

The northwest quadrant of the city is similar to the south hill. The area closest to downtown is mostly lower-income and rentals. They've had problems with crime, but the Community Oriented Policing program has been a great success in this neighborhood, pulling people together and fostering community pride. Further north, the Shadle neighborhood has its own shopping district on Garland Avenue. It's a very family-oriented area of nice, well-kept older homes. In the northwest corner of the city, the Indian Trail neighborhood is filled with large, newer homes.

It's easy to find a cute, well-kept bungalow for sale on Spokane's South Hill, like this one near Manito Park. PHOTO: ELLIE EMMANUEL

Mead

Bordering Spokane on the north, Mead has a mixture of rural and semi-rural properties, plus many new high-quality subdivisions. The Mead school district has a good reputation, a strong selling point for homes lying within its boundaries. The main problem with Mead is transportation for those who work in Spokane. The two main routes to the area, Division and Market Streets, are crowded.

Spokane Valley

The formerly agricultural Spokane Valley extends from Spokane to the Idaho border. Old-timers remember fondly when it was filled with farms and Spokanites would go out on the weekends to buy produce from stands along the roads. Those days are gone; as land prices escalated many farmers were able to retire by selling out to developers, and the valley is now filled with subdivisions. It's still less crowded than the city and the Spokane River and Centennial Trail run through it. There are many semi-rural areas with homes on an acre or more of land.

Liberty Lake

One of the fastest-growing parts of the Spokane Valley is the newly-incorporated town of Liberty Lake. Several of the region's high-tech businesses are located here, and beautiful lakeside condos and homes are complemented by new golf-course developments further from the lake. Brand new shops, a new elementary school, and a new community walking path add to the upscale feeling. Liberty Lake has long had the county's highest per-capita income, and home prices reflect that with an average price of $181,000. However, the new developments are also building homes in the $130,000 range.

Real estate brokerages in the Spokane area cover the whole area, including Spokane, Mead, and the Spokane Valley. See the Real Estate Agencies section of this chapter for an overview of the major firms in the area. Any of them will be happy to send you a relocation packet with photo listings of currently available homes.

North Idaho Communities

Post Falls

The closest Idaho community to Spokane, Post Falls offers a viable residential alternative for those who prefer to live across the border. The formerly sleepy little mill town has experienced tremendous growth in the last ten years. Houses tend to cost about $10,000 less than in the nearby Spokane Valley, and many new developments have lured young families who like the small-town feeling yet proximity to jobs in Spokane. Idaho also has a lower sales tax rate, although Idaho has a state income tax and Washington doesn't. Idaho used to have a major advantage in much lower automobile registration fees, but a revolt by Washington voters recently brought fees in line with Idaho's.

Post Falls has grocery stores, hardware stores, and an outlet mall for most shopping needs. One drawback is its lack of a cohesive, pretty downtown, however it does offer small-town living within commuting distance of two larger cities.

Coeur d'Alene/Hayden

The small city of Coeur d'Alene is one of those special places that consistently win awards for their location, beauty, and livability. Sitting right on the shores of one of the world's most beautiful lakes, Coeur d'Alene also has a great downtown filled with wonderful little shops, proximity to

outdoor recreation, and friendly, laid-back people.

Homes around Lake Coeur d'Alene are, naturally, some of the priciest in this area, with few listed under $200,000. Homes in Coeur d'Alene range from some small mobile homes listed for under $20,000 to large homes with acreage for $400,000 and up. Site-built home resales generally range from about $90,000 to $140,000.

The city of Coeur d'Alene has quite a mixture of homes, from huge, early 1900s mansions (many of which are now bed-and-breakfasts) to modest two-bedroom affairs on small lots. Many people enjoy living close enough to walk to downtown shops and the lake. Further out, the community of Dalton Gardens borders the city of Hayden. It is a semi-rural area with many new subdivisions. Average home prices in the Hayden/Hayden Lake area

Many new homes in the Inland Northwest have three bedrooms, two baths, and a two-car garage.
PHOTO: COURTESY SANDPOINT CHAMBER OF COMMERCE

130 / **Real Estate**

are higher than Coeur d'Alene, at $138,000. Almost the entire shoreline of Hayden Lake is privately owned.

Sandpoint

A small arts and outdoor sports community on the shores of Lake Pend Oreille, picturesque Sandpoint has really seen the price of housing skyrocket over the last decade. It is a lovely town, with all kinds of recreation possibilities, a new library, active music and theater programs, and unbelievable scenery. However, good jobs are fairly hard to come by, and it is a little isolated. Average home sale prices average around $150,000.

Silver Valley

The Silver Valley offers some of the best real estate deals in the Inland Northwest. With the loss of many good-paying min-ing jobs and the stigma of the huge Bunker Hill Superfund Site, real estate prices here have been depressed for years. The average home sales price in the Silver Valley is still under $60,000, and there are many nice homes to choose from. The toxic metals left in the soil from 100 years of mining operations, especially near rivers and streams, may pose a danger to children who tend to play in the dirt, but single people, older families, or retirees may want to check out this part of the country. The people are very friendly and determined to keep their towns viable by switching to a tourism/recreation-based economy. Between them, the Silver Valley towns offer most services, and there are many organizations to join to make you feel at home. For recreation buffs, the mountains around the Silver Valley offer unlimited hiking, fishing, mountain biking, and all-terrain-vehicle and snowmobile riding.

Real Estate Agencies

Spokane Area

Century 21 Premier Service
315 West 9th, Spokane
(509) 483-2100, (800) 481-0021
www.century21.com

Part of the nationwide Century 21 network, Premier Service Realty is a full-service firm offering every kind of real estate.

Gregg Jones & Associates
2975 East 29th, Spokane
(509) 535-8400, (800) 726-2124
www.gregg-jones.com

With a target market that includes all of Spokane County, Gregg Jones is a full-service realty listing single family homes, residential acreage, duplexes and multiple unit housing, lake property, and new construction developments.

John L. Scott Real Estate
1500 West Fourth Avenue, Spokane
(509) 455-8600, (800) 872-7268

A northwest company, John L. Scott has offices in Washington, Oregon, and Idaho. They sell all kinds of property and offer a free relocation kit introducing the northwest.

Windermere Real Estate/Valley
12929 East Sprague, Spokane
(509) 995-4675
www.windermerespokane.com

With Multiple Listing Service access to all Spokane properties, Windermere also lists every type of real estate. They have a feature called Premier Properties, dedicated to selling homes in some of the "oldest, most refined Northwest neighborhoods."

Temporary Housing

Solar World Estates
1832 South Lawson Street, Airway Heights
(509) 244-3535, (800) 650-9484
www.solarworldestates.com

While you are looking for a home or waiting for one to be built you may need a temporary place to stay. Solar World Estates offers fully furnished townhouse apartments and corporate suites by the day, week, or month, at affordable rates. The daily rate ranges from $25 to $70, depending on the length of stay, and includes washer and dryer, local phone, televisions with cable, linens and maid service, all utilities, etc. They even have two- and three-bedroom units.

Coeur d'Alene

Century 21 Beutler & Associates
1836 Northwest Boulevard, Suite 100
(208) 773-8303, (800) 786-4555
www.century21beutler.com

Beutler lists many fine waterfront and residential homes in and around Coeur d'Alene. They also show new developments like Treaty Rock Estates in Post Falls.

Coldwell Banker Schneidmiller Realty
1924 Northwest Boulevard
(208) 665-5234
(800) 829-2555

Offering every type of home or property in the Coeur d'Alene/Post Falls area, Schneidmiller Realty also sells homes in new developments like Hunter's Glen in Coeur d'Alene or Forest Hills in Hayden.

National Associated Properties
1111 Sherman
(208) 664-8161
www.napland.com

Northwest Associated Properties sells only land—homesites, campsites, recre-

ation, ranch, or retirement property. They own all the land they sell, and can provide financing.

Prudential Acuff Northwest Real Estate
315 West Dalton Avenue
(208) 661-6053, (800) 667-8441

Listing every type of property in the Coeur d'Alene area, Acuff also sells luxury condos in the new McEuen Terrace highrise, with spectacular views of Lake Coeur d'Alene.

ReMax Masters
400 Northwest Boulevard
(208) 664-1190, (800) 662-1190

ReMax Masters lists commercial, residential, farm, ranch, waterfront, and properties with acreage.

Sandpoint

Coldwell Banker Resort Realty
202 South First
(208) 263-6802, (800) 544-1855
155 Village Lane (Schweitzer office)
(208) 263-9460
www.sandpoint-coldwell-banker.com

With two offices to serve you, including one specializing in ski properties on Schweitzer Mountain, Resort Realty can help you find any type of land or home.

Evergreen Realty
321 North First Avenue
(208) 263-6370, (800) 829-6370
www.evergreen-realty.com

Located in downtown Sandpoint, Evergreen is a full-service realty featuring homes, vacation homes, lake, and ski properties.

Lake Country Real Estate
226 North First Avenue
(208) 263-5454, (800) 653-3454

Offering a wide selection of homes in town and in the country, plus building sites and acreage, Lake Country is also promoting Ravenwood, a new development near Sandpoint.

Mark Hall Real Estate
102 Church Street
(208) 263-0507

A full-service realtor serving Sandpoint and Bonner County since 1978, Mark Hall Realty offers residential homes, acreage, waterfront, and vacation properties.

Panhandle Kaniksu
121 North First Avenue
(208) 263-5101, (800) 282-6880
www.pankanrealty.com

In Sandpoint since 1972, Panhandle Kaniksu is a full-service realtor listing every type of property from unimproved acreage to premier north Idaho retreats.

Silver Valley

Miner's Hat Realty
300 East Cameron, Kellogg
(208) 784-1202

Offering commercial and residential property, Miner's Hat specializes in the Silver Valley.

Tomlinson Black Silver Valley
501 Bunker Avenue, Kellogg
(208) 783-1121

Multiple Listing Service members, Tomlinson Black can show you any type of property in the Silver Valley, from mobile homes to waterfront retreats.

Total Realtors
414 6th Street, Wallace
(208) 752-1181

Total Realtors lists homes, land, and commercial properties in the entire Silver Valley. They are part of the Coeur d'Alene Multiple Listing Service.

Spokane, with a population of 200,000, is the cultural, educational, and business hub of the Inland Northwest. PHOTO: COURTESY SPOKANE CONVENTION AND VISITORS BUREAU

Media

We have our share of award-winning newspapers and radio stations here in the Inland Northwest. The *Spokane Journal of Business* recently won a gold award for "Best Newspaper: Small Tabloids" in an awards competition for national business publications. In 1998 *The Spokesman-Review* newspaper won the Batten Award for Excellence in Civic Journalism for its part in a multimedia study of runaway prison costs. Many of our newspapers, television stations, and radio stations have a strong online presence too, so we can get plenty of local news whenever we like via the Internet. The excellent Edward R. Murrow School of Communications at Washington State University trains many of our local journalists, and other local universities also have strong journalism programs.

In Spokane, the major newspaper is *The Spokesman-Review*. *The Seattle Times* is also available at many outlets, especially on the weekends, and *The Wall Street Journal* is sold in a few newspaper vending machines downtown. Visitors will find many out of town newspapers, as well as the city's largest selection of magazines, at **Jimmy'Z Newsstand,** 521 West Sprague, in downtown Spokane.

Newspapers

Spokane Area

The Spokesman-Review
999 West Riverside, Spokane
(509) 459-5000

Spokane's major newspaper is the primary news source for many in this area, and despite conservatives complaining that it's too liberal, and liberals complaining that it's too conservative, the newspaper attempts to provide balanced coverage of most issues. National and international coverage can be a little slim sometimes, so some people get a big city newspaper instead. *The Spokesman-Review* has headline news, regional news, and in-life sections, a weekly food section, an "Our Generation" feature for local teens, and a section on Friday that tells what's happening over the weekend.

Spokane Journal of Business
112 East First Avenue, Spokane
(509) 456-5257

You'll learn everything you wanted to know about Spokane's business community in this comprehensive bi-monthly news magazine. Throughout the year the journal also publishes a series of special magazines, including the *Book of Lists,* which gives statistical information on area businesses, *Spokane Woman,* a lifestyle magazine for working women in Spokane, the *Market Fact Book,* with demographic information on Spokane County, and *Luxury Living,* with photos, articles, and ads featuring executive home design. If you're looking for a job in Spokane or thinking of starting a business here, this is an excellent publication to read first.

The Inlander
1003 East Trent, Spokane
(509) 325-0634

You can find the free *Inlander* weekly at local bookstores, coffee shops, grocery stores, and the like. With excellent in-depth regional reporting and coverage of stories the mainstream newspapers ignore, *The Inlander* has become a popular alternative Spokane paper. Look here also to find every type of event, from sports gear exchanges to banjo concerts, that you might not hear about otherwise.

North Idaho

The newspaper business was a contentious one in the early days of northern Idaho. The first two newspapers in the area were *The Coeur d'Alene Press,* a paper backed by the Democratic Party, and the *Kootenai County Republican,* edited by John F. Yost. The *Republican* was four pages long and cost $1.50 per year. The outstanding feature of both papers was the editorials, which often conflicted in vitriolic terms.

Today, area newspapers still get involved in local causes, but their language is much toned down. More than big city papers these tomes tend to feature news about local people and small-town doings, so if you're looking for extensive national or international coverage, you'll want to pick up a copy of *The Spokesman-Review* or even *The Seattle Times.*

The Coeur d'Alene Press
201 North 2nd Street, Coeur d'Alene
(208) 664-8176

The Coeur d'Alene Press is published Monday through Saturday (*The North Idaho Sunday* takes its place on Sunday, see below) with a circulation of almost 17,000. It features north Idaho news, sports, business, and human interest stories.

Idaho Spokesman-Review
608 Northwest Boulevard, Coeur d'Alene
(208) 765-7100

The Idaho version of *The Spokesman-Review* is north Idaho's largest circulation paper. It has the same news and information as the Spokane version, but with a regional flavor.

Bonner County Daily Bee
310 Church Street, Sandpoint
(208) 263-9534

Published on Tuesday through Saturday mornings, the *Bonner County Daily Bee* has a circulation of about 6,200.

Kellogg Shoshone News-Press
401 Main Street, Kellogg
(208) 783-1107

Serving Idaho's Silver Valley with news of local interest, high school sports, recreation, and births and deaths, the *Shoshone News-Press* has a circulation of about 4,300.

The North Idaho Sunday

Serving the five northern counties in Idaho, *The North Idaho Sunday* is a combined effort of three dailies and three weeklies: *The Coeur d'Alene Press,* the *Bonner County Daily Bee,* the *Kellogg Shoshone News Press,* the *Priest River Times,* the *Bonners Ferry Herald,* and the *Post Falls Tribune.* For contact information, see the listings for *The Coeur d'Alene Press,* the *Bonner County Daily Bee,* or the *Kellogg Shoshone News Press.*

Television

Several local television stations are based in Spokane but have north Idaho offices. Each area has its own cable television provider, but because so many people live in rural areas, satellite dishes are also popular.

In Spokane, you can get three or four local stations with just a rooftop antenna or rabbit ears. I've listed the major local stations, which carry network programming and local news.

KHQ TV Channel 6
4202 South Regal, Spokane
(509) 448-6000

KHQ is affiliated with NBC but brings you local news at 5 P.M. and 6 P.M.

KREM TV Channel 2
4103 South Regal, Spokane
(509) 448-2000

The CBS affiliate carries network programming and local news at 5 P.M., 6 P.M., and 11 P.M.

KSPS TV Channel 7
3911 South Regal, Spokane (509) 354-7800

The local public television station serves a wide area, including British Columbia and Alberta in Canada. KSPS airs many popular shows, including *Teletubbies* and *Masterpiece Theater*. It's supported with viewer donations.

KXLY TV Channel 4
500 West Boone, Spokane
(509) 324-4000

Spokane and Coeur d'Alene's ABC affiliate carries all major ABC programming with local news at 5 P.M., 9 P.M., and 11 P.M.

Radio Stations

Spokane and north Idaho are served by a variety of music and news stations. I've listed the major station in each category to make it easier for you to find the type of station you want.

CAT Country 94
1601 East 57th, Spokane
(509) 448-1000

Cat Country is country music at its best, with all the latest hits and some oldies, too. This is one of Spokane's most popular stations, at 94 FM on your radio dial.

KAEP-FM The Peak 105.7
1601 East 57th, Spokane
(509) 448-1000

The Peak is Spokane's alternative rock station targeting the 20-something crowd. If

you want to hear music by Dave Matthews or find out when Smashing Pumpkins will be coming to the northwest, tune into FM 105.7.

KISC/KISS 98.1
300 East 3rd Avenue, Spokane
(509) 459-9800

KISS features easy-listening pop and rock music at FM 98.1, with news, contests, and call-in music request shows.

KKZX 98.9
5106 South Palouse Highway, Spokane
(509) 448-9900

The classic rock station at 98.9 FM, KKZX has the popular Radio Men personalities on weekday mornings.

KPBX
2319 North Monroe, Spokane
(509) 328-5729

FM 91.1 is Spokane's only listener-supported public radio station. Carrying a wide variety of music, news, and other features you won't find on commercial stations, KPBX also sends a monthly program guide to subscribers.

KXLY NewsRadio 920
500 West Boone Avenue, Spokane
(509) 328-6292

KXLY is a news and talk radio station at 920 AM. Regular programming includes morning news, coverage of local sports games, and popular talk-radio personalities. On winter mornings this station always gives road conditions and lists school closures. In times of emergency, like the ice storms and fire storms of recent years, KXLY has suspended regular programming to bring vital news to people worried their homes were going to burn down or wondering when electricity would be restored.

KZZU 93 Zoo FM
500 West Boone Avenue, Spokane
(509) 323-9393

Spokane's Top-40 music station, the Zoo is especially popular with kids and teens. You'll find it at 93 on your FM dial.

Education and Child Care

With the Inland Northwest's family orientation, education and programs for children are a top priority. Spokane students consistently score above average on national achievement tests, and over 92% of Washington State adults have a high school diploma. North Idaho is also dedicated to ensuring students are prepared for higher education and a changing work environment.

Many area school districts have passed bonds in recent years to expand and update facilities to accommodate increasing enrollments and changing technology. Spokane School District made updates to facilities in several area schools, including a complete remodel of Lewis and Clark High School. Mead School District, north of Spokane, built another high school. East Valley School District built a beautiful new, modern high school, and so did Post Falls and Sandpoint, in Idaho. Coeur d'Alene added another elementary school.

Child Care options in the region are varied. In Spokane, there are day care centers, before- and after-school care programs, and certified in-home care providers. In smaller towns and outlying areas there aren't as many options but available programs may be less crowded.

Spokane and north Idaho offer residents many opportunities to continue their education beyond high school. In the Spokane area residents may attend community college, public four-year universities, private universities, or technical schools. Coeur d'Alene has a popular two-year community college, which also offers programs in Sandpoint. Several of Idaho's four-year colleges also offer selected programs in Coeur d'Alene, and colleges and universities in the Spokane/Coeur d'Alene area are working together to offer educational opportunities to the entire region.

Elementary and Secondary Education

Spokane Area

In addition to each district's unique offerings, there are several area-wide programs available to all students. Spokane area high schools belong to the Greater Spokane Leagues (GSL) for competitive sports. Qualifying high school students may also take classes for both high school and college credit through Running Start. This outstanding program allows motivated students to earn a high school diploma and a two-year college degree at the same time. The Spokane Skills Center, 4141 North Regal, (509) 353-3363, is open to all area high school juniors and seniors with classes in subjects like auto mechanics, cosmetology, food service, computer networking, electronics, and graphic design.

Public Schools

Spokane School District
200 North Bernard, Spokane
(509) 354-5900
www.sd81.k12.wa.us/

The Spokane School District is the largest in the region, with five high schools, five middle schools, and 25 elementary schools. The district recently won a major grant from the Bill and Melinda

Spokane's Summer Parks Program keeps kids busy. PHOTO: COURTESY SPOKANE PARKS & RECREATION DEPT.

Gates Foundation for its efforts in technology infusion, curriculum restructuring, teacher training, and extended school programs. A wide variety of educational and after-school programs is available for students. Bus transportation is provided for students involved in after-school activities and for students living further than one mile from school. More than 7,000 community volunteers donate their time to the district each year, in classrooms, offices, libraries, or wherever they're needed. For information about volunteering with the district, call (509) 354-7387.

Mead School District
12828 North Newport Highway, Mead
(509) 465-6000
www.mead.k12.wa.us

The Mead District is one of the fastest growing districts in the region, and recently built a new, state-of-the-art high school. It now has two high schools, two middle schools, and seven elementary schools serving mostly suburban and rural areas north of Spokane. Parent participation is high and the schools are academically strong.

Central Valley School District
19307 E. Cataldo, Greenacres
(509) 922-6700

Serving almost 11,000 students in a section of the Spokane Valley, including Liberty Lake, the Central Valley School District has two high schools, five middle schools, and 14 elementary schools. Parent involvement is high in the district, and a bond issue was recently passed to rebuild both high schools. Liberty Lake Elementary, a new school planned with input from the community and industry, was recently recognized as one of the top 33 elementary schools in the nation for its design and use of computer technology.

East Valley School District
12325 East Grace, Spokane
(509) 924-1830
www.evsd.org/

The East Valley district is the fastest-growing district in the Spokane area. It serves the Spokane Valley in the area north of I-90 and east of Argonne Road. Almost 5,000 students attend one high school, two middle schools, and six elementary schools. Sports participation is encouraged and is very strong at middle and high school levels. The district has strong art and music programs, and is continually upgrading its technology.

West Valley School District
2805 North Argonne Road, Spokane
(509) 924-2150
www.wvsd363.com/

West Valley School District serves Millwood and nearby areas of the Spokane Valley. It is a small district with one high school, two middle schools, and five elementary schools. Academic classes are available for college preparation and vocational and technical skills. Advanced Placement classes are offered in English, history, biology, and Spanish.

Private Schools

Gonzaga Preparatory School
1224 East Euclid Avenue, Spokane
(509) 483-8511
www.gprep.com/

Spokane's fully-accredited Catholic Jesuit secondary school serves almost 1,000 students with a college preparatory program focused on academics. Admission is selective, and considers a student's past academic performance, an entrance exam, and recommendations from teachers and counselors.

St. George's School
2929 West Waikiki Road, Spokane
(509) 466-1636
www.sgs.org/

With exemplary test scores to support its standing at the top of college preparatory schools in eastern Washington, St. George's offers a challenging K-12 academic program. All school juniors and seniors take the Scholastic Aptitude Test (SAT), with average combined verbal and math scores of 1281. In the last five years, all 117 graduates have gone on to college. Bill Gates's sister is on St. George's board of trustees, and the William H. Gates Foundation recently donated $2 million to the school.

Post Falls

Post Falls School District
206 West Mullan Avenue, Post Falls
(208) 773-1658
www.pfsd.com

Another growing district serving a fast-growing area, Post Falls School District has a brand-new high school, an alternative high school, one middle school, and four elementary schools. Preschool and Headstart programs are also offered.

Coeur d'Alene

Coeur d'Alene School District
311 North 10th Street, Coeur d'Alene
(208) 664-8241
www.sd271.k12.id.us/cda1.html

The Coeur d'Alene School District serves about 9,000 students with two traditional high schools, three middle schools, an alternative high/middle school, and ten elementary schools. The district has been recognized nationally for its successful fine arts program. High school students who qualify may enter a dual enrollment program with North Idaho College or take advanced technical and specialized courses at Riverbend Professional Technical Academy, a collaborative effort with Post Falls and Lakeland districts.

Sandpoint

Lake Pend Oreille School District
901 Triangle Drive, Sandpoint
(208) 263-2184
www.sd84.k12.id.us/index.htm

With a total enrollment of just over 4,000 students, the Lake Pend Oreille School District serves a number of small towns in Bonner County. In Sandpoint there is one high school, one middle school, and four elementary schools. Sandpoint High School has one of the 15 high-tech classrooms in Idaho and is a "Teaching With Technology" teacher learning center.

Silver Valley

Idaho's Silver Valley is served by a number of different school districts. Small schools, strong school pride, and zero anonymity are characteristics of the schools here. They offer the usual academic programs, school sports, and several high schools have Junior ROTC programs.

Kellogg Joint School District
800 Bunker Avenue, Kellogg
(208) 784-1348

Wallace School District
401 River Street, Wallace
(208) 753-4515

Higher Education

Spokane Area

Public Colleges and Universities

Eastern Washington University
526 5th Street, Cheney
(509) 359-6200
www.ewu.edu

A few years ago EWU faced declining enrollments and the possible loss of state funds. The school made a successful effort to improve programs and recruit more students and today seems to be running smoothly. Traditionally a commuter school with the majority of students living in Spokane, EWU has also had recent success filling its residence halls. A large number of international students, especially from Japan, attend EWU. It has strong programs in teacher training, social work, and business. Some classes are taught in Spokane at two different centers, and several programs offer classes in the evening.

Spokane Community College
1810 North Greene Street, Spokane
(509) 533-7000
www.scc.spokane.cc.wa.us

Offering academic transfer degrees, technical two-year degrees, community education, senior classes, apprenticeship classes, and workforce training, SCC is a comprehensive community college. The variety of technical programs cover areas such as electronics, computers, mechanics, paralegal studies, health sciences, agribusiness, and business technology. Many technical programs have excellent job placement.

Spokane Falls Community College
3410 West Fort George Wright Drive, Spokane
(509) 533-3500
www.sfcc.spokane.cc.wa.us

This comprehensive community college offers a wide variety of liberal arts courses

Eastern Washington University, rated high in job preparation, is one of several universities and colleges in the Spokane/Coeur d'Alene area. PHOTO: ELLIE EMMANUEL

for those taking the first two years of a four-year degree. The school also has two-year technical programs in graphic design, interior decorating, computer networking, early childhood education, health and fitness, and office occupations. Interesting and fun community classes are offered every quarter, and during the summer there's a youth college program for kids ages 9 to 13, with classes in popular subjects like cartooning, bowling, horseback riding, web page design, and cheerleading. See the Kidstuff chapter for more details.

Washington State University, Spokane
601 West First Avenue, Spokane
(509) 358-7500
www.spokane.wsu.edu/

Established in 1989 as an urban campus of Washington State University, WSU Spokane offers graduate studies and professional programs to working adults who cannot move to Pullman to attend classes at the main campus. Classes are offered at different times to accommodate various work schedules.

Private Schools

Gonzaga University
502 East Boone Avenue, Spokane
(509) 328-4220
www.gonzaga.edu

Founded in 1887 as a boy's boarding school, Gonzaga was named for the Jesuit Saint Aloysius Gonzaga, patron of youth. It is a comprehensive regional university offering 17 degrees in 92 fields of study, including engineering, theology, arts and sciences, business, and law. The university also maintains a study-abroad center in Florence, Italy, where many students study for a year. Many guest speakers and music and theater programs are open to the public, and Gonzaga has a perennially successful basketball team that enjoys wide support throughout Spokane. The university also hosts the Jundt Art Museum. (See the Arts and Culture chapter for more information).

Whitworth College
300 West Hawthorne Road, Spokane
(509) 777-1000
www.whitworth.edu

Whitworth is a small, Christian liberal arts college known for small classes and caring professors. An extensive study-abroad program is available to students in all majors. Strong programs include economics and business, music, and international studies.

Coeur d'Alene

North Idaho College
1000 West Garden Avenue, Coeur d'Alene
(208) 769-3300
www.nidc.edu/

North Idaho College occupies prime real estate in one of the most beautiful locations of any college anywhere. The green, walkable campus sits on the point of land where Lake Coeur d'Alene empties into the Spokane River. The college serves the community with two-year transfer and technical programs, plus a good selection of inexpensive, no-credit classes in subjects like yoga, Idaho history, and computers.

Lewis-Clark State College
Coeur d'Alene Center
715 River Avenue, Coeur d'Alene
(208) 666-6707

The north Idaho center of LCSC is located on the campus of North Idaho College. It offers students the final two years of a baccalaureate degree in business administration, communication arts, justice studies, nursing, social work, and general studies. Graduates of North Idaho College may easily transfer credits to LCSC.

Child Care

Both Idaho and Washington have regulations covering day-care centers and licensed child day-care homes. Idaho divides child care providers into five categories: in-home child care (in the children's home), family-related child care, family child care (1-6 children), group child care (7-12 children), and center child care (more than 12 children). In each type, providers must be registered, and at least one in each center must carry a current infant CPR card and current First Aid card. Providers caring for 7 or more children must be certified, which means they've had a fire inspection and criminal history check. Providers caring for more than 12 children must be licensed, which involves getting a criminal history check, fire inspection, and health inspection. All staff in both certified and licensed centers must undergo four hours of training each year.

Child CareNet, a collaboration of the Idaho Department of Health & Welfare, Mountain States Early Head Start, North Idaho College Head Start, and the Panhandle Health District, is an organization dedicated to helping parents find quality child care in north Idaho. You can reach them at (208) 667-6400.

All child care providers in Washington must be licensed except those who occasionally watch a neighbor's child, or similar situations. Allowable adult to child ratios in child care centers range from at least one adult for every four children between one and 11 months old, to one adult for every 15 children ages five and up. There are also regulations governing how many children of each age a provider is allowed to take. The Washington State Child Care Resource & Referral Network helps parents find child care that matches their needs. Contact them at (509) 484-0048 or (800) 446-2229.

Spokane Area

Creative Children's Learning Center
320 West Dalke, Spokane
(509) 484-0036

This 24-hour center serves USDA approved breakfast, lunch, and dinner, has toddler and preschool education programs, after-school activities, summer field trips, and offers transportation to and from nearby schools.

Fantasy Farm Child Development Center
3222 East 28th Avenue, Spokane
(509) 534-9360

Located in the Lincoln Heights area of Spokane's south hill, Fantasy Farm takes children from one month to 11 years old. They're open from 6:30 A.M. to 6 P.M., Monday through Friday, and offer programs in language development, reading, math, arts and crafts, and music.

North Wall Child Development Center
9408 North Wall, Spokane
(509) 466-2695

This center is accredited by the National Academy of Early Childhood Programs, and it offers an early childhood program for the gifted. Age-specific classes introduce children to reading, math, science, creative arts, social studies, computers, carpentry, physical education, and handicrafts. There are enrichment classes in swimming, gymnastics, dance, foreign languages, and piano. You also have the option of keeping your child in the same facility for kindergarten through third grade in the North Wall Primary School.

Open Arms Lutheran Child Development Center
1888 North Wright Drive, Spokane
(509) 327-4441

Offering state-licensed care for children ages 2 to 12 from 6:30 A.M. to 6 P.M. In a country setting near Spokane Falls Community College, this center has a large outdoor play area and comprehensive child development programs.

Rosie's Romper Room
1918 South Markwell Court, Spokane
(509) 535-5524
www.alittleclass.com/preschool/

This preschool for children ages 2 through 5 offers four-hour morning and afternoon classes with no more than 10 children per teacher. Kids learn about computers, drama, reading, and arithmetic through fun activities that change with the seasons. A special summer program is also offered with swim lessons, fitness, and field trips.

Spokane Child Development Center
3808 North Sullivan Road, Building S-7, Spokane
(509) 924-2850
child.uswestdex.com

From 5:30 A.M. to 6:30 P.M., this Spokane Valley center cares for infants through school-age children. They have a large outdoor play area and offer gymnastics, computer, and swimming lessons, field trips, transportation to and from local schools, and a USDA food program.

Spokane School District Express Program
Spokane elementary schools
(509) 354-7266

The Express School Age Child Care program provides before- and after-school child care in most district elementary schools. Each site is open from 6:30 to 8:50 A.M. and 3 to 6 P.M. on school days.

Valley Learning Center
10909 East 32nd Avenue, Spokane
(509) 928-5031

This Spokane Valley child care center takes infants through 10-year-olds from

6:30 A.M. to 6 P.M. Kindergarten and pre-school education is available, as well as transportation to and from nearby schools. Special summer activities keep kids busy during the day.

Coeur d'Alene Area

Kidz Zone
275 West Dalton, Coeur d'Alene
(208) 762-9941

Offering full-time, part-time, and drop-in child care for infants through school-age children, Kidz Zone has an outdoor play area, preschool, and fun activities.

Trina's Just for Kids
5648 North Government Way, Suite E,
Dalton Gardens
(208) 762-4430

Trina's is located just north of Coeur d'Alene and is open seven days a week from 6 A.M. to 10 P.M. to accommodate working parents. Transportation to and from local schools is provided, and drop-ins are welcome.

Retirement

The warm southern states have been a traditional retirement destination for many years. After all, people who are no longer stuck someplace because of a job want to get away from shoveling snow and driving on slippery streets, right? For today's more active retirees, that's not always the case. Summer heat, no seasons, bugs, and overcrowding in places like Florida and Arizona have all driven some retirees to consider more varied climates like we have in the Inland Northwest. Coeur d'Alene has been named in some retirement publications as a great place to retire, and other towns have also been attracting older people in recent years. The majority of people who live and work here also remain in the area after they retire and we have a growing number of services and amenities for retirees.

If you should decide to check out this area for retirement, allow some time to look around and compare weather, amenities, taxes, housing costs, transportation, and senior services. In some parts of Spokane, the snow usually melts quickly while parts of north Idaho see accumulations of snow all winter. The tax structure in Washington differs from that in Idaho, and one state or the other may be more attractive depending on your financial situation. You'll have to decide which area best suits your needs.

Senior Centers

Senior centers can be lifesavers for older people who may otherwise have limited social contact. There are many senior centers in the Inland Northwest. Most towns now have at least a place where older people can get together and play cards or organize parties. Spokane has many centers, both private and community sponsored, that offer everything from daily meals to trips to health checkups. Coeur d'Alene, Post Falls, and Sandpoint all have centers offering a variety of services.

Spokane

Corbin Senior Activity Center
827 West Cleveland
(509) 327-1584

Corbin is one of the most active senior centers with an especially full schedule of classes and trips. Class topics range from writers' workshops and oil painting to exercise, lapidary, and bridge. If you like to travel, Corbin is the center to join; day tours go to shopping areas, casinos, on-lake cruises, out to dinner, to concerts, and many other places, while longer trips range as far as Mexico and China. The Center also offers monthly foot care, hearing and blood pressure tests, and eyeglasses adjustments. The annual cost to join Corbin is $12.

Hillyard Senior Center
4001 North Cook
(509) 482-0803

The Hillyard Senior Center serves hot meals at noon Monday through Friday for a $2 donation (or less for those who cannot afford it). There is usually a music performance, a talk, or other program before the meal, and classes, bingo, card games, and pool in the afternoons. Scheduled day trips go out to breakfast, to local festivals and concerts, and to stores. The Senior Center van provides rides locally to and from the center for $.25 each way.

Motorcoach tours and lake cruises are great ways to see our area. PHOTO: COURTESY COEUR D'ALENE CHAMBER OF COMMERCE

Sinto Senior Citizens Center
1124 West Sinto
(509) 327-2861

Sinto serves hot meals Tuesday through Friday for a $2 donation, and they also offer a site-cooked hot meal on Saturdays for $3.50. Sinto's van provides transportation on Saturdays, and the Center often schedules interesting day trips on Saturdays.

Southside Senior Activity Center
2727 South Mt. Vernon
(509) 536-0803
www.tincan.org/~shsc/

With a plethora of activities, including singing groups, classes, bridge, bingo, dancing, golf, blood pressure and hearing

aid tests, the Southside Center is a very busy gathering place. There are also several day trips offered each month, and longer trips may include whale watching in the San Juan Islands, visiting the Calgary Stampede, or touring New England in the fall.

North Idaho

Lake City Senior Center
1916 Lakewood Drive, Coeur d'Alene
(208) 667-4628

Lake City offers noon meals on Monday, Tuesday, Wednesday, and Friday. The center also offers classes, exercise programs, and a full calendar of events.

Senior Housing

We have many housing options for seniors at all stages of retirement—from duplexes and courtyard homes with garages to continuing care communities and nursing homes. There are buy-in homes and apartments in all price ranges, as well as monthly rentals and subsidized apartments for low-income seniors. I've listed some of the nicest places here, but there are dozens to choose from—it's best to visit each one and see which price, location, facilities, and atmosphere suit you best. Monthly charges vary depending on the size of the apartment, number of meals and amenities, and whether the community requires an initial buy-in or not. Generally, a one-bedroom apartment with two to three meals daily ranges from about $900 to $2,000 per month.

The Academy Retirement Community
1216 North Superior, Spokane
(509) 484-3161

This renovated brick building next to Mission Park used to be a school—hence the name. It's interesting because no two apartments are the same; the architecture of the building gives each unit a unique layout. All apartments have kitchens, and lunch and dinner are served daily in an elegant dining room. The Academy is close to shopping and transportation, and has an activities program and in-house barber and beauty shop as well as an assisted-living option.

Cooper George Retirement and Assisted-living Community
707 West 5th, Spokane
(509) 838-1797

You can't miss Cooper George, a high-rise building on Spokane's south hill near two major hospital complexes. Apartments have expansive views, and there is a heated, secure garage and storage units for each apartment. The all-inclusive monthly rental includes three meals daily, housekeeping, an activity program, and 24-hour staffing.

Fairwood Retirement Village
312 West Hastings Road, Spokane
(509) 467-2365

This beautiful community is set among pine trees in north Spokane. It's one of the area's more expensive retirement options, with amenities to match. Financing options include buy-in and leased apartments, and there is an additional monthly fee for assisted living. A sky-walk system provides handy access between buildings in the winter. Facilities include an indoor pool and Jacuzzi, walking track, gardens and greenhouses, an emergency monitoring system, and garages.

Park Place Retirement Community
511 South Park Road, Spokane
(509) 922-7224

This lovely facility in the Spokane Valley offers a continuum of housing and personal services to seniors. The monthly

Insiders' Tip

Are you planning on retiring in the Inland Northwest, or know someone who is? Pick up *The Complete Directory for Seniors and Their Families* at any local bookstore. It covers housing, health care, recreation, services, and many other topics of interest to seniors.

rental for one- and two-bedroom apartments includes full-service dining, housekeeping, scheduled transportation, and educational and activity programs. The campus also houses an assisted-living facility.

Forest Place
2340 West Seltice Way, Coeur d'Alene
(208) 765-5505

Located near the Centennial Trail, Forest Place offers a variety of apartment sizes, activities, a spacious and elegant dining room, housekeeping, security, and recreation activities. There's an on-site beauty salon and convenience store, too.

The Bridge Assisted Living
1123 North Division Street, Sandpoint
(208) 263-1524

Residents of the Bridge enjoy very pretty surroundings and the security of 24-hour assisted living. The monthly cost includes three meals daily, a wellness program, personal assistance, and laundry service.

Learning Opportunities

Spokane Area

Spokane Community College
1810 North Greene Street, Spokane
(509) 533-8006

Spokane Falls Community College
3410 West Fort George Wright Drive,
Spokane
(509) 533-3512

Both community colleges offer senior citizen tuition waivers for residents age 60 and older. A fee of $2.50 is charged per class (with a maximum of two classes per quarter), plus any charges for class fees and parking. To take advantage of this waiver, seniors must wait until the third day of the quarter to register, on a space-available basis.

Spokane's Manito Park is popular with all ages. PHOTO: COURTESY SPOKANE PARKS AND RECREATION DEPARTMENT

Community Colleges of Spokane Seniors Program: Institute for Extended Learning
3305 West Fort George Wright Drive, Spokane
(509) 533-3393

The IEL offers a wide variety of noncredit classes to seniors 55 years and older, held at locations throughout Spokane. Tuition ranges from about $12 to $40. Tuition waivers may be available to qualified applicants (if funding is available). Classes range from photography and computers to foreign languages, history, and fitness.

Gonzaga University Senior Citizen Audit
502 East Boone, Administration Bldg., Room 229, Spokane
(509) 328-4220, ext. 3192

This private, Jesuit university offers seniors ages 62 and older the opportunity to audit classes on a no-credit, space-available basis at no charge. Contact the registrars office (listed above) for more information.

Eastern Washington University
EWU Registrar, Cheney
(509) 359-2321

Located about 20 miles west of Spokane, EWU is a public university with about 7,000 students. Washington residents age 60 and over may enroll under a tuition and fee waiver program on a space-available basis.

Whitworth College Elder Scholar Program
300 West Hawthorne Road, Spokane
(509) 777-3222

Seniors can take courses for credit at reduced rates from this small, private college in north Spokane.

Whitworth College Elderhostel
300 West Hawthorne Road, Spokane
(509) 777-4521

Elderhostel is an educational program for seniors over age 55 that operates summer programs in colleges and universities around the world. The Whitworth program is highly rated, and accepts commuters also. Classes are taught by faculty members and require no grades, exams, or homework.

Coeur d'Alene

North Idaho College
1000 West Garden Avenue, Sherman Administration Bldg. #106, Coeur d'Alene
(208) 769-3316

NIC offers inexpensive noncredit continuing education classes in a variety of subjects like computers, crafts, and natural history. In addition, seniors can receive a 50% tuition discount on regular credit classes.

Senior Volunteer Opportunities

Retired and Senior Volunteer Program (RSVP)
507 North Howard, Spokane
(509) 838-3577

RSVP organizes volunteer opportunities for people age 55 and over. There's something for every interest—health care, education, the environment, the court system, etc. RSVP also has a Reading Corps to help Spokane County students with reading skills, tutor people studying for high school equivalency tests, and help students who speak limited English improve speaking and reading ability in English. Call 344-7787 ext. 157 for more information.

Spokane Public Schools' BRAVO! Program
200 North Bernard, Spokane
(509) 354-7387

The schools always need more volunteers to help teachers in the classrooms. You might find yourself designing bulletin boards, helping students with math or a science project, or organizing a party.

Spokane Police Department Senior Volunteer Program
1100 West Mallon, Spokane
(509) 625-4085

The Spokane Police Department is a leader in community policing, and this program involves senior volunteers in traffic and crowd control, vacation home checks, and other specialty police programs. One week of police training is provided.

Spokane Valley Meals on Wheels
11704 East Montgomery, Suite 3, Spokane
(509) 924-6976

Volunteer drivers are needed between 11 A.M. and 1 P.M. Monday through Friday to deliver hot meals to homebound elders who have difficulty preparing nutritious meals on their own.

Service Corps of Retired Executives (SCORE)
1020 West Riverside, Spokane
(509) 353-2800

Have you owned your own business or have extensive business management experience? SCORE volunteers are either active or retired business men and women who provide assistance to developing entrepreneurs. Spokane's SCORE is located in the Chamber of Commerce as part of the new Business Information Center. Volunteers counsel new business owners, help with business plan development, and teach workshops.

Recreation

One of the primary reasons Insiders love this area is the variety of recreational opportunities so close at hand. Even in the big city of Spokane, lakes, forests, rivers, and mountains aren't far away. There are outdoor activities for every season, from mountain biking, hiking, river tubing, and rock climbing to playing golf and tennis. When you tire of the outdoors, there are amusement and recreation centers to keep you entertained.

Amusement Parks/Recreation Centers

Kids Play Indoor Fun Park
233 East Lyons Avenue, Spokane
(509) 484-2102
www.kidsplay.com

Rated the best place to have a kids party by area residents, Kids Play provides enough excitement to wear out even the most energetic kids. A giant 3-level playground where kids can climb, crawl, slide, swing, bounce, play in plastic balls, and drive small electric cars, Kids Play is a great value, especially on rainy or snowy days when the young ones are going stir-crazy inside. A snack bar offers standard favorites like pizza, corn dogs, pop, and ice cream. Admission is $5.95 for children and $3.95 for toddlers, who can play in a separate toddler area.

GoKart Family Fun
West 3585 Seltice, Coeur d'Alene
(208) 667-3919

Go-karts are the main attraction here, but there's also laser tag, ice skating, miniature golf, bumper boats, and a video arcade.

LaserQuest
202 West 2nd Avenue, Spokane
(509) 624-7700

The first LaserQuest center opened in 1989 in England, and since then it has become popular around the world. It is an action adventure game played in a darkened, 12,000 square foot, three-level, fog-filled maze. Kids love it, but people of all ages are welcome and can have fun. Hours

of operation change with school holidays and summer vacation, but generally Laser-Quest is open in the evenings on weeknights and from about noon until midnight on Saturday.

Nascart Indoor Speedway
1224 East Front Avenue, Spokane
(509) 568-1065

Have you always wished you could drive a racecar? Speed limits on the roads just aren't fast enough? Then come to the "House of Speed" and race your friends on over 1,000 feet of go-kart track. There are forty, sixty, and one-hundred lap races on the exciting track featuring hairpin turns and a 35 mph straightaway.

Players & Spectators
12828 East Sprague, Spokane
(509) 924-5141
www.playersandspectators.com

Players & Spectators is a huge family amusement center with an excellent bowling alley, restaurant, billiards, and a video game room with enough games for everyone. The facility also houses a casino for adults only (see the listing under Casinos, below).

Triple Play
Corner of Highway 95 and Orchard Avenue, Hayden Lake
(208) 762-PLAY
www.3play.com

This big, new family amusement center just a few miles north of Coeur d'Alene provides a smoke-free venue for all kinds of fun activity. There's a kid's soft play gym, a rock climbing wall, virtual golf, 20 lanes of bowling (including laser and blacklight bowling at night), miniature golf, laser tag, and an arcade. As if that wasn't enough, they're also working on batting cages, a golf driving range and an indoor soccer arena, expected to be finished in the fall of 2001. All this exercise will make you hungry, so a pizzeria and grill are on the premises to help take away hunger pangs.

Wild Waters
2119 North Government Way, Coeur d'Alene
(208) 667-6491

Coeur d'Alene's waterslide park is easy to find—just take the Hwy. 95 exit off of I-90 and you'll see it right in front of you. (The entrance is around the block, on Government Way.) With a variety of slides, hot pools, an indoor video arcade, gift shop, and lawns for lying in the sun and watching the action, this is a popular place on hot summer days. Admission is $15.99 for people 48 inches and over, $12.99 for under 48 inches. The senior rate is $5.99 and kids under 3 are free. A twilight rate starts at 3 P.M. and costs $9.99.

Wonderland Family Fun Center
10515 North Division, Spokane
(509) 468-4FUN

There's enough here to keep a family busy for several hours. First, play a round of indoor or outdoor miniature golf, then hit the arcade games. The go-karts and bumper cars are fun, and some will enjoy trying out the batting cages. When you get hungry, order a pizza and pop at the restaurant.

Casinos

Coeur d'Alene Tribal Bingo/Casino
Highway 95, Worley
(800) 523-2464
www.cdacasino.com

The Coeur d'Alene Indians have enjoyed huge success with their casino, located thirty minutes south of Coeur d'Alene. It's open 24 hours a day and features concerts and sporting events, high-stakes bingo, off-track betting, and a restaurant, in addition to traditional casino gambling. Customers must be 18 or older to play bingo, gamble, or stand near gambling tables or machines. However, children under 18 may accompany adults to the restaurants, hotels, and recreation facilities associated with the casinos.

Northwest Quest
100 North Hayford Road, Spokane
(509) 242-7000

Northwest Quest, operated by the Kalispel Tribe, is the closest casino to Spokane. It opened in late 2000, and has blackjack, craps, roulette, keno, gaming machines, pull-tabs, and a poker room. A buffet restaurant is open for lunch and dinner every day. All customers must be 18 or older, including those going to the restaurant.

Players & Spectators
12828 East Sprague, Spokane
(509) 924-5141
www.playersandspectators.com

Fifteen tables offer games like Caribbean Stud, Pai Gow, and blackjack, and pull-tab tickets are available for those who enjoy simpler gambling. Players isn't just a casino—the huge facility also houses a bowling alley, restaurant, billiards, and a game room. Customers must be 18 or older to gamble, and children under 18 must be accompanied by an adult in the other areas of the facility after 5 P.M.

Two Rivers Casino and Resort
6828 B. Highway 25 South, Davenport
(800) 722-4031

Located on the banks of Lake Roosevelt, the 10,000-square-foot casino has over

400 slot machines, blackjack tables, Pai Gow, craps, and roulette. The casino also operates an RV park and restaurant. Children under 18 are not allowed in the casino, which includes the restaurant. Children are allowed in the RV park.

Biking and Skating

With the Centennial Trail connecting Spokane and Coeur d'Alene and many smaller trails being built in communities around the area, cyclists and in-line skaters have great recreation possibilities here. Our terrain is hilly, even mountainous in some places, but many major trails have been built along low-lying, flat areas so enjoying them needn't be too strenuous. Of course, there are plenty of places to get a good workout—riding up Mount Spokane comes to mind.

Please be sure to wear a helmet when cycling and all safety gear when using in-line skates. People, pets, cars, and obstacles can all cause an unexpected spill, and helmets are so lightweight and comfortable now there's really no reason not to wear them. Bicyclists should also be sure to follow the rules of the road and watch out for automobiles; many of our roads weren't designed to carry the heavy traffic we have now, and distracted drivers may not notice people on bikes. (See the Getting Here, Getting Around chapter for a list of bike rental companies.)

Idaho Centennial Trail and Spokane River Centennial Trail

Essentially one trail that changes names at the border, this has become one of our most popular recreational amenities. Everyone from families with strollers to senior citizens use the trail to get out and connect with the outdoors. In Spokane the trail runs through Riverfront Park and is heavily used by in-line skaters, lunchtime joggers, and walkers. Further out, the trail borders the Spokane River and is especially popular with walkers and bike riders.

The Centennial Trail may be accessed from many trailheads along the Spokane River. In Spokane, it's easiest to catch the trail right in Riverfront Park, where it runs along the south side of the river. In the Spokane Valley there is a trailhead with parking on the north side of the river off Sullivan Road; it's right next to the Spokane Valley Mall. In Coeur d'Alene the trail runs through City Park, going southwest along the lake. A big municipal parking lot next to the Coeur d'Alene Resort is a good place to park your car; City Park is just south of the resort.

Route of the Hiawatha Rail Trail
Near Wallace, Idaho
(208) 744-1301

To really get a look at Idaho's wilderness, you can ride your bike along a scenic section of abandoned rail-bed between Montana and Idaho. Thirteen miles of the trail on the Idaho side are open now, which goes through nine tunnels and over seven high trestles. A long (1.8-mile) tunnel connecting the Idaho trail to 31 miles of Montana trail is under repair and is expected to open in summer, 2001. The best part, besides the breathtaking scenery, is that you can take a shuttle bus to the top and ride your bike back down! It's safe and easy enough for families.

The trail is open from late May through early October (when hunting season begins). It is maintained and operated by the Taft Tunnel Preservation Society with fees collected from users. A one-day pass for adults is $6, and $3 for children ages 3 to 13. The shuttle bus is $9 one way for adults and $6 for children (it transports your bike too). You can also rent bikes, helmets, and lights (for going through the tunnels). Reservations are recommended and they

The scenic route of the Hiawatha Rail Trail is easy enough for beginning riders. PHOTO: COURTESY COEUR D'ALENE CHAMBER OF COMMERCE

can also give more detailed directions. The Wallace Inn (Exit 61 off of I-90 in Wallace) has maps to the trailhead.

Silver Mountain
610 Bunker Avenue, Kellogg
(208) 783-1111

Bring your bike and take the gondola up Silver Mountain, then ride an extensive trail system back down. Chairlift-served mountain biking is available even higher, up to Kellogg Peak. Silver Mountain trails are recommended only for true mountain bikes with fat tires, and you should bring an extra tube and tools along. Also bring plenty of water and some food; although you'll be riding mostly downhill, it's a long hill. An all-day mountain bike pass costs $10.95 and includes bike and rider transportation on the gondola and chairlift. Bike rentals are available; call (208) 786-3751.

Golf

Most people may not know the Inland Northwest as a golf mecca, but there are several high-quality courses here, many of them public. A 1997 issue of *Golf Magazine* gave high marks to the quality, price, and concentration of Spokane's public golf courses. The golf tradition in Spokane goes back eighty years, when the first public course was built. Downriver Golf Course opened in 1915, and it's still one of the city's most popular courses. Indian Canyon Golf Course opened in 1935 and has been the site of many major tournaments. It has consistently been rated one of the top twenty-five public golf courses in the United States by *Golf Digest* magazine. And of course, Coeur d'Alene is home to the famous floating green, located at the Coeur d'Alene Resort Golf Course.

In this section you'll find courses in and around Spokane, Coeur d'Alene, and the areas north of Coeur d'Alene. Summer is the golf season here, although dedicated golfers head out to the courses as soon as the snow melts and play late into autumn. In the winter, many courses groom trails for cross country skiers and a few have steep hills popular for sledding.

Most golf courses in the region prefer soft spikes, but will allow shoes with metal spikes if that's all you have. At most courses you can either walk or use a cart. The Coeur d'Alene Resort course is the exception; see its listing below for cart and spike rules.

Downriver
3225 North Columbia Circle, Spokane
(509) 327-5269

Rolling terrain with tall pines characterizes Downriver Golf Course, a Spokane favorite. Downriver is surrounded on three sides by the Spokane River and has challenges for all golf skill levels. Eighteen holes cost $18.50, or $11.50 for seniors (ages 65 and older), every day except Saturdays, Sundays and holidays until 3 P.M. Kids (ages 17 and younger) can play for $8.

Indian Canyon
W. 4304 West Drive, Spokane
(509) 747-5353

This unique course was built in and around a canyon with a vertical drop of 240 feet. It was designed in1930 by H. Chandler Egan and has hosted many major tournaments. Greens fees are $22.50 for eighteen holes and $13.50 for nine holes; kids pay $8. The senior rate is $13.50 except weekends and holidays during the day.

The Creek at Qualchan
301 East Meadowlane Road
(509) 448-9317

Spokane's newest golf course, Qualchan is located in a unique natural setting. Hangman Creek meanders through the course, and there are ponds, wooded and hilly areas, and well-protected greens. The Creek at Qualchan is a sanctuary for many species of birds and wildlife. Greens fees are $22.50 for adults, $13.50 for seniors, and $8 for juniors.

MeadowWood
24501 East Valleyway, Liberty Lake
(509) 255-9539

Managed by Spokane County, Meadow-Wood is a modern links-style course. Rolling hills with scattered trees and six ponds make it a pleasant golf experience. Lots of doglegs and hazards add risk and excitement. The Robert M. Graves designed course is well-maintained and easy to walk. Greens fees are $12 during the week and $16 on weekends. Rental carts are available.

The Highlands Golf and Country Club
North 701 Inverness Drive, Post Falls
(800) 797-7339

Sitting atop a 250-acre bluff, the Highlands offers panoramic views of north Idaho. In addition to the eighteen-hole course (open to the public), the club features a driving range, restaurant, and pro shop. Greens fees are $27.

Coeur d'Alene
900 Floating Green Drive, Coeur d'Alene
(800) 688-5253
www.cdaresort.com/golf.htm

The Coeur d'Alene Resort has been named by several magazines as one of the top golf resorts in the world, and the course has also won awards. Its most unique feature is the movable Floating Green signature hole—the ultimate water hazard. If you're skilled enough to hit the green on this 100 to 175 yard par-three hole, you'll have to take the shuttle boat out to the island green. Golf packages are available at the Resort (see the Guest Ranches and Resorts chapter for more information). Greens fees begin at $99 per person depending on the time of year. Greens fees include the cost of cart rental; if you prefer to walk the course, you must pay an additional fee for a caddy. The Coeur d'Alene Resort course does not allow metal spike shoes.

Hidden Lakes
89 Lower Pack Road, Sandpoint
(208) 263-1642
www.hiddenlakesgolf.com

Rated as one of the top courses in Idaho and one of the northwest's most beautiful and challenging, Hidden Lakes Golf Course winds through the lush Pack River delta outside of Sandpoint. Water comes into play on seventeen of the eighteen holes, and the championship tees, strategically placed bunkers, and bluegrass fairways make this course interesting for all skill levels. Greens fees are $38 with a $10 discount for seniors (ages 60 and older) on Mondays and Tuesdays.

Hiking

With so much public land, the Inland Northwest offers prime hiking in a variety of terrain. There are easy hikes close to town where you can see wildflowers, birds, turtles, and sometimes deer and other animals. There are long hikes as well, requiring several days and overnight gear, where you can really get away from civilization.

Safety and courtesy are important when hiking. Always come prepared, with enough water, warm clothes, and other necessities depending on the season and conditions. Be aware of private property, and only use the official trailheads or access points. Keep pets leashed, and allow room for others to pass safely on crowded trails. Take proper precautions in bear country.

Organizations

Spokane Mountaineers
P.O. Box 1013, Spokane
(509) 838-4974
www.spokanemountaineers.org/

Dedicated to promoting safe and responsible outdoor activities, as well as environmental awareness and activism, the Spokane Mountaineers offer outdoor education, trips, and social activities.

Hikes

Dishman Hills
8th Avenue and Park Road, Spokane

A natural area right in the city, Dishman Hills is interesting to explore. It's not really a large enough area to get lost, but it's easy to not know exactly where you are. Closed to motorized vehicles and bicycles, the area is quiet and peaceful, never crowded. The terrain is surprisingly dry and rocky, and it can be very hot in the summer.

Little Spokane River Trail
Off of Rutter Parkway, Spokane

This is a marvelous, easy trail close to the city yet peaceful and relaxing. The Little Spokane River remains in its natural state, and you can see many waterfowl, small animals, and maybe even deer. Note the Indian painted rocks at the trailhead. No dogs allowed in this pristine area.

Tubbs Hill
Next to downtown Coeur d'Alene

The very popular trail around Tubbs Hill quickly takes you away from the city and into a nearby wilderness. Only 2.5 miles around, this trail is popular with families and joggers, and with people looking for secluded swimming areas. Wildflowers abound in the spring, and the trail is usable most of the year.

Farragut State Park
East off of Idaho Highway 95 at Athol

There are many trails winding their way through the forest in Farragut State Park, but the easy 3 to 5 mile lakeside trail gives the best views of the lake. The trailheads are at the swimming beach and Willow Day Use Area. The campgrounds also have trails that lead down the hill to the lake; when you reach the trail at lakeside, that's the one.

Horseback Riding

Indian Canyon Riding Stables
Indian Canyon Drive, Spokane
(509) 624-4646

With Indian Canyon you don't just rent a horse, you get a guide who will take you to the best historical sites and help you with your horse if you need it. Close to the city yet secluded, the Indian Canyon trails lead through wooded areas, up onto plateaus, and to Indian Canyon Falls. You'll also see the last tepee homesite of Chief Spokane Garry. Tours are $12.50 per hour per person. Call ahead to reserve a time.

Rider Ranch
South 4199 Wolf Lodge Road,
Coeur d'Alene
(208) 667-3373

Escape the city and go riding in the clean mountain air at Rider Ranch, a family-owned working cattle and timber ranch just east of Coeur d'Alene. Their horses are gentle and well trained, and their guides will take you through the best scenery. Typical rides last from one to one and a half hours and costs $20 per person.

An evening dinner ride meets a horse-drawn chuckwagon for a truly western meal. The ranch also offers a family barn night and hayrides.

Mountain Horse Adventures
Schweitzer Mountain Road, Sandpoint
(208) 263-TROT
www.mountainhorseadventures.com

Guided rides in the beautiful mountains near Sandpoint with views of Lake Pend Oreille, are the main offering here. There are also "Eco" rides with a naturalist, gourmet breakfast and dinner rides, and overnight rides. The standard two-hour ride costs $45 per person.

Rock Climbing

Minnehaha Rocks
Upriver Drive, Spokane

Very popular for beginning as well as more advanced rock climbers, Minnehaha Rocks is an outcrop of granite along the Spokane River near Upriver Dam. Many bolted anchors have been installed at the top. This area is easily accessible and close, and it can get crowded on summer evenings and weekends.

Riverside State Park
Deep Creek Area, north of State Park Road
(509) 456-3964
www.riversidestatepark.org/rock_climbing.htm

Deep Creek offers dozens of routes for experienced climbers in a narrow, deep

canyon with basalt walls. You'll have to walk a short way to the cliffs but it's worth the effort.

Wild Walls Climbing Gym and Pro Shop
202 West 2nd Avenue, Spokane
(509) 455-9596

Discover how fun and safe climbing can be at Wild Walls' state of the art 40-foot-high indoor climbing gym. The gym offers memberships, lessons, birthday parties, youth programs, competitions, and a pro shop.

Day Trips

Emerald Creek
U.S. Forest Road 447,
south of St. Maries, Idaho
St. Maries Ranger District
(208) 245-2531

Idaho and India are the only two places in the world where star garnets are found. If getting out in the country to dig for unique

gems sounds like fun, this is the place to do it. The star garnets range in size from sand particles to as big as golf balls, and are often found with four- or six-ray stars. Digging for them is dirty work, but fun and rewarding for both adults and children. Some families bring a picnic lunch and make it an all-day outing, and there is